The EDGAR® Online® Guide to Decoding Financial Statements

Tips, Tools, and Techniques for Becoming a Savvy Investor

Tom Taulli

EDGAR Online Analyst

ISBN 1-932159-28-2

Printed and bound in the U.S.A. Printed on acid-free paper
10 9 8 7 6 5 4 3 2 1

Library of Congress Cataloging-in-Publication Data

Taulli, Tom, 1968–
The EDGAR online guide to decoding financial statements : tips, tools, and techniques for becoming a savvy investor / Tom Taulli.
p. cm.
Includes bibliographical references.
ISBN 1-932159-28-2
1. Financial statements. 2. Investments. I. Title.
HF5681.B2T32 2004
332.63′2042—dc22 2003023673

EDGAR Online, Inc. is not affiliated with or approved by the U.S. Securities and Exchange Commission.

Direct all inquiries to J. Ross Publishing, Inc., 6501 Park of Commerce Blvd., Suite 200, Boca Raton, Florida 33487.

Phone: (561) 869-3900
Fax: (561) 892-0700
Web: www.jrosspub.com

Dedication

The book is dedicated to the USC Trojan network.

Table of Contents

Table of Contents

Foreword

My accountant says I did this at a very bad time. My stocks are down. I'm cash poor or something. I got no cash flow. I got no liquid or something is not flowing. But they just got a language all their own those guys.

—Woody Allen in *Manhattan*

The investor needs to know. With Enron now part of our vernacular, market transparency is now more important than ever. Since its founding in 1995, EDGAR Online has built products and services that help stock markets, global financial institutions, and investors see public companies clearly.

That's why we were particularly excited about Tom's book. With a better-educated investor, we will all be better served.

Tom shows us — in plain English — the basics of financial statement analysis in a way even the number-phobic among us will embrace. It is a straightforward, nontechnical, no-nonsense approach we celebrate in our own products and services. And it is why we were so pleased to collaborate with Tom on this book.

We hope you enjoy the book and that you put your newfound knowledge to work as a better, smarter investor.

Jay Sears
Senior Vice President
EDGAR Online, Inc.
sears@edgar-online.com

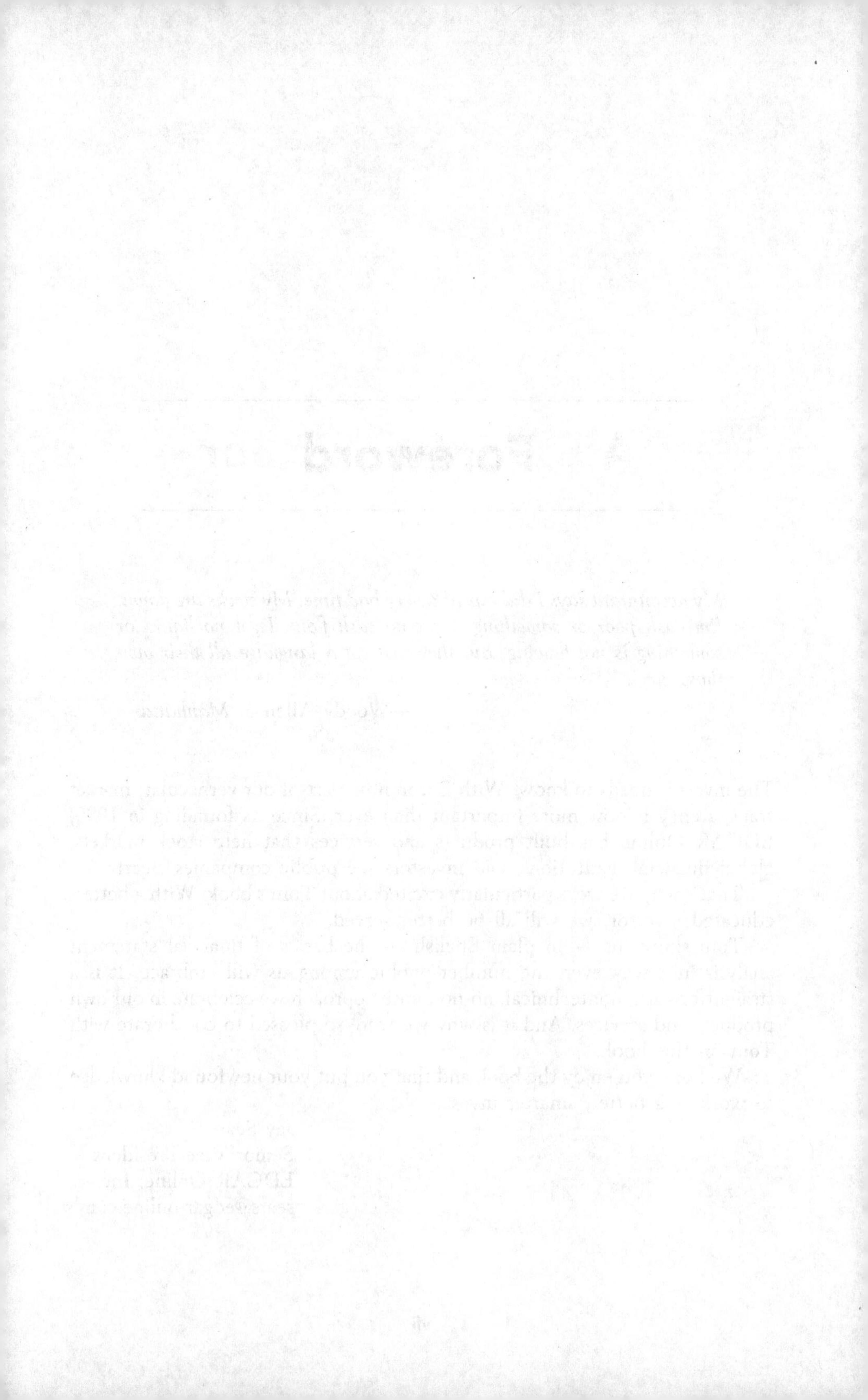

About the Author

Tom Taulli, Esq., EDGAR Online Analyst, is an attorney, accomplished angel investor, and financial writer who has authored such books as the *Complete M&A Handbook* (Random House) and *Investing in IPOs* (Random House). He has written numerous articles for such prestigious publications as *Business2.0, CBS MarketWatch, MSN Investor,* and *Forbes*. In addition to his writing efforts, Mr. Taulli has appeared on high-profile television venues such as CNN, CNBC, and Bloomberg TV and has been quoted in the various print media sources including the *Wall Street Journal, Barron's, USA Today,* and *LA Times*. Besides his publications on M&A and IPOs, he has written five other books on finance, with publishers such as Bloomberg Press and McGraw-Hill.

Mr. Taulli founded several successful businesses, of which Hypermart.net was sold to InfoSpace (NASDAQ:INSP). He has a Bachelor of Science degree in Finance from Cal Poly, Pomona, and a law degree from Whittier School of Law. Currently, Mr. Taulli owns and operates the MergerForum.com (www.mergerforum.com).

About the Author

About EDGAR Online, Inc.

EDGAR Online, Inc. (http://www.edgar-online.com) is a financial information company that specializes in making complex regulatory reporting by public companies actionable and easy to use. The company makes financial information and a variety of analysis tools available via online subscriptions and licensing agreements to professionals in financial institutions, corporations, and law firms.

The EDGAR System

EDGAR is an acronym that stands for Electronic Data Gathering, Analysis, and Retrieval. EDGAR is the name of the electronic filing system run by the U.S. Securities and Exchange Commission (SEC). Companies use this system to submit, or file, their reports with the SEC.

Prior to the introduction of the EDGAR system, SEC filings were only available on a delayed basis in costly paper or CD-ROM format from a limited number of document providers or from SEC public reference rooms. The SEC established the EDGAR system to perform automated collection and acceptance of submissions by companies and others that are required to file disclosure documents with the SEC. In 1996, the SEC universally required all U.S. public companies to file compliance documents such as prospectuses and annual and quarterly reports via electronic format through the EDGAR system.

Since 1994, over three million documents have been submitted electronically to the SEC. These documents are submitted by over 12,000 public companies, over 2,200 institutions, over 8,000 mutual funds, and over 60,000 corporate executives and other company insiders. On a typical day, up to 10,000 documents might be filed with the SEC, representing over one million pages of data.

Information Derived from SEC Filings

Since the inception of the EDGAR system, and even before electronic reporting, companies in the financial information business have built various distinct databases based on mandatory reports to the SEC that have commercial value to various customer segments. These databases include information on initial public offerings, normalized financial data, and stock ownership. The electronic EDGAR system has enabled EDGAR Online to apply proprietary technological know-how to extract extremely complex information and present it in a real-time user-friendly database format.

For instance, institutions managing over $100 million are required to submit a quarterly list of their holdings to the SEC. A recent filing by the institution FMR Corporation shows over 4,500 rows of data. Companies such as EDGAR Online use technology to place this information into a relational database to make a product that can be easily accessed by the end user. Customers that view EDGAR reports and databases built from this raw data are also often interested in other financial information such as U.S. and global annual and interim reports, call transcripts, and events calendars.

Seat-Based Subscriptions

EDGAR Online offers subscription services to meet the demands of professionals researching and making investment decisions on public companies. Its client base currently is largely within the financial services sector, including investment bankers, asset managers, credit risk managers, compliance officers, hedge fund managers, market data professionals, and others.

The company's flagship product is EDGAR Online Pro (http://www.edgaronlinepro.com). This product offers complex fundamental ownership, initial public offering and secondary offering datasets, and advanced search tools — all of which were previously offered only to large enterprises as part of the EDGAR Online Explorer product (via XML API data feeds for intranet integration). There are currently more than 8,000 subscribers to our EDGAR Online Pro service.

If you are interested in additional information on EDGAR Online, Inc., visit http://www.edgar-online.com to see the latest company news and product offerings.

Free value-added materials available from the Download Resource Center at www.jrosspub.com

At J. Ross Publishing we are committed to providing today's professional with practical, hands-on tools that enhance the learning experience and give readers an opportunity to apply what they have learned. That is why we offer free ancillary materials available for download on this book and all participating Web Added Value™ publications. These online resources may include interactive versions of material that appears in the book or supplemental templates, worksheets, models, plans, case studies, proposals, spreadsheets and assessment tools, among other things. Whenever you see the WAV™ symbol in any of our publications, it means bonus materials accompany the book and are available from the Web Added Value Download Resource Center at www.jrosspub.com.

Downloads available for *The EDGAR Online Guide to Decoding Financial Statements* consist of spreadsheets to conduct ratio analysis and sample financial statement analysis spreadsheets using techniques outlined in the book so readers can use them for their own target companies, as well as a checklist of red flags to look for within a company's financials and PowerPoint slides that detail the financial statement analysis process.

Introduction

Being a successful investor was easy from 1982 to 2000. Pick a mainstream mutual fund and you would see 20 percent returns every year, or more. Pick a stock — even a company that looked bad — and it might well increase 20 percent per year. Although the market did drop from time to time — most dramatically in October 1987 — those who stuck with it were generally made whole and more than whole relatively soon.

The psychology of the day was simple: The stock market is the only place to be. You're a fool not to be playing the game.

In many ways, I believe this is still true. Every investor needs exposure to the markets. Yet at the same time, every investor needs to do some direct analysis. It is a big mistake to rely completely on the advice of others. You spend many hours every year making money. Shouldn't you spend time making sure it grows?

This do-it-yourself message may not sit well with mutual fund managers. After all, the theory of the mutual fund is that — for a small fee — you get diversification and professional management. This is true. Despite this, of the more than 5,000 mutual funds, do you know which ones to pick? You see, even if you decide mutual funds are your bag, you still need to do some homework.

A Cautionary Tale

I once ran into a friend of mine, a consummate dealmaker, while he was talking rapid-fire on his cell phone. The sun flashed off his black sunglasses as he opened the door of his BMW 740 IL. He was not even 30.

"Hey, Tom-buddy, guess what?" he said, putting away his phone. "I was just talking to this heavy hitter in New York. He manages about a billion bucks and he says he has a great stock tip."

Always interested in a tip, I of course said, "Yeah? Let me in."

"It's Enron. It's a real company and it's ready to bounce."

Well, I would not normally invest solely on a tip. But this time it was tempting. I had known about Enron for several years and knew that it looked like a solid and fast-growing company.

Something else: My friend had given me a similar tip several months before and the stock climbed 400 percent. Unfortunately, I did not act on it.

Should I act on Enron?

I almost did. Then I decided I wanted to look at the financials (the financial statements that a company issues to show investors what it's doing) first before making a decision. Rushing into a stock had always been a mistake for me.

Good thing I did. Enron started dropping out of control within a couple of months, and — as everyone knows — wound up the laughingstock of the market, trading at pennies a share. Many investors rode it to the bottom, hoping against hope that it would somehow magically turn itself around. Others asked the right questions — the tough questions — and found their way out of the morass. Enron and the questions it generated (or should have generated) provides a useful lesson for every investor, and its adventures form a thread that carries throughout this book.

Asking the Tough Questions

It's unfortunately common, despite the fact that they are putting their hard-earned money at risk, for investors to fail to ask questions. They will accept a rumor as truth and buy a stock based on it. They will listen to an analyst on CNBC and buy stock based on what they think of as private and intimate tips, which the expert just shared with a few million other viewers.

Well, if you want to be a successful investor, you need to start asking questions — lots of them. And that means focusing on the company's financial statements.

The problem for many investors is: What questions do I ask? Yes, even the professionals have problems asking the right questions. Financial statements often look very complex, and they can *be* very complex, especially when they describe widely diversified businesses — or when their authors hope no one will study them closely.

The ultimate goal of this book is to help you ask the right questions and to be able to see and understand the answers when you get them. No one will tell you this stuff, so you need a solid foundation in understanding financials so you can recognize what the company is doing, what it wants you to think it is doing, and whether the two differ in any material way.

Big, Big Changes

Unless you were living in a cave during 2002, you've probably noticed that the U.S. financial disclosure system is undergoing tremendous change. In fact, the changes now in progress are the most significant since the 1930s.

The legislation that has brought this about is the Sarbanes–Oxley Act, which was passed on July 30, 2002. True, there are other changes, such as new rules from the New York Stock Exchange and the NASDAQ. There are also rule changes from the Securities and Exchange Commission (SEC).

But by far the most sweeping impact is from the Sarbanes–Oxley Act. There was little resistance to the bill, and even high-profile D.C. lobbyists could not stop the stampede. The vote in the Senate was 99 to 0 and in the House was 423 to 3. In his speech to the nation, George W. Bush declared that the bill would help end the "era of low standards and false profits." Here are the bill's main provisions:

- It requires the CEO and CFO to *certify* (that is, sign off on) the company's financial statements. (This means that if the statements turn out to be fraudulent, it could mean prison time for the top execs.)
- It provides safeguards for corporate whistleblowers.
- It prohibits auditors from performing certain types of consulting services that may pose conflicts of interest.
- It requires insiders to report buying or selling any company stock within two business days.
- It establishes an accounting oversight board to help fashion new accounting rules.
- It bars companies from making loans to their corporate executives.
- It extends the time allowed to file corporate fraud lawsuits of up to two years from the date the fraud has been discovered or five years after the fraud occurs.

This legislation has many goals. One is to promote *transparency* (disclosing more information to investors so they can tell what's really happening in a company). Another key element is reducing conflicts of interest, both within a company and between the company and its auditors.

It is too early to tell what the impact of these reforms will be. The bill is quite vague in some parts (such as with the ban on corporate loans). But vagueness is always part of landmark legislation, and you can be sure we'll be seeing unintended consequences from it.

Ultimately, the SEC, the Justice Department, and the federal courts will be the ones to sort things out and try to establish a system that works.

But there is already much evidence that corporate America isn't waiting for the legal situation to settle down before instituting new systems to improve its own financial reporting and credibility to investors. For example, Citigroup has adopted some significant policy changes, such as expensing employee stock options, eliminating off-balance-sheet debts, and forming a new special corporate governance committee. The CEO, Sandy Weill, said his executives have a blood oath not to sell more than 25 percent of their personal stock holdings.

You Still Need to Do Your Homework

No doubt, the changes will be very good for the U.S. capitalist system. As trust builds again, investors will warm up to stocks, and this means more funding for companies and, yes, more economic growth. It is a virtuous cycle. However, this does not mean you can sit back and not do your homework. Despite the reforms, financial statements will still be complex. Perhaps they will be even more complex because of the increased disclosure requirements.

Besides, government reform will not change human nature. Greed is a powerful drive, and it's far from absent among hard-charging corporate executives. This can easily lead to fraud and criminal behavior. In addition, rules themselves form a sort of temptation for many people, leading them to see what they can get away with.

Something else that has been lost in the debate: Financial statements are the result of a process of substantial judgment. Just having more disclosure does not mean everything will be revealed or that investors will have a clear picture of a company's operations.

Keep in mind that the basic procedures of accounting were set hundreds of years ago. The word *auditor* actually means just what it sounds like, *listener*, because financial records used to be so personal that only the one who wrote them could tell what they contained; the auditor's job was to listen to a recital and try to spot inconsistencies. Double-entry bookkeeping was hailed as a dramatic improvement in financial reliability, but — like all the innovations that followed it — it didn't put a stop to creativity and concealment.

What's more, the Industrial Revolution has had a tremendous impact on what financial statements look like, because of its overwhelming focus on physical assets and means of production. Many companies list assets like "plant and equipment" in their financial statements, but make little mention of the intangibles (things like brands, intellectual property, or good standing in the global community) that may well provide a major part of a company's value. You cannot touch these assets — that's what *intangible* means. Yet their value can be substantial. This is certainly the case with such high-growth companies as Microsoft, Amgen, and Cisco. Do such assets as "plant and equipment" adequately reflect the market value of these companies? Certainly not. This book will show you some techniques for assessing intangible values.

Financial statements always have another inherent problem: They reflect the past, not the future. Financial statements are recordings of history, and successful investors need to find ways of gauging the future. But it turns out that, despite their firm roots in the past, financial statements can be used to look into the crystal ball and see where a company is heading. I discuss those techniques throughout this book.

Why You Need This Book

This book helps you do your own homework. It lays out the structure of the financial marketplace and describes the kinds of information you can find and where to find it — and what to do with it when you've got it.

Chapter 1: You're On Your Own. In this chapter, I set the scene for the way the financial system really works. Unfortunately, it is not kind to individual investors. But, by using strong research skills, you will have the edge. In fact, you may have some advantages over the institutional Wall Street pros!

Chapter 2: What Do Investors Need to Know About Accounting? Accounting may sound like a boring subject, but the basics are absolutely critical to understanding financial statements. I will show you the history and the evolution of accounting principles, which makes them easier to follow, and give you an aerial view of the accounting process.

Chapter 3: Filings and Other Vital Company Communications. For more than 70 years, the federal government has required disclosure of many details of public companies. This chapter covers the many types of filings and how to use them effectively.

Chapters 4 and 5: Balance Sheet. The balance sheet gives a snapshot of the assets, liabilities, and capital of a company, showing you what it owns and how it is financed. A look at real-life examples will help you understand the financial statement.

Chapters 6 and 7: Income Statement. Does the company make any money? This is what the income statement reveals. You have to be wary, though. It can be manipulated easily — but an alert investor can usually spot the manipulations.

Chapter 8: Cash Flow Statement. The phrase "cash is king" may seem overused. But it should be used a lot. Cash analysis is absolutely essential for the success of an investor. Besides looking at the statement, this chapter will show you how to calculate free cash flow (often a mystery to investors) — and why you want to do so.

Chapter 9: Ratio Analysis. Ratios help you interpret all the financial statements. Is the company taking on too much debt? Is its profitability deteriorating or growing? Find out before you buy!

Chapter 10: Proxy Statements. Proxy filings often include juicy information — things like the details of executive compensation and the existence of sweetheart deals, known as *related-party transactions* — that can help put the rosiest financial statements into perspective.

Chapter 11: Insider Buying and Selling. Executives must disclose whether they are buying or selling stock. What if they are grabbing up lots of stock or dumping it? You'll see how to make use of this vital source of information.

Chapter 12: IPOs, Spin-Offs, and Tracking Stocks. These are specialized transactions and have their own types of filings. In this chapter, you'll learn how to spot the winners and avoid the duds.

Chapter 13: Rating System. The world of investing is full of so much information that it can seem overwhelming. In this chapter, you'll learn ways to use automated screeners to fish out the best potential prospects, then develop a systematic approach to picking out the ones you want to follow — and monitoring the ones you actually buy to make sure you don't ride them too far down if they start to slide.

Appendix: Financial Statement Resources. Both online and in print, you'll find many useful resources designed to help investors. The Appendix will help you figure out which ones are best for you.

Throughout the book, you'll see sidebars that provide more detail on cases that illustrate the main concepts and on the major players in the financial game, such as Warren Buffett and Bill Miller. There will also be many hints and tips to guide your investment success.

Looking Ahead

Many analysts believe that we will no longer see the kinds of sustained bull markets we witnessed during the 1980s and 1990s. This may be true, but I'm not about to make any predictions about it. Rather, my philosophy is that you should use strong analysis in any market. Whether the trend is up or down, you can still make money. It just takes common sense.

So let's get started!

Sources

1. Osterland, Andrew, No more Mr. Nice Guy, CFO *Magazine*, September 1, 2002.
2. Murphy, Cait, D.C. gets it almost right, *Fortune*, September 2, 2002.
3. Waggoner, John and Fogarty, Thomas A., Scandals shred investors' faith because of Enron, Andersen and rising gas prices: the public is more wary than ever of corporate America, *USA Today*, May 7, 2002.

1

You're On Your Own

What Every Investor Needs to Know About the "System"

The U.S. stock market calls to mind Winston Churchill's view of democracy: It's the worst of all economic systems — except for all the others people have tried. Wall Street has done a lot of good. For more than 200 years, the stock market has been the driving force behind many great innovations — the telephone, the railroads, the software and biotech revolutions. As long as people come up with innovations, Wall Street will be ready to take a bet.

But Wall Street earns its position among the "worst" rank as well, rife with misunderstandings, abuses, and outright fraud. The late 1800s isn't known as the era of the robber barons for nothing! Speculators like Daniel Drew, Jim Fisk, and Jay Gould cornered markets, manipulated stock prices, and launched bear raids — anything to make a buck. In fact, these wily speculators thought it was their god-given right to make money because they were, well, better adapted than others. They took Darwin's concept of survival of the fittest, turned it on its head so that whatever they did to survive proved their fitness, and applied it to Wall Street.

Fast forward to the Roaring Twenties. True, some companies of the day were truly revolutionary and deserved high valuations. But in many cases, the stock price of a company was the result of manipulation. The era had its own crew of speculators — men like Joseph Kennedy and Will Durant — who continued to apply Darwin's theories to Wall Street.

Like all bubbles, this one eventually popped. The market began to drop dramatically in 1929, and the Great Depression followed. With massive bank failures, the American public lost confidence and thought the safest place for their hard-earned money was under the mattress. This change of heart was absolutely deadly for the stock market, which plunged more than 90 percent from 1929 to 1933 (to a low of 41 on the Dow, a level the market has never reached again).

The beauty of the American system is democracy and flexibility. President Franklin D. Roosevelt and Congress took significant action to bring back confidence in the financial system. They clearly understood that if Wall Street failed, so would the whole system. The governmental initiatives resulted in the passage of the Securities Act of 1933, which basically mandated that no stock could be sold to the public without certain minimum disclosures.

A year later, Congress passed the Securities Exchange Act of 1934, which set new rules against stock market manipulation (banning insider trading, among other ploys) and required that companies make quarterly and annual disclosures to shareholders. The legislation also created the Securities and Exchange Commission, the federal agency that enforces the securities laws. Ironically enough, the first chairman of the SEC was Joseph Kennedy, who certainly knew everything would-be manipulators were likely to try and how to spot their efforts.

For the most part, the system has worked. Since the 1930s, the U.S. economy has shown tremendous growth and innovation. Great companies like Microsoft, Amgen, and Wal-Mart grew out of the combination of great ideas, hard-working entrepreneurs, and risk capital. Without confidence in the financial system, these companies would not have become global leaders. It is that simple.

The 1960s was a time of tremendous economic growth fueled by new innovations. (If a company had a name that ended in "onics," it was bound to soar.) True, the economy suffered problems, especially during the 1970s with grueling *stagflation* — the combination of high inflation and high unemployment — a cycle recognizable to all of us who invested happily through the 1990s and saw the plug pulled in the early 2000s: The prior decade had been one of the most bullish in U.S. history.

Investors got too greedy and pushed prices to unsupportable levels. The markets crashed amid a round of scandals. Perhaps the most visible fraud was Equity Funding Corporation, a Wall Street darling that had more than $1 billion in assets. These assets turned out to be mostly a mirage and the company entered bankruptcy in 1973. Employees and auditors were indicted and the president was sentenced to eight years in prison.

But the system survived. It did take time to heal, but by 1982, with interest rates falling, we saw a substantial bull market. Inflation and unemployment collapsed and companies became more competitive. Every year, the market rewarded loyal shareholders. New technologies were everywhere —

and they led to new financial techniques and products, such as junk bonds and program trading. Increasingly, Wall Street was entering the Computer Age.

We all know that the 1980s also became the decade of greed. In fact, a popular movie during the 1980s was *Wall Street*, which starred Michael Douglas as the amoral financier Gordon Gekko. Gekko was loosely based on a real financial wizard, Ivan Boesky, who made his fortune by using insider information on takeovers during the 1980s. He even wrote a book about his strategies called *Merger Mania* (published in 1985). He paid a $100 million fine and was sentenced to prison in 1986. For a reduced sentence, he implicated junk bond king Michael Milken, who paid a $600 million fine and was also sent to prison.

Investors pushed things too far yet again. The market collapsed in the early 1990s, as the economy slipped into a recession. Inevitably, examples of corporate fraud abounded. One of the most prominent was from the once-staid savings and loan, or S&L, industry. Because of high-risk investments (especially in junk bonds), U.S. taxpayers had to spend $300 billion to clean up the mess. The symbol of the excess was Charles Keating, whose S&L wiped out the savings of 23,000 seniors and cost the taxpayers $3.4 billion. Keating spent five years in prison and paid a $125 million fine.

The system then proved its resiliency yet again. After the early 1990s, the U.S. economy underwent an unprecedented bull run. Even more sophisticated technologies emerged, both outside the market and within it.

In a way, investing became too easy. It was as if all laws of economics were thrown out the window. Gravity? Forget it. It had somehow been repealed on Wall Street. Serious advisers propounded theories that said the new online giants were actually better off *not* making profits, so their continuing losses were a reason to invest.

Speaking of ignoring the laws of economics, the emergence of the Internet greatly fueled the surge in stock prices. Now, with cheap access to computers and connectivity, all investors had the same types of tools that institutional investors had been using, which led to the new profession of day trading.

What next? Of course, history does seem to repeat itself.

This Time It Is Really Different

The markets peaked in early 2000 and continued to slide. Times were particularly tough on technology stocks and even the so-called tech blue chips, such as Cisco, Dell, and Sun, fell hard.

But it was not just the day traders or individual investors who lost money. Well-heeled experts did as well. One striking example is Bernie Ebbers, who founded the telecom giant WorldCom. In the late 1990s, he borrowed about $800 million in margin loans to purchase stock in the company. Unfortunately, the stock price collapsed and he was unable to pay back the loans. His company loaned him a hefty $430 million when the stock price was $20 per share. A few months later, the company was bankrupt and the stock was worthless.

But wait a minute. What about the other shareholders of WorldCom? Did they get any loans to bail out their positions? Of course not.

And WorldCom was not an aberration (for a humorous look, see Figure 1.1). Throughout 2002, it seemed that company after company announced similar sweetheart deals that catered to corporate insiders and stomped on all other shareholders.

Look at Global Crossing, another high-flying telecom company. It filed for bankruptcy in early 2002, but the executives were able to cash out $1.3 billion in stock sales before its demise. In the company's entire history, it was never a profitable enterprise — that is, except for corporate insiders.

And all this is nothing compared to Enron. It's hard to believe now, but *Fortune* once called the company one of the most innovative in the United

Figure 1.1 As 2002 showed us, even the big companies can become worthless. (From *The Oregonian*, ©2002 Tribune Media Service)

States — and meant to praise it. By 2001, Enron was the seventh-largest company in the country.

Enron and the Story of the 1990s

The mastermind behind Enron was Ken Lay, who grew up in a modest family in Missouri. Hard work and ambition were constants in his life. As a kid, he was a good student and president of his class in high school. He had three paper routes, worked at the school newspaper, and sang in the choir. While in college, he studied economics and became captivated by the power of free markets.

He started to apply these free-market principles when he got a job at the Federal Power Commission (later revamped as the Federal Energy Regulatory Commission). During this time, he got his Ph.D. in economics at night school.

He then started to work for a variety of natural gas pipeline companies — but continued to be a vocal political networker, warmly espousing deregulation. Lay's company was bought out in 1985; within a year he, was CEO of the new organization, which he called Enron. He was only 44 years old at the time.

But Lay had boundless ambition and wanted to make Enron a huge power. To this end, he hired the "best and the brightest." Perhaps the most important hire was Jeffrey Skilling, a Harvard MBA and McKinsey & Co. consultant. It was Skilling's work that generated the substantial growth in the company during the 1990s. He thought the key to this goal was to make Enron "asset lite," so he focused on esoteric things like futures and derivatives trading. In his many statements to the press, he would mention the "New Economy" and the "high velocity of capital" and how Enron was at the forefront of these high-powered concepts. Skilling promoted an aggressive company culture and instituted a "*rank and yank*" policy; that is, if you were not pulling your weight, you would be asked to leave the company.

By August 2000, Enron's stock price hit an all-time high of $90.75. However, to fuel this hypergrowth, Enron executives found they needed to adopt practices that were more and more dangerous.

Wall Street grew spoiled on Enron's growth in earnings and revenues. The appetite was ravenous, and it became clear that any disappointment would spell disaster for the stock. Skilling realized it was an absolute priority to make it clear throughout the organization that all steps needed to be taken to boost growth. For example, he set up training courses that showed employees how to draft contracts to speed up the recognition of revenues while minimizing debt exposure. Another ploy was "The Sting," in which Skilling and Lay would make a large office space — full of people pulled in from other jobs to pretend that they were trading energy futures — look like an active trading room so as to impress analysts.

But what damaged Enron most were the complex partnership subsidiaries known as *special purpose entities* (SPEs). With an SPE, Enron was able to transfer large amounts of debts off its balance sheets. This helped maintain Enron's high credit rating, thus keeping its borrowing costs low.

Enron's CFO, Andrew Fastow, helped devise many of the SPEs, and on several occasions he owned positions and was general partner in these vehicles. He made $40 million on these deals, while Enron lost billions. The conflict of interest was quite disturbing: Was Fastow looking after the shareholders' interests or his own, which were tied up in the SPE investments?

In 2001, Enron's stock began to crumble. Even though senior management made confident statements about Enron, they were nonetheless selling

Jim Chanos Spotted Enron

Everyone seemed to be fooled by Enron. Even well-known mutual funds such as Janus, Fidelity, and Alliance Capital had big positions in the company. Did anyone figure out that Enron would collapse? Yes, some spotted the disaster and even made money off of it. Who? The short sellers.

Short selling is not new. In fact, it has been in existence since the establishment of the first stock market in the Dutch Republics in the 1600s. Short selling is the process of borrowing stock and selling it immediately. Then, the short seller waits for the stock price to fall, buys back the stock, and closes out the position. Thus, a short seller makes money when a stock price falls.

One of the top short sellers is James Chanos, who started as a stock analyst in the early 1980s. Since he had no problem making "sell" recommendations, he was not like other analysts. One of his calls was to go negative on Baldwin-United, a fast-growing financial firm. It was a gutsy call, and Chanos had to withstand strident criticism from fellow analysts and the CEO of Baldwin-United. (Chanos even received several death threats.) But Chanos engaged in extensive analysis of the company's financials and saw many problems. Within a year, the company was bankrupt.

After this, he started his own short-only fund, which did quite well during the 1980s, making money on failed leveraged companies and savings and loans. His performance in the Soaring Nineties, though, was terrible. After all, one of his biggest shorts was none other than the mighty AOL. The stock went up and up, greatly damaging Chanos's portfolio.

substantial stakes. Between February and October 2001, Lay sold $70.1 million in stock.

Interestingly enough, in the fall of 2001, Enron had a "lock-down" of its employee retirement account, which meant that its employees could not sell any stock. Lock-downs are not illegal; they give companies a way to keep things stable during administrative changes to a retirement account. But in this case, it was terrible timing.

By December 2001, Enron was the biggest bankruptcy in U.S. history, wiping out billions in shareholder value and retirement accounts. Thousands lost their jobs.

In the wake of this disaster, the markets swooned. The public was outraged, as was Congress. Wall Street called it the "Enron Effect," as many other companies came under scrutiny. Were there any other Enron-style time bombs ready to go off?

But in early 2000, his luck turned. Every year, Chanos holds a small convention for short sellers — called "Bears in Hibernation" — and everyone votes on their top three short sale candidates. Most of the crowd voted for Enron. Despite this, he was reluctant because he had been burned so many times on New Age companies. But could all the short sellers be wrong?

Chanos went through the hundreds of filings of Enron, and even though he is a financial whiz, he had trouble understanding many of the footnotes (interestingly enough, a Goldman Sachs analyst once said he had to take the company's word on its numbers because they were so complex).

Later in this book, I will return to the expert techniques that Chanos employs to spot problems in financial statements. Here are some of the red flags he noticed at Enron:

- The company was bragging about its big investment in broadband in 2000–2001. At the same time, Chanos made lots of money shorting failed broadband companies.
- Enron said it was similar to an investment firm. But, according to Chanos, Enron was selling at six times its book value. Typically, a financial firm would sell at two times its book value.
- He noticed a vague footnote that indicated a senior-level executive was a general partner in several SPEs that Enron was dealing with. Later, he would find out it was Fastow.
- Most important, he really did not know how the company made money. (Of course, the answer turned out to be that it did not make any money.)

The Players and the Game

The suspicions triggered by Enron's collapse led to a substantial crisis in confidence, and the markets continued to fall and fall. Just as in the 1930s, Congress and the president offered bold reforms. These reforms will ultimately lead to a system that will be more robust and help promote growth in the U.S. system.

This does not mean you should not be vigilant. The fact is that many of the players in the financial system have interests that diverge from your own. The next several sections will give you a look at the main players in the financial system — which should underscore the key theme of this book: You need to make your own decisions. And this means reading, understanding, and analyzing financial statements for yourself.

Investment Bankers

An investment bank is a financial adviser for a company. Its services include raising money through a public offering of stock or debt and structuring merger and acquisition (M&A) transactions. For these services, an investment bank can generate hefty fees. It thus has an incentive to encourage its clients to, well, engage in offering stock or debt or buying or selling companies.

Investment banks can also be crucial in structuring financial instruments that achieve the goals of companies. One of the most influential was from the premier investment bank of Goldman Sachs. Basically, the firm developed a security called a Monthly Income Preferred Security (MIPS) that could be classified either as a debt or as an equity instrument. Also, it was tax deductible. Certainly, this seems like a CFO's dream. The U.S. Treasury, IRS, and SEC made several attempts to eliminate this security throughout the 1990s, but they were beaten back by the strong lobbies of the financial community and corporate America.

Enron was one of the early users of the MIPS, employing it in late 1993 for a Caribbean tax haven. This ploy allowed Enron to increase its credit rating by effectively hiding its real status.

Investment bankers also helped Enron structure its SPEs. In fact, some of the investment bankers who structured these deals were also directors of the SPEs.

Such conflicts are not uncommon. Actually, they permeate the investment banking community and are not likely to go away. This is not to say that investment bankers are shareholders' natural enemies. However, investment bankers have a big incentive to engage in many transactions given the fact that their compensation is based primarily on the transactions of their corporate clients, and this is apt to give them a rosy view of any given transaction.

Stock Analysts

In general, Wall Street analysts study stocks, forecast earnings, and provide recommendations. That's established knowledge among investors, but relatively few investors realize that analysts come in three flavors — sell-side, buy-side, and independent — and that the different types make their services available to different kinds of clients.

Sell-Side and Buy-Side

Basically, a sell-side analyst is one who works for a brokerage firm such as Merrill Lynch or Morgan Stanley, one that gets commissions from selling stock. If you are a client of a full-service brokerage firm, you will often get research reports from your stockbroker, who is assuredly in the sell-side camp. You will also see sell-side analysts on television and quoted in the press — they're in the business of promoting sales, and the more people who take their advice, the happier they and their employers are.

A buy-side analyst, on the other hand, is employed by a money management firm (a mutual fund, pension fund, or similar institution). You are likely not to get buy-side reports or even see these analysts on television or quoted in the press. Why? A buy-side analyst is essentially developing research to support better investment decisions on the part of the people paying for the service. Firms that hire buy-side analysts use the advice for competitive advantage and have no interest whatsoever in sharing that advantage with anyone else, including you. For example, one of the hallmarks of the success of the Fidelity funds has been its deep bench of strong analysts, and Fidelity makes its money when people buy into its funds, not when they follow its lead in the market.

Most sell-side analysts will have a rating system for a stock. Typically, these ratings are very positive, such as "buy," "strong buy," "trading buy," and so on. In fact, the rating system is different from one firm to the next — making it difficult for even professional investors to decipher the recommendations. Firms like Zack's and First Call, which follow consensus analyst estimates, will have sophisticated numbering systems to try to standardize analyst recommendations.

However, the biggest problem with sell-side research is the conflict of interest. Here's an example: Suppose the management of Fast Co. retains Finance Co. to take the company public. Finance Co. loves this sort of business; the initial public offering (IPO) will net it a hefty fee of $5 million. Besides, Fast Co. is likely to need more investment banking services in the future, and if it's happy with this deal it will bring Finance Co. its M&A plans and secondary offerings for years to come.

But Finance Co. doesn't just set up deals like this one. It also has a team of sell-side analysts who advise eager would-be investors on what's hot and what's not. Now, suppose one of those analysts has done enough homework to know that Fast Co. really ought to be called "Fast and Loose Co." What happens to that information? If it gets out right when Fast Co. is hoping everybody will flock round to buy its stock, what do you think the response will be? No doubt, the CEO of Fast Co. will be angry — probably angry enough to take the business to another firm. So Finance Co. analysts always have an incentive to slant research reports in favor of investment banking clients.

And it's not just a matter of hiding negative information. The analyst may love Fast Co. — love it enough to buy lots of its stock and therefore have a strong interest in seeing its price climb and climb. And the more positive the research report, the easier it will be for Finance Co.'s stockbrokers to sell the stock to clients, thus generating commissions.

For example, consider this charming exchange of e-mail notes between an outside institutional investor and an analyst who had made about $12 million in banking fees in 2001:

> From: John D. Faig [outside institutional investor]
> To: Henry Blodget [Merrill Lynch analyst]
>
> What's so interesting about GoTo except the banking fees???
>
> From: Henry Blodget
> To: John D. Faig
>
> Nothin.

That was part of a bombshell that hit the analyst community in early 2002. New York Attorney General Eliot Spitzer had been investigating the securities industry and struck pay dirt with a subpoena issued to Merrill Lynch in January 2002. Merrill Lynch's stock price fell 12 percent on the news. Spitzer called analysts' reports "biased," "distorted," and "misleading" and announced that he believed that the reports were mere attempts to get investment banking clients.

Other correspondence showed analysts were often privately negative on a stock, but still kept their positive recommendation for the public. An analyst at Merrill Lynch called InfoSpace a "piece of junk" even though it had the highest rating of 1–1.

The brokerage industry has always denied any connection between investment banking and analysis. It claimed to maintain a so-called Chinese Wall between the two. But a May *Wall Street Journal* article uncovered written agreements in which analysts were compensated based on attracting investment banking clients. One contract showed that an analyst could get anywhere from 1 to 3 percent of the firm's net profit per transaction. (Of course, the poor analyst had to put up with a cap of $250,000, but that's enough to cover a lot of fancy donuts at coffee break.)

In response to the investigation, Merrill Lynch agreed to pay a fine of $100 million and make a variety of reforms. But, in the end, it is still in the interest of sell-side analysts to be on the side of investment banking clients, and you can assume that this interest will tend to influence their thinking even when they don't actively embrace and promote it.

Independent Research

OK, what about independent research? An independent researcher works for a firm that has no investment banking ties. During the 1960s, boutique research firms of this type were common, but the investment bankers and brokerages swallowed them up over the next couple of decades. These days, with the much-publicized problems of sell-side research, we are likely to see a growth of such boutique firms again.

ChangeWave Investment Research is a good example of an independent firm. It publishes an advisory service that involves daily contact with a network of 3,500 members, which include top analysts as well as senior managers at companies. ChangeWave sends these members surveys, asking questions such as, "Are you increasing your purchases of Sun servers?" and so on. Speaking of Sun, ChangeWave was ahead of the curve when its survey showed that companies were shifting toward lower end applications.

The problem for individual investors? Well, these types of products are geared for hedge funds, private pension portfolio managers, and institutional portfolio managers. As a result, they carry a hefty price tag; these services can cost $5,000 or more per year. As for ChangeWave, its reports cost $15,000.

Keep in mind, though, that if you want quality research information, you will probably need to pay for it. Research always costs somebody something. If someone offers to give it to you for free, assume it has strings attached.

Another approach for individual investors is to consider a ratings service such as Morningstar (more on these in Chapter 13). The fees are affordable and the research is top-notch.

Regulators

Many government agencies appeared to be quite lax during the late 1990s. In fact, Enron was masterful in taking advantage of this open atmosphere. Some of the wins for Enron included:

Sell-Side Research

Despite the problems, sell-side research does have some value. In fact, some top-notch sell-side analysts have great reputations — and deserve them. Prudential Securities, for instance, is known for being more willing than most to make "sell" recommendations. The firm put a "sell" recommendation on Enron when it was at $20 per share. It put one on Kmart, even saying it thought the company would go bust (it did). At the time, the stock was at $4.75. Within a few months, it was a penny stock. Then again, Prudential sold its investment banking business in December 2000.

Here are some tips for evaluating the potential usefulness of sell-side research:

- Look at the performance history of the analyst, and figure out how much money investors would have made or lost by following the recommendations for the past several years.
- Avoid analysts who do lots of interviews for the press and CNBC. How much time can they have left to devote to research? You can figure their main purpose is to hype stocks.
- Ignore price targets and overall recommendations. These are highly subjective. Does an analyst really know what a stock price will do in the next six months or year? Probably not.
- Be wary if the analyst provides investment banking services for a company on the recommended list.
- Go ahead and read research reports even if you're not keen on following the analyst's advice, as they can provide some insight into overall industry trends. It's good background information.
- Pay attention when analysts go against the grain of the market. Even with Enron, some analysts had a negative view of the stock. It is definitely a good exercise to look at these reports and see what you think about the rationale they offer.

- Partial deregulation of the national electricity marketplace.
- The passage of the Commodity Futures Modernization Act of 2000, which exempted Enron's electronic trading system from regulatory oversight.
- Hundreds of millions in subsidies for overseas investments.
- Exemption from the Public Utility Holding Company Act.
- Exemption from the Investment Company Act of 1940. This helped the firm create the more than 3,000 limited partnerships, which were important for hiding liabilities off the balance sheet.

Ken Lay also used his corporate board in political ways. For example, in 1992, the chair of the Commodity Futures Trading Commission, Wendy Gramm, helped pass a rule that exempted energy futures from government regulation. A few weeks later, Lay placed Gramm on the board of Enron. Lay also named Mack McLarty — a top adviser to President Clinton — to the board. In fact, Lay played golf with President Clinton and President Bush (and spent a night at the White House during the Bush term). Bush's economic adviser, Lawrence Lindsey, and Trade Representative Robert Zoellick were advisers to Enron.

Enron also benefited from lack of oversight from the SEC. For three years before the Enron bankruptcy, the SEC did not perform any review of the company's filings — even though the filings were both complex and questionable. Of course, the SEC has had budget cuts and turnover in its workforce, and it has jurisdiction over 12,000 public companies — so by necessity it must be selective. The policy at the SEC is to engage in extensive reviews of a company's financial statements every three years (a policy that may change because of the Enron debacle).

Then again, the SEC was quite aggressive in terms of setting new policy during the late 1990s. The chair of the SEC at this time was Arthur Levitt, who spent 16 years on Wall Street and also chaired the American Stock Exchange. Some of the reforms he was responsible for include plain English rules for financial statements, better sales practices and compensation for brokers, the introduction of better communications for investors (called the Fair Disclosure rule or Regulation FD), and requiring the disclosure of compensation for auditors.

One of his most important initiatives was to investigate aggressive accounting for financial statements. Levitt highlighted this in his September 1998 speech, which has come to be called "The Numbers Game." Among his prescient comments in that speech, Levitt said:

> Increasingly, I have become concerned that the motivation to meet Wall Street earnings expectations may be overriding common sense business practices. Too many corporate managers, auditors, and analysts are participants in a game of nods and winks. In the zeal to satisfy consensus earnings estimates and project a smooth earnings path, wishful thinking may be winning the day over faithful representation.
>
> As a result, I fear that we are witnessing an erosion in the quality of earnings, and therefore, the quality of financial reporting. Managing may be giving way to manipulation; integrity may be losing out to illusion.

It is likely that the focus of the SEC on financial statements allowed for the eventual uncovering of the many abuses on Wall Street, especially Enron.

The *Wall Street Journal's* Best Analysts List

Every June, the *Wall Street Journal* publishes a comprehensive report titled "Best on the Street Analysts." In the report, the *Journal* really looks at one criterion: Which analysts do best at picking stocks? The report not only looks at the big firms but also at the obscure ones. In all, the *Journal* analyzed the performance of over 4,000 analysts from more than 200 firms. Of these, 242 analysts made the cut. The report is divided into 49 different industry sectors, which makes it particularly helpful in homing in on an analyst who is looking at the fields you want to consider.

Despite a tough year for stocks in 2001, many analysts were still able to pick winners. The *Journal* report had such highlights as these:

- Peter Benedict, a specialty retail analyst at CIBC World Markets, thought there were some good retailers at great valuations and essentially zero expectations of performance on Wall Street. One of his picks, Global Sports, saw its stock surge 579 percent.
- Then there was Internet analyst Mark Rowen, with Prudential Securities. In February 2001, he recommended getting rid of Amazon.com (a good call), but then recommended buying Digital River, which went up 570 percent.
- Mercedes Sanchez, an apparel analyst at Raymond James & Associates, selected fashion chain Chico's FAS. She thought women would not stop shopping even in a recession and she was right. The stock climbed 185 percent.
- Investing is often called an educated form of gambling — and you can invest *in* gambling if you want to. Todd Jordan, who covers the casino industry for Dresdner Kleinwort Wasserstein, made a gutsy call and recommended buying Harrah's Entertainment after the 9/11 tragedy. The result was a 166 percent gain.

Plaintiffs' Attorneys

A shareholder lawsuit is something that is not preventive; rather, it is the response when a company engages in fraud or even criminal activities. (Such suits cannot be filed over bad decisions or even stupid ones.) Basically, a shareholder suit, which is also known as a derivative suit, is brought on behalf of shareholders against a company, its executives, and its board members.

Perhaps these suits could, in a sense, be a deterrent to company misconduct. So why was this not the case in the late 1990s? Simply put, in the mid-1990s, Congress passed legislation that made it tougher to launch shareholder lawsuits. The main reason for the law was the assertion that too many frivolous lawsuits were hampering corporate America. In light of the recent scandals, such as Enron, it seems likely that at least some of the legislation will be rolled back.

In a shareholder suit, a law firm will issue a press release and attempt to get investors to join the case. Typically, many of these suits are filed, then consolidated into a broad class of investors. But the process can be long, lasting several years.

In most cases, a suit is settled. As an investor, do not expect to get all your money back — perhaps you will get 10 to 20 cents on the dollar. Of course, the plaintiff's attorneys will get a big chunk of the money in fees. There are also administrative fees.

As for Enron, the fact that the company declared bankruptcy threw a wrench in the works. That is, a bankruptcy filing stays any outstanding litigation. If the company is liquidated, the suits will be worthless, as any assets will go to the company's creditors. Then again, the shareholder actions against the executives and directors and the auditor are still extant; the firm's bankruptcy doesn't affect them.

Finally, the SEC may also fine a company and set up a restitution fund for shareholders. Unfortunately, the amounts paid out will typically be nowhere near the amount shareholders lost.

Credit Agencies

A credit agency is an independent company that analyzes the debt structure of a company. The two main agencies are Moody's and Standard & Poor's (S&P). These agencies did not spot the problems of Enron — as well as other major bankruptcies — until it was too late. Moody's and S&P claimed that these companies provided fraudulent information, but the SEC believes that the credit agencies should have looked deeper. In fact, the SEC is considering regulating these agencies.

Auditors

Basically, the SEC requires that all public companies have audited financial statements for annual reports, IPOs, and debt offerings.

It would be impractical for an auditor to analyze all the information flowing through a company. Just imagine trying to decipher all the deals of a multinational such as General Electric. It would be impossible. As a result, an auditor will take samples of various departments and see if things match up. If matters look askew, the auditor will analyze further.

So sampling necessarily includes the risk that the auditors will miss something. Also, in some cases, public companies have not been forthright with their auditors. Sometimes a company will even lie to its auditors — as ZZZ

Best did when it showed its auditors boxes of "inventory" that were really full of bricks. (It wasn't in the brick business!)

And some auditors have been lax or even downright dishonest. They have allowed matters to slide past that they should have reported. In fact, Enron has not been the only case of major auditor blow-ups. Other examples:

- After HFS merged with CUC, HFS learned that its merger partner inflated earnings by $500 million. The newly merged company, Cendant, received a $335 million settlement from CUC's auditor, Ernst & Young.
- The SEC charged the management of Sunbeam for inflating earnings. The company's auditor, Arthur Andersen, settled a shareholder lawsuit for $110 million. The high-profile CEO of Sunbeam (known as "Chainsaw Al" Dunlap) paid a $500,000 fine to the SEC.
- Waste Management inflated earnings by $1 billion. The auditor, Arthur Andersen, settled a shareholder lawsuit for $229 million.
- Investors lost $570 million in a fraud scheme that was part of the nonprofit Baptist Foundation. The auditor, Arthur Andersen, agreed to settle civil suits for $217 million.

One the major problems with auditing is the pressure for the firms to get new business — or maintain current accounts. Young auditors always hear this old story: A company wanted to inflate its earnings and interviewed many auditing firms. When the company asked, "What is 2 plus 2?" the answer was always 4, except for one firm — the one that got the job — whose answer was, "What did you have in mind?" In other words, the conflict is that a company pays an auditor. If a company does not like the results, it can get a new auditor.

Another problem is consulting. The top accounting firms have consulting arms, which provide services for IT integration and corporate strategy. This gives the firms an incentive to low-bid auditing services as a way to get contracts for lucrative consulting gigs. For example, in 2001, Arthur Andersen received $25 million in auditing fees and $27 million in consulting fees for its work on Enron.

However, the new reforms passed in 2002 make it more difficult for auditors to receive consulting fees.

The Media

The media have devoted more and more coverage to financial matters since the beginning of the bull market of the 1990s, with many specialized magazines, newspapers, and even television shows on the market. But the media are not perfect. A journalist may write one or two stories a day — making it nearly impossible to do extensive research.

Or look at television shows such as CNBC, *Wall Street Week*, CNN *Moneyline*, and Bloomberg TV. Televised interviews simply do not have enough time to cover a subject in a deep manner. Rather, they go in for catchy phrases and sound bites — fun to watch, but not nutritious.

Besides, the press tends to reflect the general sentiment of the market. When the market was surging in the late 1990s, the press was quite bullish. Then again, when the markets turned down in 2000–2002, the press turned decidedly negative.

Financial Adviser or Stockbroker

For the most part, financial advisers are not stock pickers. Instead, they rely mostly on their firm's research department for this (which, as noted earlier, is not particularly great). Moreover, a financial adviser may have a hundred or more clients to handle. If you have a small account, will your financial adviser pay much attention to you? Chances are slim.

An interesting case came up at a Morgan Stanley office. The branch manager — who was in charge of the regulatory compliance issues for the branch — was also a broker and handled the account for a CFO. The CFO decided to sell large amounts of stock, which would have put pressure on the price. So the branch manager told other brokers in the office to recommend that their clients start *buying* the stock.

Financial advisers work under an interesting regulatory structure. For major cases, the SEC will handle matters. However, for most matters, the brokerage industry polices itself. This is done on two levels:

1. The National Association of Securities Dealers (NASD) is a self-regulatory organization funded by the industry to regulate the industry.
2. Each brokerage firm is also required to have a compliance department to oversee the branch offices, and each branch office has a branch manager who enforces the rules.

Unfortunately, the NASD tends to be far away and out of sight, and if a branch manager is also a broker, there is a potential conflict of interest, as seen in the example described earlier.

Another problem is that compliance may take a hands-off approach to top-producing brokers who generate substantial profits for the firm. This may have been the case at Lehman Brothers, where a broker bilked clients out of $125 million over a 15-year period. (See the sidebar titled "Taking Precautions with Your Broker" for advice on ways to avoid problems with a rogue broker.)

Taking Precautions with Your Broker

Your broker has a fiduciary responsibility to look out your for interests. Unfortunately, some brokers may be tempted to look after their own interests instead — even defraud you. The first step in picking a broker is doing a background check. You can do an Internet search with one of the major engines, such as Google.com. In the search query, use terms such as "lawsuits," "judgments," "disciplinary actions," and "complaints." You also should visit the NASD Web site at http://www.nasdr.com, which includes a comprehensive database of the history of licensed stockbrokers (see Figure 1.2). It will provide info on pending arbitrations and civil suits, formal criminal or regulatory investigations, judgments and liens, bankruptcies, and complaints of forgery, theft, or misappropriation of funds.

It is also a good idea to use the site to do a background check on the brokerage firm — especially if the firm is small.

Once you hire a broker, pay attention. Do you get answers to your questions?

Also, always check your mail. Are you getting confirmations of trades you did not authorize? If so, the broker may be *churning* your account — that is, making unnecessary trades for the sole purpose of increasing commissions.

Finally, beware if your broker says things like "guaranteed" or "sure thing." There is no such thing in the investment world.

Attorneys

The beauty of the U.S. judicial system is that everyone has the right to counsel. In addition, it provides special protections for clients, such as the attorney–client privilege. This means that information clients disclose to their attorneys is kept confidential unless certain exceptions are triggered. Only the client can waive the privilege.

Because of this privilege, it is difficult for an attorney to be a whistleblower when a client is engaging in illegal behavior. In fact, the ethics rules may be different from one state to the other. Besides, an attorney has a duty to represent the interests of a client, and putting a client in jail would definitely not be in the client's interest.

This was the tough situation for Enron's outside counsel, Vinson & Elkins. Enron was the firm's biggest client, with about $35.6 million in fees in 2001. Moreover, Vinson & Elkins developed tremendous expertise in the complex and innovative energy deals that Enron was creating. When Enron was struc-

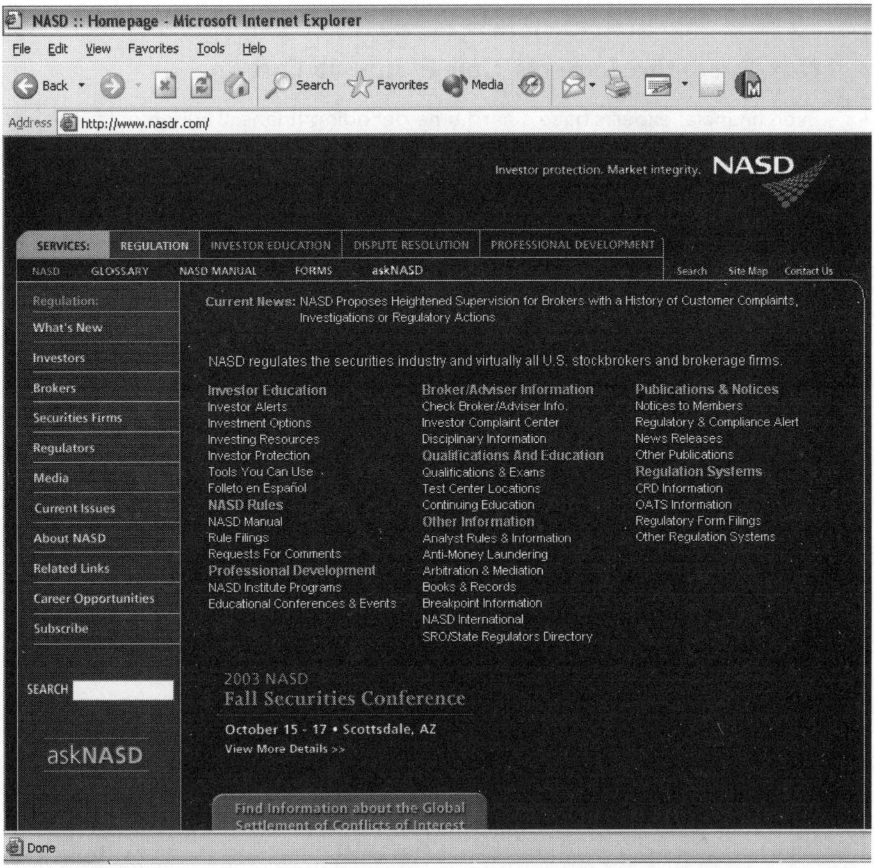

Figure 1.2 You can do a background check on your stockbroker by going to www.nasdr.com.

turing its complex partnership deals, Vinson & Elkins did raise many concerns (especially about conflicts of interest), but Enron's management did not want to hear this. They were paying their attorneys to make their wishes come true, not to tell them what they could not or should not do.

Something else interesting is that the board of Enron twice waived conflict of interest policies to allow for Andrew Fastow's transactions, without consulting Vinson & Elkins. With no such policy, would it then be OK for Fastow to have these partnerships? Again, it was a murky situation for the law firm.

In light of the Enron scandal, it is likely that we will see some changes to the ethical requirements of attorneys. But these changes will probably be small. For the most part, do not expect a company's corporate counsel to protect its shareholders.

Not Even the Experts Can Figure It Out

Even financial experts have a hard time decoding financial statements. This was the case with Jim Chanos, as described earlier.

Often, the complexity level is high with multinational corporations. For example, insurance company American International Group (AIG) has more than 250 subsidiaries. What's more, the insurance industry is based on estimates. How many people will die? How many claims will need to be paid? There is certainly a large degree of fuzziness.

Such companies are known as "black boxes." In light of the accounting scandals, these complex companies are trying hard to make their financials clearer (a goal called *transparency*) but it could be an impossible task. As an investor, can you really track a company with 250 subsidiaries?

And, as a general rule, if you cannot understand the financials, do not invest in the company — even if the company is a brand name.

Interestingly enough, even apparently simple businesses can be made quite complex. A prime example is Coca-Cola. What can be simpler than selling sugar water? Well, if you dive into the financials, you will quickly realize that the company knows how to create complex corporate structures. Basically, Coca-Cola has spun off its bottling companies as public entities, shifting debts from the parent company to the subsidiaries. Yet Coca-Cola still has strong control, owning hefty percentages and keeping board seats. Coca-Cola itself has $1.4 billion in debt. However, if you factor in the debt of the bottlers, the figure soars to $11.2 billion.

Finally, be wary of companies that rely heavily on derivatives as a source of income. As the name implies, a *derivative* is an investment vehicle that derives from the value of an underlying asset, such as stocks, bonds, or real estate. These derivatives have many names, including options, futures, or swaps. For the most part, derivatives are extremely complex. In fact, the accounting rules are hundreds of pages long.

Enron relied heavily on derivatives — and it was OK. That is, it was OK until the markets started to fall.

Conclusion

I do not want this chapter to scare you. But when talking about the system, it doesn't do to sugarcoat things. The fact remains that it is tough for investors out there, especially if you do not have large amounts of money and clout.

But this does not mean you will ultimately fail. Far from it. Individual investors have many advantages: Unlike a mutual fund or other institutional investor, you are not required to meet quarterly targets for your portfolio.

Individual investors can invest for the long term. You don't have to deal with pressures like the ones a fund's board of directors can apply. Most important, individual investors have access to the same types of information that institutions have — and much of the information is affordable if not free.

When it comes to your money, it is ultimately your responsibility. Thus, do not take information from those in the system on blind faith. They have agendas that can run counter to your interests. The decision to buy, short, or sell a stock needs to be yours — and only yours.

Finally, I do not want to imply that attorneys, CPAs, analysts, and other professionals are all scumbags. Many are honest and hardworking. Their dedication is part of what has made the United States the world's most powerful country.

But during the late 1990s, excesses were prominent and there were some that crossed the line. It has been a painful process, but it will be good in the end.

Enough with the system. Time to start finding out how to make some money!

Sources

1. Gold, Howard R., Merrill bombshell shows corruption runs deep, *Barron's*, April 11, 2002.
2. Maremont, Mark, Tyco director says monitoring of management is stepped up, *Wall Street Journal*, May 1, 2002.
3. Gasparino, Charles, Morgan Stanley branch draws scrutiny for trading of Voicenet, *Wall Street Journal*, May 23, 2002.
4. Elgin, Ben, E*Trade: CEO pay isn't the only problem, *BusinessWeek*, May 17, 2002.
5. Hamilton, Walter, Scandals pave way for Wall St. reforms, *Los Angeles Times*, May 5, 2002.
6. Beckett, Paul, Stecklow, Steve, and McKay, Peter A., For the auditors, metals scheme is another too-interesting story, *Wall Street Journal*, May 16, 2002.
7. Gasparino, Charles and Craig, Susanne, Watchdogs of brokers face scrutiny amid mounting investor complaints, *Wall Street Journal*, May 23, 2002.
8. Schroeder, Michael, SEC mulls curbs on credit agencies amid its probe of the Enron collapse, *Wall Street Journal*, March 21, 2002.
9. Accounting failures aren't new — just more frequent, *BusinessWeek*, January 28, 2002.
10. Craig, Susanne, Amid the stock market's slide, top analysts spot big gainers, *Wall Street Journal*, June 17, 2002.
11. Saporito, Bill, How Fastow helped Enron fall, *Time*, February 12, 2002.
12. Gasparino, Charles, Analyst's contracts link pay, *Wall Street Journal*, May 6, 2002.

13. Drinkard, Jim and Farrel, Greg, Enron made a sound investment in Washington, *USA Today*, January 24, 2002.
14. Fergus, Mary Ann, Ken Lay known as man of humble beginnings, *Houston Chronicle*, January 24, 2002.
15. Weil, Jonathan, Andersen agrees to pay $217 million to settle suits over audits of Baptist Church, *Wall Street Journal*, May 6, 2002.

This book has free materials available for download from the Web Added Value™ Resource Center at www.jrosspub.com.

2

What Do Investors Need to Know About Accounting?

When does a guy decide to become an accountant?
When he realizes he doesn't have
the charisma to succeed as an undertaker.
—Anonymous (and rightly so)

Although the accounting profession is the target of constant jokes, and accounting trails the list of topics most people outside the field want to think about, accountants and accounting are nonetheless the mainstay of modern business. And many accountants leave the stereotype in broken shards; they're lively and passionate people, and they have a lot of fun both off the job and on it. Of course, I'm biased — some of my best friends are accountants, and I actually took Accounting 101 as an elective in college. But I'm right, too.

Without accounting, it would be impossible for companies to function. It is absolutely critical that managers know where they are and where they have been — that is, what their company owns and owes, what it spends (and on what), and what money is coming in and from what source. That makes attention to detail incredibly valuable to companies when selecting accountants to generate the numbers and auditors to verify them.

Integrity is also vital. For investors to plunk down their hard-earned money, a company's numbers need to be free of gimmicks. Investors want to know the real story.

In this chapter, I'll give you the proverbial "30,000-foot airplane view" of the accounting industry. You won't learn enough to be able to do the books for a friend's business and earn some extra money on the side, but you'll pick up the essential foundation that you need for deciphering a company's financial statements.

First, a step back in time....

Great Moments in Accounting History

People have been making attempts at accounting for thousands of years. In the earliest agrarian societies, landowners wanted to keep track of their wealth, and of course governments wanted to make sure they were collecting enough taxes generated from that wealth.

Even in these early days, accounting required a certain degree of literacy, as well as a way to create records and a financial system that had a standard of value. In ancient times, this was not easy and the accountant, usually known as a scribe, was in a noble profession.

Although writing and recordkeeping did improve somewhat, the accounting profession underwent very little change until the emergence of economic growth during the Renaissance in the 14th century. The major innovators of what would become modern-day accounting were Italians. For example, it was the Italians who first used Arabic numerals (certainly much easier than the unwieldy Roman numerals) to keep business records.

The biggest innovation was double-entry bookkeeping, which was invented in the 1300s but wasn't widely publicized until the late 1400s, when Luca Pacioli published a summary of everything then known about the arcane and high-tech topic of arithmetic. Pacioli brought forward other innovations, such as the general journal, credit and debit entries, trial balances, and so on. Of course, Pacioli's system was geared mainly for small businesses. Then again, in his era, there were mostly small businesses.

It was during the 1800s, with the emergence of the Industrial Revolution, that accounting underwent much change to account for large commercial organizations. To this end, the Institute of Chartered Accountants was established in England and Wales in 1880 to help bring standardization to the accounting industry. For instance, an accountant had to take an exam and meet certain ethical requirements.

U.S. business was also undergoing tremendous growth, and accountants were beginning to form their own societies. The most influential was the American Association of Public Accountants (which is now known as the American Institute of Certified Public Accountants or AICPA).

Even though these organizations introduced some standardization, this did not mean that published financial statements were common. Unless investors demanded detailed reports, companies would rarely provide them. The lack

Accounting Highlights

Pacioli tends to get much of the fame in accounting, but many others helped build the profession. For example:

- The first corporations, known as *joint stock companies,* were started in the 1600s. But when the South Sea Bubble broke and the financial markets crashed in 1720, there was tremendous anger. The public wanted to know the cause. As a result, Charles Snell started to review the financial records of the various companies and is considered perhaps the first modern auditor.
- Josiah Wedgewood, who lived between 1730 and 1795, was a true entrepreneur (he was also the grandfather of Charles Darwin). He developed new production techniques and built a thriving pottery company. However, when an economic depression hit in 1772, his business suffered tremendous losses and he really did not know their exact sources. So he began to analyze every aspect of his business: inventory, expenses, wages, internal controls, and so on. What he realized was that different products had different cost structures — and pricing had to be adjusted accordingly. In the end, he developed what we still call "cost accounting." (He also discovered that his head clerk was embezzling money — then as now, an all-too-frequent factor in unexpected losses.)
- By the beginning of the 20th century, industrial corporations were becoming increasingly complex and clearly there was a need for sophisticated accounting techniques. One such company was DuPont, which had the foresight to hire a smart financial officer, Donaldson Brown. Brown helped DuPont develop return on investment (ROI) analysis, long-range planning, extensive monthly financial reports, and make-versus-buy decision analysis. Then, in 1920, DuPont purchased a substantial portion of General Motors. Brown was brought in to restructure the operations, which involved flexible budgeting, pricing formulas for products, profit sharing plans, and modern-day cost accounting systems.

If you're interested in learning more about the history of accounting, a good Web site is http://accfinweb.account.strath.ac.uk/df/contents.html.

of standardized disclosure no doubt made it easier for unscrupulous traders to manipulate stock prices.

By and large, the U.S. government was heavily procapitalist and refrained from attempts to regulate business. With the rise of monopolies and several depressions, Congress did pass some major federal regulation such as the antitrust laws, but there was little in terms of federal requirements for public company disclosures until the Depression of the 1930s. (The next chapter will look at the effects of these laws on corporate America.)

Where Do Accounting Rules Come From?

A key part of accounting is consistency. If one company reports a transaction a certain way and another company in the same industry reports the same type of transaction in another way, it's nearly impossible for people to compare the financial statements. It is the age-old problem of apples and oranges. How do you know which company is doing better or worse? This is absolutely critical for investors.

Consequently, all public companies must publish their financial statements according to standards known as Generally Accepted Accounting Principles or GAAP. Don't rush to the store to buy a handbook that publishes the rules — they run to thousands and thousands of pages of material, and accounting firms have many shelf-feet of library space devoted to them. GAAP standards come from a variety of sources:

- *AICPA (American Institute of Certified Public Accountants)*. As noted earlier, this is the association for accountants in the United States. The AICPA is also very influential in setting accounting policy and works closely with the Financial Accounting Standards Board (described in the next paragraph). However, some critics believe that this should not be the case; they point to a conflict of interest because, in a sense, accountants are setting rules for themselves to follow. Are the resulting rules strong enough to protect investors? In light of the many scandals of 2002, the Sarbanes–Oxley Act took action to deal with this by setting up an accounting oversight agency. The AICPA also regulates the process for someone to become a CPA, which has stringent requirements: an accounting degree from a college or university, a tough five-part exam, and minimum work experience in auditing. In many companies, the CFO and other high-level finance executives are CPAs. Moreover, only a CPA can sign off on a public company.
- *FASB (Financial Accounting Standards Board)*. This is a private organization, established in 1973, that promotes accounting and reporting standards. Any FASB statement is considered authoritative by the SEC and the AICPA.
- *SEC (Securities and Exchange Commission)*. The SEC has the authority, under the Securities Exchange Act of 1934, to establish accounting and reporting standards for public companies. However, the SEC tends to rely on private pronouncements, such as those from the FASB. The next chapter will look at the SEC in much more detail.

Accounting and Global Issues

For multinational corporations, accounting can be a nightmare because of varying standards from one country to the next. Under German accounting standards, for example, DaimlerChrysler earned $733 million in 2001; under GAAP, the company reported a loss of $589 million.

To help with the situation, the International Accounting Standards Board (IASB), founded in 1973, has the ambitious goal of establishing a single standard for all companies to comply with. Such international efforts often result in very little, but the IASB may be a different story. In fact, it appears that the FASB wants to cooperate, as does the European Union.

It does help that both GAAP and the IASB standards are approached on the basis of principles. That is, the rules state a general standard and then auditors and companies apply the standard.

It is easy to see the benefits of global standards:

- Comparisons are easier to make.
- Financing can come from more than one country's marketplace.
- Companies only need to deal with one standard (no need to reconcile different systems on the financial statements).

- *PCAOB (Public Company Accounting Oversight Board)*. This has a broad mandate to deal with setting standards for auditing, quality control, and accounting ethics. The agency also has the power to inspect registered accounting firms and even bring disciplinary action. The agency, though, is under the purview of the SEC. Funding comes from public companies and not from the accounting profession.

Note: You will often hear people use the words "accounting" and "finance" interchangeably. Well, they are very different concepts. As stated earlier, accounting is about the collection, recording, and reporting of past information about a company. Finance is the process of interpreting the information and making decisions.

The Rules in Action

The best way to see how the rules of accounting operate is to look at a very basic hypothetical company: Simple Co., which develops a component for vending machines. Jane, the founder of the company, puts together the $25,000 capital she needs by cashing out her 401(K) and selling all her stock. (She didn't have much, so it's a good thing this tale begins before the crash

Financial Statements in the Digital World

It is not something that rolls off your tongue — Extensible Business Reporting Language (XBRL) — but it is likely to be extremely influential in financial statement analysis. XBRL is a set of standards that make it easier to digitally transmit and analyze financial statements. It is not just for public companies, but any company. This is a great benefit for the many users of financial statements, such as analysts, lenders, investment bankers, accountants, and regulators.

With XBRL, a company creates a standard digital tag for each piece of financial information (revenues, costs, and so on). Once this is done, a computer system can process the information and do analysis.

It should be no surprise that the tech giant Microsoft was the first company to use XBRL. So, do not be surprised to see the standard widely adopted. For more information, you can check out www.xbrl-express.com (see Figure 2.1).

of 2000–2001.) These moves bring in $20,000, and Jane also has a good friend who likes the business concept and lends her $5,000.

Jane files the necessary papers to incorporate her business and opens a company bank account. An accountant would say that she has fulfilled the requirements for one of the most basic principles of accounting: the *entity concept*. In order to generate financial statements, you have to have a separate defined entity.

The first financial statement Jane sets up is a balance sheet, which harks back to the first great chronicler of accounting, Pacioli. As the name implies, a balance sheet must be *in balance* — the basic concept of the double-entry accounting system.

Here's the fundamental formula (known as the *balance sheet formula*):

$$\text{Assets} = \text{Liabilities} + \text{Capital}$$

Basically, with the double-entry system, after every transaction, the left side (assets) must always equal the right side (liabilities + capital). If not, the difference is an error.

Assets are all the things a company owns, such as equipment, land, buildings, desks, pencils, and so on. To increase assets, a company must either borrow money, which creates liabilities, or raise money from investors, which adds capital. Another source is profits (which become part of the company's capital). Of course, a company can reduce its assets by paying for expenses or withdrawing money.

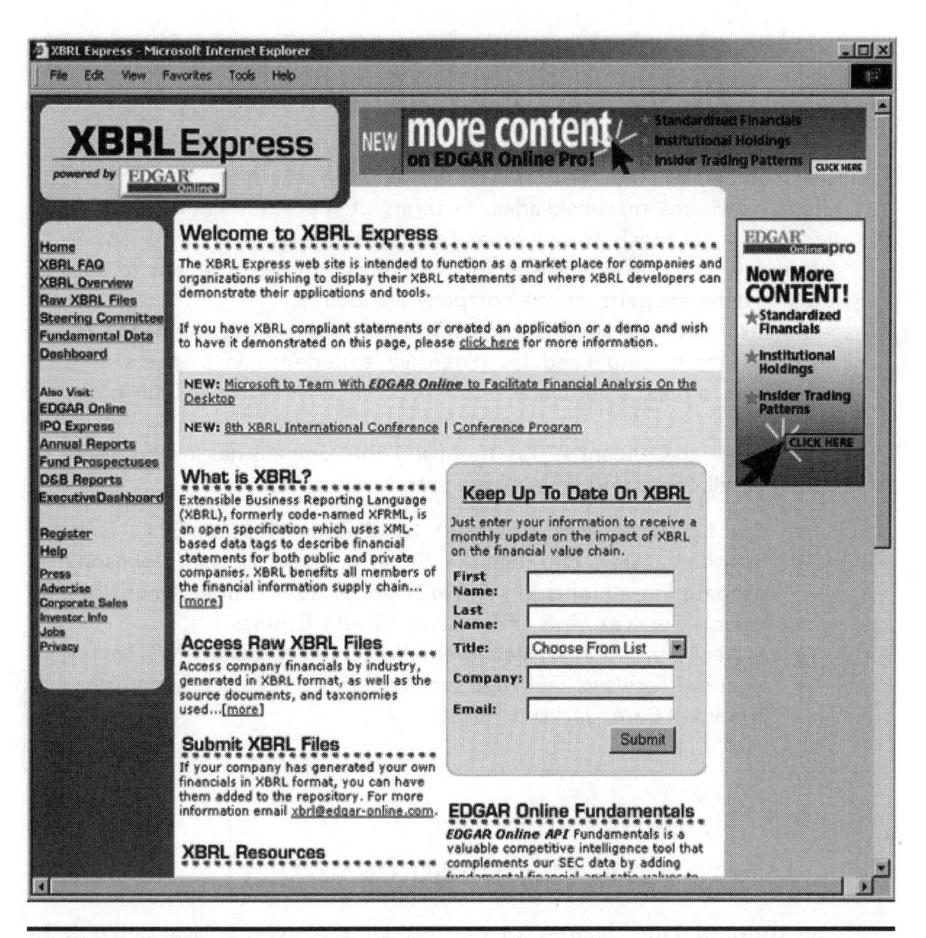

Figure 2.1 XBRL-Express.com provides a wealth of information on the emerging standard for financial statements, XBRL.

Even though Simple Co. has no sales or even products, Jane still has enough information to fill in the balance sheet formula. The assets are $25,000 in cash, the liabilities are $5,000, and the capital is Jane's investment in the business, her contribution of $20,000, which makes the formula look like this:

$$\$25,000 = \$5,000 + \$20,000$$

The formula will change often as the company engages in transactions. For example, if Jane gets another loan for $5,000, then liabilities will increase by $5,000 and cash will increase by $5,000:

A Company May Have Many Entities

As a company grows, it will often add new product lines or even purchase other companies. The result is that a company may have a variety of different divisions or subsidiaries. In terms of the entity concept, each division or subsidiary is its own separate operation and has its own financial statements. This makes it easier for the company's management to see how the different parts of the company are doing.

For example, consider Cendant. The company is the brainchild of Henry Silverman, who used his extensive experience in mergers and acquisitions to build a company with 70,000 employees and $15 billion in revenues.

According to Cendant's 2001 10-K filing, the company has five business segments, all containing several separate business units:

- *Real Estate Services.* CENTURY 21, Coldwell Banker, ERA
- *Hospitality.* Days Inn, Ramada, Super 8 Motel, Howard Johnson, Wingate Inn, Knights Inn, Travelodge, Villager Lodge, AmeriHost
- *Vehicle Services.* Avis, PHH Arval, Wright Express
- *Travel Distribution.* Galileo International, Cheap Tickets, WizComm
- *Financial Services.* FISI*Madison, Benefit Consultants, Long Term Preferred Care, Jackson Hewitt

$$\$30{,}000 = \$10{,}000 + \$20{,}000$$

Now suppose Jane decides to pay off all the loans. Cash will fall by $10,000 and liabilities will fall to zero. Again, the equation will be in balance:

$$\$20{,}000 = \$0 + \$20{,}000$$

Then Jane can withdraw $5,000 from the business, in which case the cash falls by $5,000 and equity falls by $5,000. Yep, the equation is in balance:

$$\$15{,}000 = \$0 + \$15{,}000$$

Currently, the company is not very dynamic. To get things moving, Jane needs to build a real business. Forget about paying off the loans and withdrawing cash; those were just illustrations of the way the formula works, not something someone starting a real business would do. Rolling back to the point where Jane took out that extra $5,000 loan, she has assets worth $30,000 and a corresponding amount of liabilities and capital. She decides to buy supplies for $10,000 so she can build the components she plans to sell. These components are called inventory.

As is the American way, Jane does not immediately write a check to pay for the $10,000 in supplies. Instead, she agrees to pay off her suppliers in 30 days. In a sense, she is getting a loan from her suppliers, which is a short-term loan of the type called an *accounts payable*. Since this is a liability, it must be recorded on the right side of the balance sheet.

She also purchases equipment for $10,000 to allow her to make the components, for which she signs a check. As a result, the cash balance falls by $10,000 but the equipment is recorded as an asset on the balance sheet.

Assets		*Liabilities*	
Cash	$20,000	Loan	$10,000
Inventory	$10,000	Accounts payable	$10,000
Equipment	$10,000	Equity	
		Capital	$20,000
Total assets	$40,000	Total liabilities and equity	$40,000

Suppose Jane got a great deal on the equipment and it is really worth $15,000. Shouldn't she record this as a $15,000 asset on the balance sheet? Nope. Accounting sticks to the *historical cost method*, which means that assets must

Historical Cost Breakdown

Inflation can distort the historical cost method. For instance, suppose a company purchased land in southern California in 1950 for $100,000. On the balance sheet, it would still be booked at $100,000 in 2000, but of course the value would be much higher. In fact, some investors will try to delve into a company's balance sheets and find these undervalued assets.

This was especially the case during the surge in hostile takeovers of the 1980s. With easy financing (such as junk bonds), a raider could purchase another company at a low price, sell off its assets at a higher price, and then pay off most of the debt. This is what the Gordon Gekko character did as a career in the movie *Wall Street.*

Some countries suffer from *hyperinflation,* that is, a general price increase of 100 percent or more over a three-year period. This obviously makes historical valuations look ludicrous on a company's books. When Brazil ran into hyperinflation during the early 1990s, Brazilian accounting standards were changed to allow for "inflation accounting," making a correction that washed out the effects of inflation and made financial statements easier to understand.

be recorded at what the company paid for them. That's the only objective measure — anyone can name any value for a thing, and allowing estimates of value would make financial statements too subjective to be useful. Besides, when calculating the profitability of a company, you have a truer gauge if a company uses the actual costs for its purchases.

Jane has managed to build her product all by herself, paying herself a salary barely enough to eat on (lots of peanut butter sandwiches), and now she has $10,000 of inventory to sell — and she'd better sell it soon, as her creditors want their money back. Her balance sheet can't track sales for her properly, so it's time set up the next part of the company financials: an *income statement*. The income statement shows what a company generates in profits or losses over a period of time. This brings up another accounting concept known as *periodicity*. That is, for financial statements to be meaningful, they must be completed on a regular basis, such as every year, or every quarter, or even every month. If not, a company can hide problems until it is too late.

Back to the income statement. The basic formula is easy:

Profits (or Losses) = Revenues – Expenses

That $10,000 on the balance sheet is what Jane *paid* for her inventory, not what she needs to sell it for; if she just gets her money out, she's no worse off than when she started. Jane works hard and is able to generate $30,000 in sales, but to do this she incurs a variety of expenses. First, there were the costs of producing the goods (called the "cost of goods sold") — the $10,000. Next, her salary was $5,000, rent $2,000, advertising $5,000, and interest on the loan $400.

The income statement looks like this:

Revenues	$30,000
Cost of goods sold	$10,000
Gross profits	$20,000
Salaries	$5,000
Rent	$2,000
Advertising	$5,000
Interest	$400
Total operating expenses	$12,400
Income before taxes	$7,600
Taxes (30%)	$2,280
Net income	$5,320

On an income statement, the top always shows revenue items, which is why revenue is often called the *top line*. If you hear analysts say a company has "strong top-line growth," they mean the company is showing nice revenue increases. At the end of the income statement is the *net income* item, which indicates whether a company has generated a profit or a loss. This is called the *bottom line*.

As you can see, it is not easy for a company to generate a profit because of the myriad expenses. A change in any of its expenses, such as advertising or salaries, could easily mean losses for the company. Thus, it is important for a company to have accurate accounting so it can track its progress.

Fortunately, Jane is able to generate a decent profit. However, do not be misled into thinking that net income is the same thing as cash. In fact, it is possible for a company to be profitable yet have negative cash flow. How is this strange result possible? Companies operate on a system called *accrual accounting,* which separates business events from transfers of cash following these basic principles:

- Recognize revenues when they are earned, not when you get the cash.
- Recognize expenses when they are incurred, not when you pay out cash for them.

Example: As noted earlier, Jane's customers have bought her products for a total of $30,000. Of this amount, only $10,000 arrives in cash (well, in checks she can deposit, but that's the same thing in accounting terms); the rest of the amount is payable in 30 days — most of her customers expect the same kind of terms she got from her own suppliers. But according to accrual accounting, she has *earned* the whole $30,000 now and must report this total on the income statement.

To help sell these goods, she spent $5,000 in advertising but did not pay the invoice right away as it wasn't due for 30 days. But since she incurred this cost — by agreeing to an invoice — she must expense this item now.

This brings into play another important accounting concept called the *matching principle*, which means that a company must report all expenses that relate to its reported earned revenues. If not, a company could artificially increase its profits by deferring the recognition of certain expenses (just imagine if the company reported its advertising expenses a year later). In fact, the income statement section of this book (Chapters 6 and 7) will give you a look at tricky methods a company can use to manipulate the matching principle.

Something else to realize is that the balance sheet and income statement will interrelate. When Jane earned the $30,000, $20,000 was owed to her company within 30 days. This is an asset to her company and must be recorded on the balance sheet as an account receivable. The $10,000 in cash received is also recorded as an asset in the cash line item. When she takes care of these income items, her balance sheet would look like this:

Assets		*Liabilities*	
Cash	$30,000	Loans	$10,000
Accounts receivable	$20,000		
Inventory	$0	Accounts payable	$10,000
Equipment	$10,000	Equity	
		Capital	$20,000
Total assets	$60,000	Total liabilities and equity	$40,000

Does something look wrong with this balance sheet? Definitely. It violates the balance sheet formula because the assets are now $20,000 higher than the liabilities and capital. What's wrong? Jane has failed to make some important adjustments.

First, to generate the revenues, the company had expenses. Some of these expenses were paid from the company's cash and others were borrowed in the form of accounts payable. Let's suppose that of the total expenses of $14,680, $5,000 is cash and $9,680 is accounts payable (including the $2,280 in taxes due, which would actually be reported on a different line, but I want to keep things simple for the moment).

The revised balance sheet looks like this:

Assets		*Liabilities*	
Cash	$25,000	Loans	$10,000
Accounts receivable	$20,000		
Inventory	0	Accounts payable	$19,680
Equipment	$10,000	Equity	
		Capital	$20,000
Total assets	$55,000	Total liabilities and equity	$49,680

It still does not balance! What is the problem? Jane's company made a profit — and profits increase a company's equity. So she needs to add the profit on the right side of the balance sheet in the equity section. This requires a new item that is called *retained earnings*, since the profits are kept in the company (unless the company decides to pay them out to shareholders in the form of a *dividend*). Revising the balance sheet by adding $5,380 in retained earnings means everything is in balance:

Assets		*Liabilities*	
Cash	$25,000	Loan	$10,000
Accounts receivable	$20,000		
Inventory	0	Accounts payable	$19,680
Equipment	$10,000	Equity	
		Capital	$20,000
		Retained earnings	$5,380
Total assets	$55,000	Total liabilities and equity	$55,000

A Self-Professed Accounting Skeptic

With over 30 years' experience in investing, Charlie Dreifus has seen many fads come and go. Through it all, he has kept a very strong value approach to investing. The success is evident in his fund, Royce Special Equity, with over $500 million in assets.

Dreifus is an avid reader of company financials. His criteria, in fact, are quite strict. He looks for companies with high return on assets, low debt, and a competitive niche. Interestingly enough, he approaches investments as if they were M&A candidates. In other words, is this company cheap enough that another company would want to buy it?

A big factor that Dreifus focuses on is cash flow. While many analysts talked about *burn rates* (the amount of negative cash flow) of high-tech companies in the 1990s, Dreifus looked for companies that had substantial cash *build rates* instead.

A company that met Dreifus's criteria was Benjamin Moore. Ironically enough, it was another famed value investor, Warren Buffett, who bought out the company for a nice premium.

A big advantage for Dreifus is that he studied under Abraham Briloff during the 1970s. Briloff was one of the first to develop techniques to uncover aggressive accounting. He wrote an influential book on the matter called *More Debits Than Credits: The Burnt Investor's Guide to Financial Statements* that is still worth reading. (Unfortunately, it has gone out of print, but you may still find it via interlibrary loan or a used book dealer.)

Accordingly, Dreifus spends a great deal of time analyzing a company's accounting. He refers to the process as "deep value with accounting cynicism." He maintains that when sifting through the publicly available data on a specific company, it's essential to insist on ample indication that conservative accounting practices are being followed. He recognizes that the statements are never fully cut and dried, and he doesn't look for any one single disclosure or item. But the drudgery of poring through financials and reading all the footnotes produces a useful mosaic: "a sense as to the overall veracity and integrity of the numbers, and whether the company is conservative or aggressive in its accounting practices."

Jane isn't quite finished with her first set of financials, but this is enough to go on with for now. To round out the set, she'll need to make something called a *cash flow statement*. Basically, this adjusts the balance sheet and income statement to see how much money a company generated or spent during a period of time — information that can be crucial for wise investing.

I'll get back to the cash flow statement in Chapter 8, after you've had a chance to get comfortable with balance sheets and income statements.

Conclusion

Remember that accounting is not a perfect science. The fact that financial statements have numbers that look exact gives the impression that they are a true reflection of a company's worth. However, companies have a great deal of discretion in how they report their financials, and even when they try to be conservative in all their choices, outside conditions can warp the statements — as with the effects of inflation on the historical cost method. In the rest of this volume, I will show you many techniques to uncover the gray areas and the environmental effects. In the end, keen awareness here can mean the difference between picking a winner or a dog.

The next chapter will look at the main types of filings required for public companies in the United States.

Source

1. Kahn, Jeremy, Accounting's white knight, *Fortune*, September 30, 2002.

3

Filings and Other Vital Company Communications

"Buyer beware" was the philosophy of securities regulations until the early 1930s, such as they were. In this anything-goes environment, it is no surprise that many traders engaged in outright fraud, let alone such questionable practices as price manipulation and insider trading. As an investor, if you were the victim of any of the shenanigans, you were simply out of luck. Your money was gone forever.

With the crash of 1929 and the bear market and Great Depression that followed, the American public was understandably outraged. Why invest in a system that was rigged? Why give your money to make the rich even richer?

President Franklin Delano Roosevelt and Congress understood clearly that swift action was needed to fix the ailing financial system.

The big question was: How should the reform be carried out? Two approaches were considered. One was to use a system known as *merit review;* that is, the federal government would review the financials of each company and determine if the investment was appropriate for investors. A bill based on this concept was actually proposed on Capitol Hill, but it was quickly rejected. The rationale for abandoning the approach was that securities laws should not be paternalistic — and besides, the federal government should not be in the business of judging what is a good or bad investment. (Another drawback was that it would result in a huge and expensive bureaucracy of its own.)

The preferred concept involved *disclosure* in place of review, and the main proponent of this alternative was Supreme Court Justice Louis Brandeis. He said: "Sunshine is said to be the best of disinfectants; the electric light the most efficient policeman." That is, the goal of the securities laws should be to require companies to disclose material information so that investors can then make up their own minds. The disclosure philosophy became the bedrock of the most influential federal securities laws: the Securities Act of 1933 and the Securities Exchange Act of 1934.

Amazingly enough, a group of great legal thinkers — James Landis (a Harvard law professor), Thomas Corcoran (a government lawyer), and Benjamin Cohen (a securities lawyer) — helped Brandeis draft the Securities Act of 1933 over a weekend. The legislation primarily concerns disclosure requirements for public offerings of securities. To this end, a company is required to file extensive disclosures to the Securities and Exchange Commission (SEC) (the registration process), as well as provide a prospectus to potential investors.

The Securities Exchange Act of 1934, on the other hand, concerns regulation of securities that are currently trading in the marketplace. For example, it provides for regulation of stock exchanges and brokerage firms, as well as for prohibition of stock market manipulation and insider trading. The law also created a federal agency to enforce the securities laws: the SEC.

Required Filings

Another key aspect of the Securities Exchange Act of 1934 is the mandatory requirement for public companies to make periodic disclosures. In this chapter, I introduce these key filings:

- 10-Q
- 10-K
- Annual report
- 8-K

Later in the chapter, I'll discuss the way these filings can give you insight into debt that doesn't show up in its assigned place on the balance sheet. I'll also give you a look at press releases and investor conference calls. Companies are required to make other filings as well, but I'll leave them for later chapters. Here's the rest of the set, to give you a list in one place:

- Proxy Statement: The form for important shareholder votes (Chapter 10)
- Form 4/Form 144: The forms for insider buying and selling (Chapter 11)
- S-1: The form for filing for an initial public offering (IPO) (Chapter 12)

10-Q Filing

A public company reports its results for the first, second, and third quarter of each year on the 10-Q. (The fourth quarter is covered in the 10-K, which is discussed in the following section.) As a result of the Sarbanes–Oxley Act, the deadlines for filing a 10-Q are as follows:

For Fiscal Years Ending On or After	*Deadline*
Dec. 15, 2003	45 days after fiscal quarter end
Dec. 15, 2004	40 days after fiscal quarter end
Dec. 15, 2005	35 days after fiscal quarter end

The above is for so-called "accelerated filers." These are companies with public market values in excess of $75 million. For those public companies that do not meet this status, the filing deadline is 45 days.

The 10-Q provides valuable information about the finances of the company, and its footnotes may shed more light on the status of the company than do the financials themselves. Here is some of the soft but endlessly useful information that you can glean from these disclosures.

First Page

The first page of the 10-Q provides the name and contact information for the company, and shows the last day of the quarter covered in the report.

I like to see a company that is incorporated in the United States (a favorable area is Delaware, which has a long history of welcoming corporations). On the other hand, I'm instantly wary if a company is incorporated in Nevada (unfortunately, a variety of frauds occur in this jurisdiction) or in some exotic foreign location — especially in the Caribbean, where the rules make Nevada look like a pillar of rectitude.

At the bottom of the page, you will see the following question:

> Indicate by checkmark whether the registrant (1) has filed all reports required to be filed by Section 13 or 15(d) of the Securities Exchange Act of 1934 during the preceding 12 months (or for such shorter period that the registrant was required to file such reports), and (2) has been subject to filing requirements for the past 90 days.
>
> YES [ ] NO [ ]

If the answer is no, then you should be concerned. Did the company file a late report? If so, why? See the sidebar titled "Oops — We're Late" for the significance of this.

Oops — We're Late

What if a company misses the filing deadline? Stay away!

Credibility is crucial on Wall Street. If a firm is unable to file its 10-Ks or 10-Qs on time, investors will wonder: Is the company in trouble? Are the operations in disarray? Who is in charge? Such questions can be deadly for a stock even if the underlying conditions turn out to be OK — and chances are, they won't.

An example is Adelphia Communications. In April 2002, the company announced that it had large amounts of undisclosed liabilities. How much? Unfortunately, the company was not certain, so it asked the SEC if it could delay the filing of its annual report. As a result, the stock price plunged 13 percent, to $12.90.

Actually, it would have been a good time to sell even after the plunge. A few months later, the family that ran the company was indicted and the stock was nearly worthless.

Legal Proceedings

The 10-Q must report on pending legal proceedings, which raises a potential red flag to a cautious investor when it does so. Litigation is a wild card. How do you know what a judge or a jury will decide? What's more, an adverse judgment can cost a company huge amounts of money. One area to be particularly mindful of is environmental lawsuits — just think of asbestos claims, which bankrupted several major companies.

Moreover, look carefully at patent litigation. Take the case of Gemstar, which spent millions to protect lucrative patents on its technologies for interactive television. The courtroom can often be a lottery, especially for patent cases. It was extremely clear that Gemstar felt confident about its patent infringement case against several competitors. In fact, its confidence was so high that it even recognized $107.6 million in unpaid revenues from one of the alleged patent violators, Scientific-Atlanta. But in late June 2002, a judge for the International Trade Commission ruled against Gemstar. Shareholders were aghast, and the stock fell 39 percent — to $5 (a five-year low) — on the news. Investors ignored the fact that a substantial proportion of Gemstar's revenues come from its flagship *TV Guide* magazine, which wasn't affected by the legal action, and they were right to do so because the company's growth had been coming from interactive technologies while the *TV Guide* business was beginning to slide. (Its revenues dropped by 15 percent in 2001.)

Stock Repurchase Program

The 10-Q also reports on stock repurchase programs, that is, announced intentions to buy back a certain number of company shares on the open market. If a company is strong and has healthy cash flows (more on that in Chapter 8), then a buyback can be good for its long-term position. On the other hand, if a company is not performing well — and there is no hope it will perform well — then a buyback should mean very little. And even when conditions are favorable for a buyback, according to a study by professor David Ikenberry of Rice University, the result is usually not an immediate increase in the stock price. Instead, it's apt to be a gradual one. How long? It can take about four years.

Other Useful Tidbits

All the fine print in the 10-Q will reward a careful reading. Here are some additional things to look for:

- *Defaults*. If a company is unable to pay its debts or meet the requirements of its debt agreements, then the company is *in default*. This may mean that the creditors will demand immediate payment of the loan or perhaps even bankruptcy. So if you see any defaults on the 10-Q, be particularly wary. Usually, things only get worse and worse.
- *Labor negotiations*. Some industries have unionized workforces (for example, airlines). The 10-Q will disclose if there are current negotiations or disputes awaiting settlement. Pending negotiations could pose a risk to a company, in terms of either a potential strike or higher wages.
- *Seasonality*. Sometimes results differ from quarter to quarter without regard to changes in the company's business or environment — products may be available or in demand only at certain times of year. The 10-Q will give you an idea about the significance of changes in bottom-line results, a point explained in more detail in Chapter 6 (see the sidebar titled "Don't Be Fooled by the Seasons").
- *Management's discussion and analysis*. This is where the company's top management presents its formal view of the results. It's always worth reading, but is even more interesting in the context of the 10-K, so I'll save the detail for the next section.

10-K Filing

The 10-K provides results for the whole year, including the periods covered by the preceding 10-Q filings as well as the fourth quarter. The Sarbanes–

Oxley Act makes the following changes for the deadlines of the filing of a 10-K:

For Fiscal Years Ending On or After	*Deadline*
Dec. 15, 2003	75 days after the fiscal year end
Dec. 15, 2004	60 days after the fiscal year end

Again, these deadlines apply to accelerated filers. If a company does not meet this requirement, the deadline is 90 days.

Basically, it is a recap of the prior year's activities. However, it is not the same thing as an annual report. The annual report tends to be flashier and not as detailed, though it's useful in its own right, as I'll show you later in this chapter. The 10-K includes a number of sections that merit careful attention.

Business Summary

Despite the brevity implied by the name, the "Business Summary" can be 10 to 30 pages long, or more. It can be a great source of background to help you understand the underlying business and the industry. If you still do not understand the business after reading the summary section of the 10-K, then you should probably pass on the investment.

Things to look for in the summary:

- What products and services are offered? Any new products or services?
- Any acquisitions? Do these acquisitions fit the strategic direction of the company?
- Any major investments or expansion programs? Or are there closures of such endeavors?
- Any new alliances or joint ventures?
- What is the competitive edge of the company? Is it product design? A patented product? Brand name? Better performance? Cost effectiveness?
- What is the business model? Does it make sense?
- How does the company market its products or services? Have you seen any advertisements? If so, are they good?
- Is there a long sales cycle?
- Who are the main competitors?
- Who are the customers? Are they big companies or start-ups? Do some customers make up most of the sales? (If, say, five customers constitute 40 percent of sales, how strong are those customers?)
- Does the company make use of sophisticated information technologies to make the business more efficient?

Of all these factors, the one I'm most interested in is the business model. It drives literally everything. It must make intuitive sense and also go against the grain of the industry. Watch for an upstart entering the market with a sensible business model that turns the industry on its head — that can be a very good investment indeed. Wouldn't you be happy to have picked up a few hundred shares of Dell soon after it started taking orders? Or eBay when it was a cozy little community? (See the sidebar titled "Business Models Are Good Business" for more on this.)

As with all soft information, there is no clear-cut way of finding such a business model. The analysis is really similar to what a Supreme Court Justice said about pornography: "I know it when I see it."

Management's Discussion and Analysis (MD&A)

The MD&A section is a narrative that explains the financials. In fact, it is often referred to as the view from the "eyes of management," and it is the place to look for disclosures regarding recent developments, trends, products, competition, and financial position.

If you see rosy commentary from management in the press or in the annual report while the MD&A is negative, the disconnect may indicate an attempt to hide something. The legal filing requirements hold management's feet to the fire on the MD&A, so it's apt to be more trustworthy than what you see in other media.

In fact, according to Sarbanes–Oxley, a company must provide separate sections in the MD&A for off-balance-sheet liabilities, contingent liabilities, and related-party transactions.

Auditors' Letter

Public companies must hire auditors to review their financial statements every year, and the auditors prepare a high-level summary of their findings that appears in the 10-K and the annual report. (For more information on auditors, see Chapter 2.) In most cases, the auditors' letter will simply indicate that the financials comply with GAAP and represent the condition of the company fairly.

If you find that the auditors have provided a "qualified" opinion of the financials, it indicates that the company may be in deep trouble. It's a sign that the financials are not fair, not in accordance with GAAP, or both. If this is the case, avoid the company's stock.

In some cases, an auditor may even provide a "going concern" opinion, which means that the company is likely to go bust. For example, in August 2001, Excite@Home filed an amendment to its 10-K indicating that its auditors had doubts about the company's status as a "going concern." By October, the company declared bankruptcy.

How can you tell what type of opinion the auditor is making? It's very simple: It will indicate either "qualified" or "going concern."

Annual Report

An annual report, in a way, is an advertisement for all shareholders — or potential shareholders. It is glitzy, it highlights strengths, it talks about achievements for the past year. The language often seems mostly to be mere puffery. For example:

Business Models Are Good Business

Dell and eBay have very powerful business models. It's useful to consider some background on each company, then look at what it says for itself in its annual report.

Dell: Michael Dell started his company in 1984 as an undergrad at the University of Texas. From his dorm, he assembled PCs for customers and business boomed; he soon dropped out of college. By 2001, his company was the number-one PC maker in the world and Dell was on the Forbes Rich List.

Dell's business model has changed very little since his dorm-room workshop days. He calls it the "direct model." And the business model has been no secret over the years, as Michael Dell has repeatedly explained it (along with the profits it generates) to shareholders in his annual report. Here's what he said in the 2001 report:

> Our relentless drive for efficiency gives us the industry's lowest cost structure, and allows us to continuously redefine price-for-performance. There are no middlemen to pay. Because we only build systems after they've been ordered, inventory is kept to a minimum, and reductions in component costs can be passed to customers quickly. In fact, we ended last year with a record-low five days of inventory.
>
> The competitive advantages of our direct business model are particularly compelling in challenging times. Customers trying to get the most from their budgets more clearly understand the benefits of buying direct from Dell: great prices on the latest relevant technology, outstanding reliability, and superb service.

eBay: In 1995, software developer Pierre Omidyar started a simple Web site to allow people to trade things. At first, he offered the service for free. But when trading surged, he had to charge a price so as to cover

Why do we believe we can meet our ambitious deadlines? The answer is simple: because of the incredible building blocks we now have in place. These strengths include:

- A new world-class leadership team with passion, energy, and core beliefs to lead radical cultural change;
- The store-by-store successes we are seeing every day;
- Our 2,105 competitive locations;
- A powerful, unmatched portfolio of world-class brands;

the equipment and time required — and he discovered that lots of people were happy to pay. Before long, eBay was a real business.

Unlike many other Web companies, eBay was profitable from the beginning. Then again, the company has an inherently powerful business model. Meg Whitman has clearly explained the business model since joining the firm in 1997 (see Figure 3.1). Here's how she explained it in the 2001 annual report:

> Simply put — eBay is a marketplace manager. Our mission is to build an online marketplace that enables practically anyone to trade practically anything almost anywhere in the world.
>
> eBay's marketplace makes it fun, easy, safe, and efficient for buyers and sellers to connect through shared areas of interest and commerce transactions. Trading is part of the human experience, and eBay enables sellers to expose their products to a local, national, and increasingly global base of millions of buyers, who in turn have access to the broadest and most interesting range of goods in the history of commerce. Leveraging eBay's trading platform, sellers are able to achieve higher sales and profits than through alternative sales channels, and buyers have an unparalleled ability to find what they want, often at a significant value.
>
> In many ways, this marketplace has evolved into a dynamic and self-regulating economy all its own. Like any healthy market, the eBay economy is shaped by its millions of customers who instantly act on changes in economic conditions and trading trends every day, expanding the business across geographies, categories, buying formats, types of users and services. As the manager of this global marketplace, our job is to create the right environment for our users' success, which we accomplish through maintaining an unparalleled level of transparency, fairness, efficiency, and trust.

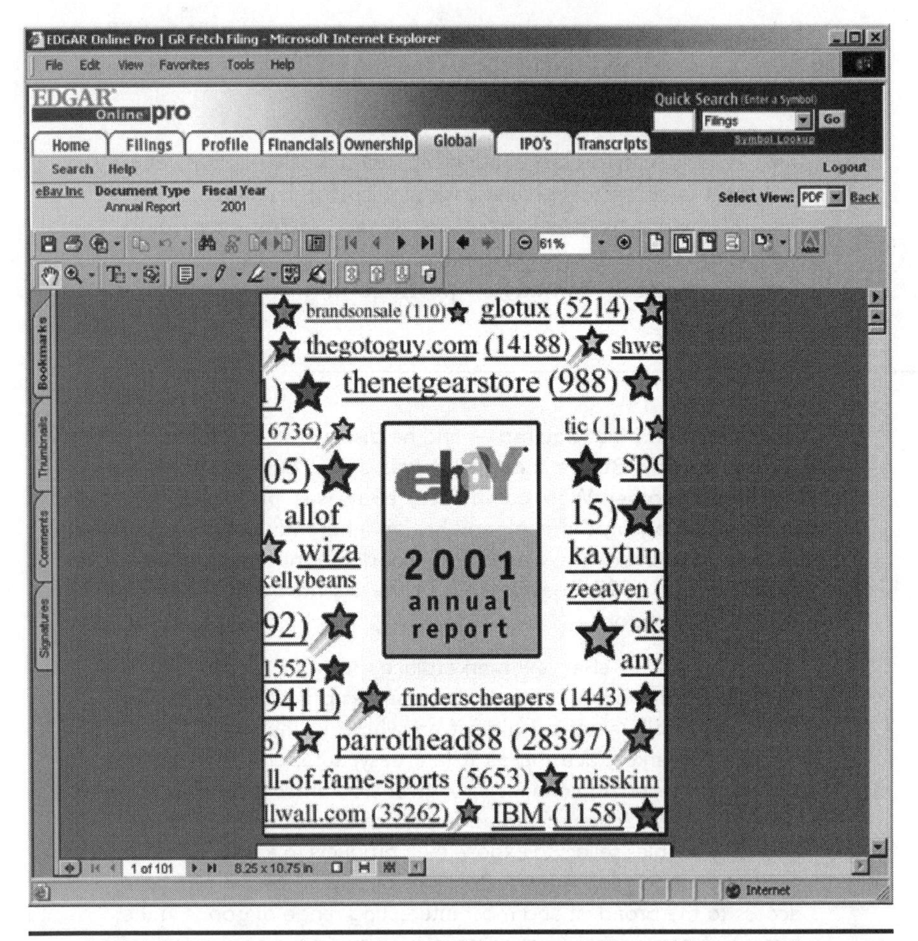

Figure 3.1 What is the company's business model? Try reading the chairman's letter from the annual report. In the eBay report, the model is quite clear — and, yes, compelling. From EDGAR Online Pro (http://www.edgaronlinepro.com).

- Extraordinary reach, with 85 percent of the U.S. population shopping at Kmart every year; and
- The re-energized, dedicated Kmart associates across the country

This was from the Kmart 2000 annual report. A year later, the company was in bankruptcy.

Despite the glitz, annual reports can be a useful tool for investors. Where should you look? A good place is the chairman's letter to shareholders, which leads off the annual report. In the letter, the chairman talks about the prior year and gives some predictions of where the company is headed. The tone is almost always very positive, as with the Kmart report just quoted, yet you can sometimes find some hints of underlying problems. And on rare occasions, the letter may be brutally honest. Consider this from Fairfax Financial Holdings in 2000: "As I write this letter to you, I must say that I am shocked at our atrocious results over the last three years and I sincerely apologize."

The letter to the shareholders in the annual report is a great place to find the essence of the business model — which, as I mentioned in the discussion of the 10-K, is one of the things that can do the most to make an investment prosper.

When you're reading the chairman's letter, watch out for words and phrases designed to put the best possible face on bad news. One of the clearest warnings is "challenging"; good news is never a challenge in business-speak. When you see it, take a look at the letters from the past few years. Have those years been challenging, too? If so, the company and its industry may be in permanent decline. Following are some more examples of statements that should have been clues to investors to stay away from the stock.

Tough Transitions

Once an icon for telecommunications, AT&T's stock price has been miserable. Even during the rush of technology during the late 1990s, the company was having troubles.

Michael Armstrong, AT&T's chairman and CEO, began his 2001 letter with these grim words:

> Transitions are tough, and 2000 was a major transition year for the communications industry and for AT&T. It was a year when the decline in long distance prices accelerated sharply throughout the industry while newer segments of our company such as data, wireless, and broadband services grew in double digits.

The problem was that — despite spending $100 billion in acquisitions to diversify its services — long distance was still 50 percent of revenues. Besides, AT&T diversified into data, wireless, and broadband just as those markets were starting to decline. Armstrong continued:

> But the economic difficulties of long distance voice are masking the progress of our growth businesses. As a result, AT&T's stock price took a pounding last year along with the rest of the long distance carriers. It was tough for our shareowners as well as all of us, but in a painful way it confirmed AT&T's decision to move well beyond long distance voice.

Uh-huh. And next year is going to be a lot better, right? Wrong. The company continued to deteriorate and began to unwind its transactions with spin-offs of its cable and wireless businesses.

Intense Competition

Steel was the epitome of U.S. growth in the 1800s and into the 1900s. Even during the 1960s, a threatened strike in the steel industry shook the stock market. But since the 1970s, steel has been in steady decline, as foreign competitors have provided better prices.

One of the giants in steel was Bethlehem Steel, a company that was founded in 1904. But just like much of the rest of the industry, Bethlehem is struggling. If you read the annual reports, this has been clear — year after year.

In the 1997 letter, the chairman hinted at the problems:

> Competition in 1998 is expected to be intense. We are very concerned about the high levels of unfairly traded imports and have appropriate remedies under active consideration. We also expect that new steel capacity will enter the marketplace during 1998. While there will be pressure on steel prices, we will continue to take actions to improve our competitiveness. We will enhance our customer service and reliability, increase the utilization of our facilities and aggressively reduce costs.

Then things got worse. The 1999 annual report said:

> The unprecedented level of unfairly traded steel imports being dumped into the United States continues to cause serious injury to Bethlehem and the American steel industry. The high levels of imports have adversely affected production, shipment levels, and prices, and workforce schedules have been reduced at all of our operations.

The outlook was even bleaker in the 2000 report:

> The year 2000 was clearly a very difficult one for the steel industry and for Bethlehem. When I became chairman last April, I was optimistic about our company's prospects for the year. At the time, it was a reasonable expectation for, during much of the first half of 2000, steel prices were being restored and production and shipments were at satisfactory levels. But by mid-year, my optimism began to wane as steel imports flooded our market at devastatingly

> low prices and energy costs began to soar. Storm clouds were gathering, and it was clear that changes in our business environment were accelerating.

By October 2001, Bethlehem Steel filed for bankruptcy.

Increasing Obfuscation

Enron's annual reports from 1998 to 2000 rarely so much as hinted at any problems; it never resorted to the sort of stiff-upper-lip forced optimism of AT&T or the outright warnings of Bethlehem Steel, but there were troubling signs. First, the company radically changed its business model. In the 1998 report, Enron was a very simple business to understand: It was a "brick-and-mortar" energy pipeline business. The vision was clear:

> Global energy franchise.
> We believe our unparalleled ability to deliver on these three words will propel Enron to become THE "blue-chip" electricity and natural gas company of the 21st century.

Well, by the 1999 report, the business model got murkier. Enron referred to itself as a "New Economy" company. The chairman stated:

> Enron is moving so fast that sometimes others have trouble defining us. But we know who we are. We are clearly a knowledge-based company, and the skills and resources we used to transform the energy business are proving to be equally valuable in other businesses. Yes, we will remain the world's leading energy company, but we also will use our skills and talents to gain leadership in fields where the right opportunities beckon.

Then, in the 2000 report, it was almost impossible to understand what the company was doing. According to the chairman of Enron:

> Enron hardly resembles the company we were in the early days. During our 15-year history, we have stretched ourselves beyond our own expectations. We have metamorphosed from an asset-based pipeline and power generating company to a marketing and logistics company whose biggest assets are its well-established business approach and its innovative people.
>
> Our performance and capabilities cannot be compared to a traditional energy peer group. Our results put us in the top tier of the world's corporations. We have a proven business concept

What Did Annual Reports Look Like in the 1800s?

It was the emergence of the railroads that brought about financial disclosure; investors wanted to track the progress of their substantial investments. But with no SEC and minimal regulations and standards, the reports were individual and often creative. For example, the April 1998 issue of the *Accounting Historians Notebook* describes the annual reports of the Minehill and Schuylkill Haven Railroad from 1844 to 1864. Here are some interesting tidbits:

- The annual reports all had a letter from the chairman.
- There were no audits.
- It was not until 1848 that the company started disclosing financial statements at all.
- The complete financials (income statement, balance sheet, and cash flow statement) were only disclosed in 1851.
- The balance sheet was called the "Summary of Debits and Credits, or Ledger Balance." One of the assets was "stock," which included horses and mules.
- The income statement was called "Statement Showing the Income of the Company for the Year 1850, and Expenses Chargeable Thereto." Most of the profits were paid as dividends to shareholders.

that is eminently scalable in our existing businesses and adaptable enough to extend to new markets.

And everyone knows what happened next....

Form 8-K

For certain material events, a company is required to file a Form 8-K with the SEC. In fact, under the reforms of 2002, the list of required filing events has increased to more than 30 (although, as of this writing, the final rule has not been released). The filing must be made within two business days of any of the following:

- Resignation of a director because of disagreements with senior management
- Change in control of the company (that is, a merger or buyout)
- Bankruptcy filing
- Purchase of a significant amount of assets

- Change from a rating agency
- Off-balance-sheet liabilities
- Resignation or firing of the company's auditor
- Sale of a significant amount of assets
- Change in the company's auditor and the reason for the change

Companies have some discretion to use the 8-K to announce developments they wish to publicize. For example, a CEO may want to disclose the details of a major strategic alliance or joint venture. So the simple fact of an 8-K report isn't necessarily a danger sign — but I would avoid a stock if the 8-K announces a bankruptcy filing or if the auditor resigned because of a disagreement.

Where Do You Get the Filings?

When a company makes a filing, an electronic version is transmitted to an SEC database called Electronic Data Gathering, Analysis, and Retrieval,

Filings That Will Keep You Awake

Most companies deliberately make their filings as dry as possible, but Expeditors International likes to play with them — often using them as a platform for jokes targeted at Wall Street. Is this a case where a company may be cutting itself off from future funding? Probably not. Expeditors International is so profitable that the last time it needed to raise outside money was in 1984. Here are some of my favorite lines:

> *Responding to an analyst who suggested the company hire an investment banker*: "We decline to learn about fairness from anybody who has worn braces within the last five years."
>
> *Describing another analysis*: "[It] strikes us as a totally meaningless observation. We advise most people to stop reading right here."
>
> *Discussing quarterly conference calls* (described later in this chapter): "We don't do conference calls, and we never follow children or animal acts."

The company is careful in one respect: it does not name the analysts that it rips up.

If you want to see filings like these, check out the company's 8-K disclosures, which it releases during the middle of every month (use the ticker symbol EXPD on EDGAR Online Pro).

How Big Is the EDGAR Database?

Bigger than it's easy to imagine.

Some think of the SEC as a huge filing cabinet of corporate disclosure documents. Besides receiving registration statements, quarterly reports, annual reports, and proxies, the SEC also receives filings for sales of restricted securities by insiders, disclosure documents of special situations (like mergers), and filings from financial firms and stock exchanges.

To deal with the huge amount of paperwork, the SEC has a staff of over 3,000 employees — lawyers, economists, accountants, and yes, software engineers who can manage complex databases.

which is always referred to as *EDGAR*. In all, the database contains more than two million filings. The best place to search and analyze the EDGAR database is one of the services provided by EDGAR Online, Inc. This public company, founded in 1995 and traded on NASDAQ, is a financial information specialist that sells subscription products, data, and services to financial institutions, corporations, and law firms. The company's best-known product is EDGAR Online Pro, its professional desktop service (see Figure 3.2). You can find out about this and other services in the Appendix, the company's Web site (http://www.edgaronlinepro.com), or by calling 1-888–870–2316. This book provides a variety of hints and tips for how to use this valuable service.

The EDGAR Online Pro service provides various features including:

- *Initial and secondary offering data.* Real-time and historical profiles on initial and secondary public offerings, including company, underwriter, auditor views, calendar information, and post-offering performance.
- *Ownership information.* Fielded data on insider trades and intents to sell, as well as equity holdings from over 2,200 institutional investors indicating asset management strategies.
- *Comparative financial tools.* Subscribers can compare financials across multiple companies and industries. Included are five years of annual and five quarters of standardized financial information (from income statements, cash flow statements, and balance sheets).
- *Real-time SEC documents and multiple search criteria.* Eleven million electronic and paper SEC documents dating back to 1966. Subscribers can now search by 18 different criteria including keyword. Also included are international annual and interim reports from more than 18,000 companies and 69 countries in full-color native PDF format.

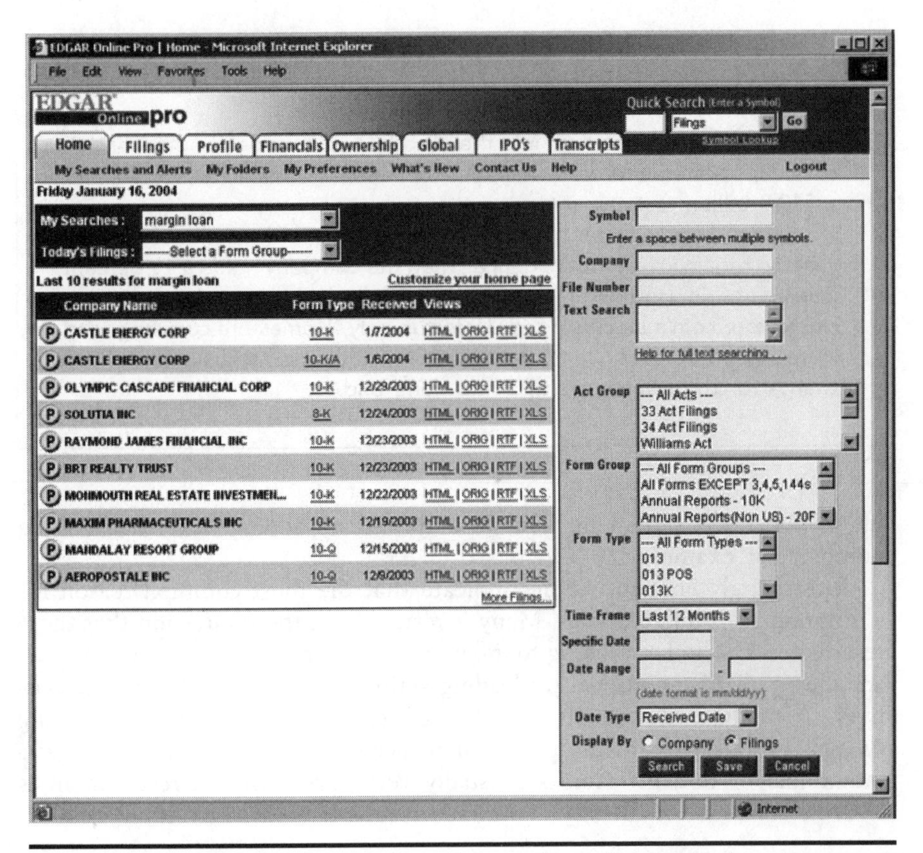

Figure 3.2 At EDGAR Online Pro (http://www.edgaronlinepro.com), you can search and download the necessary SEC filings for a public company to begin doing your homework.

Financials and text can easily be downloaded into Microsoft Excel® and Word® documents.

- *Call transcripts and events calendar*. A corporate events calendar, webcast audio links, raw transcripts, corrected transcripts, and CallStreet Reports®.
- *Watchlist capability*. Real-time e-mail, onscreen and portfolio alerting.

Restatements

Companies sometimes discover they need to revise the amounts in prior financial filings, so they issue what are called *restatements*. Some analysts call this "rewriting history." For any financial statement affected, a company must

Big-Time Restatements

WorldCom restatements ran into the billions. And even before the scandals of 2002, restatements were sometimes massive. For example, Lucent had a $10.9 billion restatement.

Another was Cendant, which restated $11.4 billion. It took several years to regain investor confidence. Then the company made a 19 percent investment in Homestore.com, which looked like a smart move, as Homestore.com's stock surged. Unfortunately, Homestore.com engaged in fraudulent accounting and yet again Cendant had to take a $285 million charge for the investment that had gone bad.

file an amended statement. This is indicated by adding "/A" to the form number (for example, 10-K/A or 10-Q/A).

Interestingly enough, studies indicate that the most common reason for a restatement is inflated sales. Many investors have the impression that these restatements, whether relating to inflated sales or underreporting of expenses, are the result of intentional misleading actions on the part of senior executives. Actually, restatements may be the result of bad internal reporting systems or mistakes in interpretation of accounting rules. Whether it was intentional or not, investors are usually very harsh when a restatement is announced. In most cases, you will see results like these:

- A significant fall in the stock price
- Shareholder lawsuits
- Loss of credibility on Wall Street
- Firing of the auditor
- Firing of top management

One industry that is particularly vulnerable to restatements is high-tech. Why? A major reason is the complexity. A tech company is in a fast-moving marketplace in which business models can change rapidly. Furthermore, demand may shift drastically, making it difficult to make accurate forecasts. A company may also have to keep track of a variety of revenue streams, such as licensing, services, subscriptions, and so on. If not careful, a high-tech company can easily mismanage its revenue and expense reporting.

Because of the complexity, some companies are using sophisticated software systems to help better manage revenue recognition. But no matter how good the software gets, restatements will not go away. So long as companies engage in complex transactions, there will inevitably be problems.

So if you have stock in a company that has announced a restatement, should you hold on? It is really a matter that should be analyzed on a case-by-case basis. If the restatement is a significant percentage of revenue — say 20 percent or more — then it is probably a good idea to sell off your position. History has shown that after restatements in that league, stocks tend to deteriorate over time.

Off-Balance-Sheet Debts

It sounds strange, but it's true: Even though the balance sheet is supposed to lay out all of a company's assets and liabilities, including its debts, many companies have debts that do not show up on their balance sheets — and, at least officially, they're not cheating. Yet these debts are still obligations and can sneak up on a company, the way Enron's did. So, where do you find them? In some cases, the situation can be almost impossible to decipher (again, just think of Enron), but they typically appear in the footnotes of the 10-Qs and 10-Ks.

The reason for hiding debts is really simple: It makes a company look more attractive. Investors don't worry that a company will be unwilling to pay its interest or principal payments because they don't think the burden will be too heavy.

When perusing the footnotes, keep an eye on what they say about special purpose entities, operating leases, and retirement funds.

Special Purpose Entities

The special purpose entity (SPE) is the clever contraption that Enron employed to shove billions in debt off its balance sheet. Enron's fate makes it likely that companies will shy away from SPEs in the future, but you should still keep an eye peeled for the device.

The best way to think of an SPE is as a joint venture wearing a mask. Example: Fast Co. decides to engage in some high-risk activities, like trading in derivatives. Because of the potential for huge liabilities, Fast Co. does not want to chance these activities' tarnishing its balance sheet. Instead, it sets up a limited partnership for the purpose, putting up most of the money for the partnership's activities. Such operations are usually called joint ventures, but if Fast Co. has more than 50 percent ownership in a joint venture, it must recognize that joint venture's debts on its own balance sheet. Well, with an SPE, this is not problem at all. In fact, Fast Co. can own up to 90 percent of an SPE and not have the debts appear on its balance sheet. And it gets better: Fast Co. will probably even be able to realize certain lucrative tax advantages by employing the structure.

This is not to imply that all SPEs are bad. As with most any financial structure, an SPE can be quite useful. But if you see more than 10 of them nestling in the footnotes, take it as a warning bell. The company may be hiding something.

How many did Enron have? Approximately 900 in all.

Operating Leases

Leases come in two flavors — capital and operating — and you'll find more discussion of them in Chapter 5, in connection with the treatment of capital leases on the balance sheet. But operating leases (those that just provide use or occupancy, not an ownership stake) do not appear there, even though they represent an ongoing obligation that behaves much like other liabilities. Example: Fast Co. signs a five-year lease for a chip facility for $1 million per year even though the company expects to use the facility for 10 years. When the lease expires, do you think the company will just abandon the facility? This would be a costly move. So, in a way, this lease appears to represent a long-term liability for the company. If the company will use the facility for 10 years, it will need to pay some level of lease payments for that period of time. This is an ongoing obligation of the company and really acts as a debt. Again, these leases are disclosed as footnotes in the 10-Ks and 10-Qs.

Retirement Funds

A company has the option of providing two types of retirement plans. The traditional plan is known as a pension. Example: Fast Co. provides a pension for its employees, promising that they will get a fixed amount per month for the rest of their lives after they retire at age 65. The amount of the benefit depends on how many years an employee has been with the company. To meet the pension obligations, a company will set aside a trust fund that invests money in the bond or stock markets. If these investments perform well, the pension plan should be overfunded (that is, enough money in the plan to pay off retirees). Then again, if the performance is not so good, the plan would be underfunded and the company will sustain losses.

The other type of plan is called a defined contribution plan. The most common is the 401(K), which allows employees to set aside a portion of their salaries in different investment vehicles (typically mutual funds or company stock). In this case, the company is not on the hook if there is a shortfall in the value of the retirement accounts. It is solely the responsibility of the employees to manage their own investments.

Investors need to look at retirement plans carefully because companies can skillfully manipulate things. In the footnotes of the 10-Ks and 10-Qs, look for the following:

- Over time, the company has been lowering the overall obligations it expects to pay its retirees. A company has much latitude in these estimates and may be tempted to be too optimistic.
- Again, a company may be too optimistic in its estimate of the future performance of the trust's investments. For example, if a company expects its return on the pension to go from 8 to 12 percent even though the stock market has actually been declining for the past few years, you should be skeptical.
- Be wary if a company has invested a substantial amount of the pension assets in its own stock. If the stock collapses, the pension plan is likely to be underfunded.

Press Releases and the Fine Art of Spotting a Fraud

Most companies tend to publish many press releases (in some cases, one every several days). For their investors, it is critical to read them all — yes, every one. Fortunately, press releases tend to be short.

For me, the press releases provide an indication of momentum in the business. I like to see:

- Formations of new joint ventures or strategic alliances
- New contracts
- New patents
- New products

I'm less fond of the companies that, for the most part, use press releases to hype their operations. In fact, some of these companies may be downright frauds. Actually, in my investment career, I have bought a handful of stocks that have turned out to be frauds. That kind of slip-up is inevitable in the investment game. Even the pros can get snookered by a fraud.

This was the case with Bre-X Minerals. Analysts at Lehman Brothers said the company had uncovered the "gold discovery of the century." How big? An analyst at JP Morgan estimated that the gold deposits, in the jungles of Indonesia, were worth about $70 billion.

Such numbers attracted big investors like Fidelity and Invesco. Even the government of Indonesia was interested enough to snap up a substantial interest in the land.

But investors seemed to forget that Bre-X was a once-obscure company that had never mined anything, much less gold. The company's management team was lackluster, and it was selling substantial amounts of stock (in 1996, the vice president of exploration sold $26.5 million in stock and then quit the company to live in the Cayman Islands). Moreover, the company had a knack for publishing hyped press releases. At first, the company reported that the estimated gold deposits were worth several million. A few years later it was over $70 million.

At its height, the stock reached a staggering $5 billion in market capitalization. But in late 1996, the scam was coming undone. Geologists from Freeport McMoRan, a company thinking of investing in Bre-X, conducted an investigation and found no evidence of gold. This was also the conclusion of a group of independent consultants.

After word began to spread, there were some mysterious events. A fire destroyed a shack in Indonesia that contained geological reports. Then the chief geologist of Bre-X fell 600 feet from a helicopter while conducting due diligence on the deposits.

In the end, geologists discovered that Bre-X was salting jungle rock so it looked like it held enormous amounts of gold. Of course, the stock price of Bre-X collapsed, making the computer system at the Toronto Stock Exchange go haywire.

Great story, right? But it does seem useless unless we can get some tips on how to avoid a scam.

Like anything in investing, nothing is certain. Some scams will always hoodwink some of the best investors. Nonetheless, it's useful to keep these scam-dodging tips in mind:

- Look at the company's past. Who took it public? Has the company changed much from its beginnings?
- Is management lackluster or involved in prior scams?
- Does the company publish hyped press releases?
- Is the company headquartered in a secretive area such as the Caribbean?
- Is the company in an industry that is prone to scams? People do make money from mining companies, companies that make huge discoveries in remote areas, technologies that will revolutionize everything (the proverbial "next Microsoft" or "next Cisco"), and medical companies that claim they can cure cancer or AIDS even though the drug has not even been submitted to the FDA — but the chances are really good that you won't be one of them.
- Does the company engage in many acquisitions? Acquisitions can be a great way to manipulate the books. See the sidebar titled "The Dark Side of M&A" in Chapter 4.

Finding Inconsistencies

The most astute financial statement analysts will try to find inconsistencies. Although it's not common, companies do slip up when they are trying to hide something. On the face of it, an inconsistency among filings may seem inconsequential — but it should raise concerns. Is the company hiding other things?

One real pro at finding inconsistencies is Herb Greenberg, who writes a widely followed column for TheStreet.com (see the Appendix for a profile). He likes to look at the management bios in the proxies for the past five years. Have details about education or experience been added? Or deleted? Greenberg will also compare the bios of the proxies to information in other sources, such as the company's Web site.

For example, when Greenberg read the bio of Nautilus CFO Rod Rice on the proxy and on the company's Web site, he saw some intriguing differences. He then did some background research on Rice. Although the proxy bio indicated that Rice was a Certified Public Accountant (CPA), Greenberg learned that this was not true. Greenberg also discovered that Rice was not an economics major either, despite claims to that effect on the proxy.

In fact, Nautilus Group filed an amended proxy to change the bio not only of the CFO but also of CEO Brian Cook. The Cook bio was expanded greatly and now mentioned that he had "various financial and managerial positions" at a company called Sea Galley Stores. Greenberg did a background check on this company and found that it had filed for bankruptcy in 1994.

Earnings Release

Another important press release to be mindful of is the earnings release, which is published every quarter during the "earnings season." Actually, proposed rules under Sarbanes–Oxley would make these statements part of a company's Form 8-K.

When earnings releases come out, you are likely to see lots of fireworks. If companies report earnings that are better than expected, their stock price will usually rise. But if the earnings fall below expectations, the stock can fall — sometimes hard. It is not uncommon to see the stock drop 20 percent or more.

The earnings release will typically have a title that emphasizes whatever positive news there is, and then describe what happened in the prior quarter, such as the release of new products, acquisition of new customers, resolution of lawsuits, and so on. After the release, the management will have a conference call. With the Internet, you can listen in to these conference calls (described in the next section of this chapter), and it is a good idea to do so. You can learn a tremendous amount of information.

Under the securities laws, an earnings release does not need to be reviewed by an auditor or the SEC (although some companies do have their auditors review them). In fact, the SEC provides no rules on how to structure an earnings release. It is really up to the creativity of the company — and, yes, companies can be quite creative.

Interestingly enough, some companies will publish only the income statement — not the balance sheet or the cash flow statement — in the earnings release. They let interested parties wait until the 10-Q or 10-K is filed to see the balance sheet. This is certainly a red flag. Does the company want to hide something? The Big Three statements (balance sheet, income statement, and

Benjamin Graham: Father of Financial Statement Analysis?

Benjamin Graham is often referred to as the "father of security analysis." To this end, he could also be the father of financial statement analysis, or even the father of value investing (a topic I turn to in more detail in Chapter 4).

Graham developed his theories in the 1930s, when investors lost faith in the system and the SEC required companies to issue honest financials in order to return confidence to the markets. Graham refined and taught his theories as a professor at the Columbia School of Business and then wrote them down in a monumental book, *The Intelligent Investor.* Even though it was published in 1949, it is worth reading today.

By delving into a company's financial statements, Graham attempted to determine the intrinsic value per share. If this value was above the stock price, he thought it was a bargain. He believed the difference provided a "margin of safety," because if the company closed shop and sold off all the assets, there would be more than enough money to make investors whole.

Another margin of safety was to focus on companies with at least $100 million in sales. (In today's dollars, that would be about $1 billion in sales.) He also wanted a company that showed steadily rising earnings.

Finally, he looked for companies that were paying dividends, especially those that had paid them for at least 20 years.

On the surface, this all sounds good. However, it is very difficult to find stocks that meet these stringent requirements (it was much easier to find such beaten-down stocks during the Depression). Consequently, devoted followers of Graham, such as Warren Buffett, have changed the Graham requirements to meet the realities of modern-day financial markets. See the sidebar titled "Knowing When to Fold 'Em" in Chapter 13 for more information.

cash flow statement) tell you relatively little on their own; you need to see how they relate to each other.

Also be mindful of so-called *pro forma earnings* in an earnings release. What's this all about? This is a very good question, because pro forma earnings are not very clear. In fact, they often provide a way for companies to make things look better than they really are. Then again, *pro forma* means "for shape" in Latin. And companies can certainly shape the numbers.

Traditionally, pro forma earnings were a way to make adjustments for unusual events such as a restructuring or a huge merger. For example, suppose Fast Co. experienced slower growth and decided to restructure its operations, which means laying off a thousand employees. To do this, Fast Co. had to make severance payments. As a result, Fast Co. had a loss of $2 million for the last quarter. But the severance payments are a one-time expense. If you exclude these expenses, the company actually made a $4 million profit. The $2 million loss is the bottom-line result the company is required to report under GAAP, but the company can claim the $4 million profit as pro forma earnings.

During the 1990s, companies were under extreme pressure to report better-than-expected earnings. Why not use pro forma numbers? No doubt, it became quite common to announce pro forma numbers in the earnings release, and often the news did result in stock price surges.

The big problem with pro forma numbers is that they're wide open — no standards govern them. It is up to the discretion of the company as to what to include or exclude. Thus, as a general rule, focus on the GAAP results. Pro forma numbers are simply too elusive — and too prone to inflate profits.

Interestingly enough, the SEC has announced that it will investigate companies that provide pro forma numbers that appear to be deceptive. In fact, the SEC has even written its own "Tips for Investors" guide to pro forma numbers. It warns:

> In contrast, "pro forma" financial results aren't prepared using GAAP, and they may not convey a true and accurate picture of a company's financial well-being. They often highlight only positive information. And because "pro forma" information doesn't have to follow established accounting rules, it can be very difficult to compare a company's "pro forma" financial information to prior periods or to other companies.

You can find the SEC article at http://www.sec.gov/investor/pubs/proforma12-4.htm

Conference Calls: The Word from the Horse's Mouth

Suppose Fast Co. announces in its earnings release that profits were up 45 percent during the last quarter. In response, the stock climbs $1.50. Then Fast Co.'s senior management has a conference call. After 30 minutes, the stock price is actually *down* $3.50. What happened?

Welcome to the fascinating world of conference calls. The conference call was once only for top analysts and investors. But with recent changes in regulations and the emergence of the Internet, now everyone can listen in on a conference. You should make an effort to tune in, too — a conference call can be more critical than the earnings release.

Many of the top financial Web sites, such as Yahoo!, the Motley Fool, and TheStreet.com, have access to conference calls (see Figure 3.3). Also, a company's Web site may have the conference call archived. You can listen to the calls through a webcast, which streams the audio over the Internet. Alternatively, you can dial a 1–800 number and listen in.

Basically, a conference call has two parts. First, senior managers, usually the CEO and CFO, will summarize what happened during the past quarter and will also usually offer some guidance for the future. That is, management may provide predictions for the next quarter or year in terms of revenues and profits. For the most part, though, management tends to stick to the information contained in the earnings release.

Next, there will usually be a question-and-answer (Q&A) session. These can be fun, especially when an analyst or investor asks a tough question. Moreover, they can be educational. After all, you can see the types of questions a top analyst will ask a company. Listen for some common phrases, like "Great quarter, guys" — which is often what an analyst says before asking a really good question. If an analyst is asking for "granularity," it doesn't mean sand or sugar in the works; it's a request for more specifics in the numbers.

Following is a guide on how to use conference calls.

Earnings. Listen for explanations. If there was a fall-off in earnings, why was this the case? Was it a one-time event? Is the company taking steps to change things to restore growth? If management is not clear, then avoid the stock.

In fact, always listen for evasiveness. Is management avoiding the question? Is management saying "we are not clear" often?

Then again, you do not want a company that appears to be overconfident. Are the company's predictions ambitious, exceeding the rest of the industry by a big margin? Is management using hyped-up words? If management is too enthusiastic, it may fail to see potential competitors or problems within its organization.

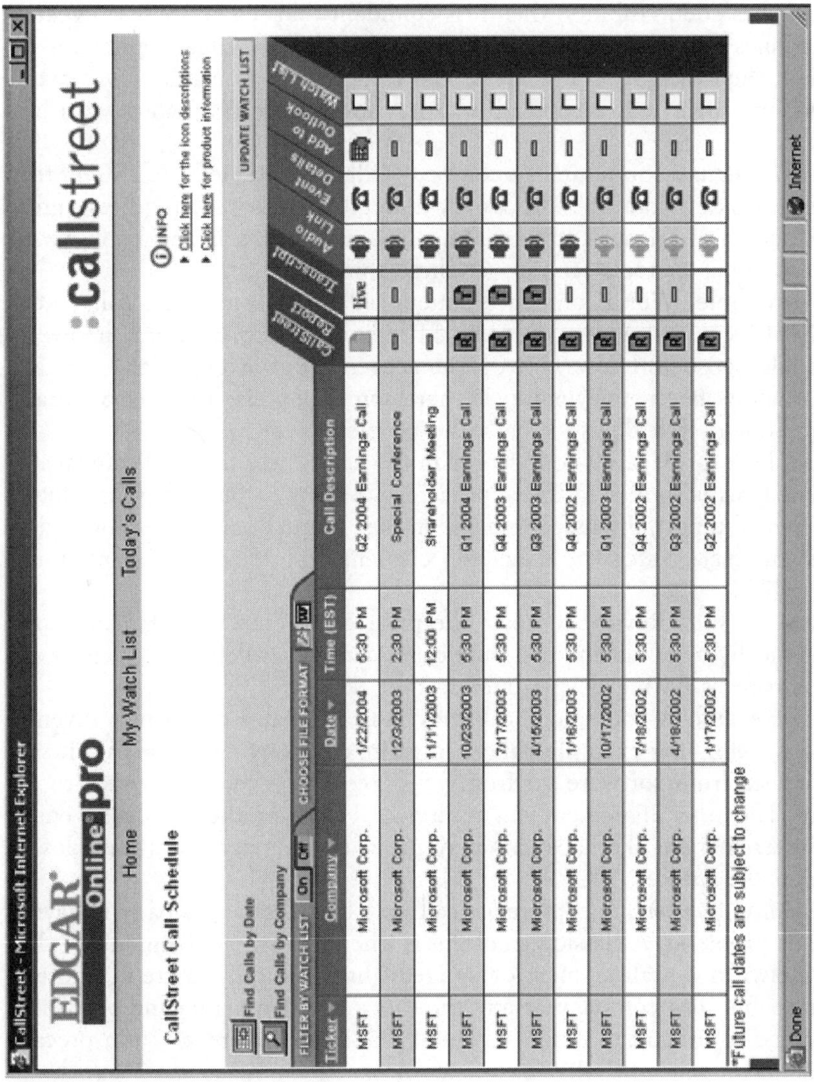

CallStreet - Microsoft Internet Explorer

EDGAR® Online® pro :callstreet

Home My Watch List Today's Calls

CallStreet Call Schedule

INFO
Click here for the icon descriptions
Click here for product information

Find Calls by Date
Find Calls by Company

FILTER BY WATCH LIST On Off CHOOSE FILE FORMAT

UPDATE WATCH LIST

Ticker	Company	Date	Time (EST)	Call Description	CallStreet Report	Transcript	Audio Link	Event Details	Add to Outlook	Watch List
MSFT	Microsoft Corp.	1/22/2004	5:30 PM	Q2 2004 Earnings Call		live				
MSFT	Microsoft Corp.	12/3/2003	2:30 PM	Special Conference						
MSFT	Microsoft Corp.	11/11/2003	12:00 PM	Shareholder Meeting						
MSFT	Microsoft Corp.	10/23/2003	5:30 PM	Q1 2004 Earnings Call						
MSFT	Microsoft Corp.	7/17/2003	5:30 PM	Q4 2003 Earnings Call						
MSFT	Microsoft Corp.	4/15/2003	5:30 PM	Q3 2003 Earnings Call						
MSFT	Microsoft Corp.	1/16/2003	5:30 PM	Q4 2002 Earnings Call						
MSFT	Microsoft Corp.	10/17/2002	5:30 PM	Q1 2003 Earnings Call						
MSFT	Microsoft Corp.	7/18/2002	5:30 PM	Q4 2002 Earnings Call						
MSFT	Microsoft Corp.	4/18/2002	5:30 PM	Q3 2002 Earnings Call						
MSFT	Microsoft Corp.	1/17/2002	5:30 PM	Q2 2002 Earnings Call						

*Future call dates are subject to change

Done Internet

Figure 3.3 Make sure you listen to the conference call, which you can access from EDGAR Online Pro (http://www.edgaronlinepro.com).

It is even more worrisome when management ignores problems. For example, if sales and earnings are falling while management brags about its products and team, you have to wonder about the disconnect.

Visibility. This is a common word in a conference call. Essentially, if a company has good visibility, then it is confident that it can predict revenues and earnings for, say, the next year. However, if a company provides no guidance, then visibility is low. True, the company may be able to grow, but the risks are high. It is a good idea to stay away from companies with low visibility.

Stealth guidance. Sometimes a company will indirectly tell Wall Street that its business is deteriorating. This is very difficult to detect and requires a great understanding of financial statement analysis. Of course, in this book, you'll learn a number of tools to uncover these things.

For example, WorldCom once announced in its conference call that it would cut its capital expenditures by $1 billion. As explained in Chapter 8, this should boost cash flow. However, management gave no guidance on cash flow. Analysts began to wonder: Is there something else that is potentially dragging down cash flows? What's the problem?

Also, look for negative-tone words in the call. These may indicate stealth guidance (this is similar to the approach to looking at the chairman's letter in the annual report, discussed in detail in the "Annual Report" section earlier in this chapter). Watchwords include "challenging," "weakness," "softening," and the like.

Same old stuff. Review some of the prior conference calls. Has management basically been making the same claims but never delivers? Chances are the company is having deep troubles.

Revenue shift. A conference call may indicate that a company's revenue mix is changing. For example, take a software company. Suppose that it saw its revenues from software go from 75 percent of overall revenues to 65 percent. The other 35 percent was in services. However, the services revenues have lower margins. Perhaps this may mean the company will have lower profits in the future.

Liquidity problems. A conference call may hint that a company is having cash flow problems. A classic sign of this is when management announces that it has drawn down all or most of its credit line. Basically, a credit line is a loan available to a company at any time. If a company is having problems, it may find it difficult to renew its credit line in the future. So, as a precaution, it makes sense to take the money now.

New product, new customers. A new product release can have a substantial impact on a company in terms of improving revenues and earnings. The conference call can be very useful in gauging the success of a new launch. Pay particular attention to whether a company is getting new customers.

Investor Filing System

Services like EDGAR Online Pro are critical for financial statement analysis, but you also need to have a filing system of your own. Over time, a company will release many documents, and it can certainly create a mess if you do not have an effective system for tracking everything.

Here is what I do on my Windows system:

- Create a file folder called "Financial Statements."
- In this file folder, I create a separate folder for each company I'm investing in or considering, such as "Wal-Mart" or "HomeDepot."
- For each company, I create file folders for the following: "10-K," "10-Q," "Proxy," and "Press Releases."
- I then set up an alert system on EDGAR Online Pro to notify me about any new filing for the companies I cover. I save the filing to the appropriate folder in the RTF file format (since I use Microsoft Word). I also use a consistent file name, such as "Quarter-3–10Q-2002."

Customers. True, the conference call may indicate that a company has many new customers. But who are these customers? Are they well-known names or start-ups? In the tech boom, high-fliers showed strong growth — but fueled by start-up customers. When start-ups failed, revenues collapsed. Also, be concerned if a handful of customers account for the bulk of sales.

Blame games. In some cases, management will lash out at the press or short sellers when on a conference call. This is taboo. A company should focus on its internal operations and how to grow its own revenues. External factors — things beyond the control of a company — should be irrelevant. Avoid companies that get into blamefests.

One of the most famous cases of lashing out occurred during an April 2001 conference call from the CEO of Enron, Jeffrey Skilling. A hedge fund manager asked a tough question. Skilling called him an "asshole."

Resignations. Be wary if a top executive resigns, especially the CEO or CFO. It is even more troublesome if the company has no immediate replacement to announce. This may indicate that the company really fired the executive and did not have time to search for a new executive.

Analyst questions. In the Q&A session, what are the analysts focusing on? If an analyst asks several questions about a particular part of the business, then he or she may have some concerns. This is probably an area for further study.

Conclusion

All of a company's filings present or at least depend on information in the Big Three financials, though they may also give you nonfinancial information that can make a big difference in interpreting the results. Useful as the latter is, however, understanding the Big Three is absolutely essential, so the next five chapters will dig into them in depth — two chapters each for the balance sheet and the income statement and one for the cash flow statement. Once you've got those nailed down, you can begin to make use of the information to protect yourself and make money in the market.

Sources

1. McGough, Robert, Seattle shipper responds to Street, *Wall Street Journal*, June 6, 2002.
2. Schlosser, Julie, He ranks and files, *Fortune*, April 15, 2002.
3. Ward, Judy, Stock buybacks make a comeback, *Board Member Magazine*, May/June 2002.

4

Balance Sheet, Part One

What Does the Company Own?

The balance sheet. The income statement. The cash flow statement. These are the Big Three when it comes to understanding a company — the foundation of financial statement analysis. And the balance sheet is the first and most basic because it describes what a company owns, owes, and has in reserve, so I'll take it up first.

People often talk about a company in terms of its balance sheet, as a sort of shorthand. A "strong balance sheet" is what all smart investors want to find: real assets growing in value and a debt load that is at least manageable. As a company's profits continue to grow, so does the shareholder equity. All things are good. By contrast, a "deteriorating balance sheet" is bad news: debts surging, assets losing value, and inventories and receivables piling up are signs that things are bad for investors and will get worse.

The Basics

Think of a balance sheet as a financial snapshot of a company — a still picture that freezes the movement of capital and goods so you can see what's what. The picture can be pretty or ugly or kind of boring, but it always shows the same three things: assets, liabilities, and equity. The balance sheet shows the values of these three categories as of a specific date, typically at the end of the last month of a quarter.

Sometimes you'll look at the reports for a big company and the numbers look awfully small: What is General Motors doing with only a few thousand in sales? What's happening is that these companies simply don't have enough room on a page for the real numbers. Just imagine putting a sales figure like $12,345,678,901 in a filing! To deal with this, financial statements will often be condensed. For example, if a statement is expressed "in millions," this means that $12,345,678,901 (or anything else over $12,345,500,000) is converted to $12,346 — that last few hundred thousand just gets lost in the shuffle; it's not worth thinking about in a pile of that magnitude.

This chapter gives you a look at the left side of the balance sheet, which discloses a company's assets. The next chapter explores the right side, which shows how a company is financed through debt and equity.

Assets

Assets are the property that a company owns. The assets may be either tangible, such as money or desks or a building, or intangible, say a patent or a trademark.

The order of the different classes of assets on the balance sheet is based roughly on liquidity, that is, how easy it would be to turn each category into cash. Of course, the cash item is the most liquid. At the bottom, you will see property, plant, and equipment, and other noncurrent assets such as natural resources. Some companies also report the value of *intangible assets* such as intellectual property and of long-term investments on their balance sheets. Each of the different types of assets is worth considering in its own right, so the following sections take them up one at a time.

Current Assets

Many mistakenly believe that current assets are expected to turn over in one year or less. Well, the real definition is a little more subtle:

> Current assets are those assets likely to be used up, converted into cash, or sold within the company's operating cycle or within one year, whichever is greater.

A company's operating cycle is also known as the *cash-to-cash* cycle. Remember Jane, in Chapter 2? She had to spend cash to purchase raw materials and develop them into products. She then sold the products for more cash. The length of this process is the operating cycle. For Dell Computer, which keeps its parts inventories under a week's supply, it's a matter of days; for other companies, it can be several years. Think of a plantation growing pine trees for the pulp and paper industry.

The main types of current assets are cash and cash equivalents, marketable securities, accounts receivable, inventory, prepaid expenses, and restricted cash.

Cash and Cash Equivalents

Cash and cash equivalents include checking accounts, savings accounts, currency on hand, and petty cash (which is additional cash for small emergencies). Over time, you will see quite a bit of activity in the cash balance, as a company will be constantly spending money on raw materials, supplies, inventory, debts, equipment, dividends, and so on.

Generally, to be considered a *cash equivalent,* the asset must be highly liquid. That means it's available right now or is in an account with a maturity no longer than three months.

Marketable Securities

Cash or cash equivalents have a very low rate of return because of the low risk involved. Thus it does not make sense to keep too much in this account. For just a little bit more risk, a company can get a higher return from marketable securities such as:

- Commercial paper
- Treasury bills
- Bonds
- Certificates of deposit
- Stock

A small difference in rate of return can mean a lot of money when a company is generating substantial cash flows. In light of this, it is no surprise that companies spend a lot of time developing sophisticated cash management systems like the one at Microsoft (see sidebar titled "The Microsoft Cash Machine").

Even though short-term commercial paper, Treasury bills, and CDs are liquid, they still change in value. Under GAAP, a company is required to make adjustments to the values of these investments. These adjustments are in the footnotes of the financials and are typically small percentage changes in values.

Stock and bond holdings require more complex adjustments. (Other debt securities, such as longer term commercial paper and Treasury bills, as well as CDs with maturities longer than three months, are classed with bonds for this purpose.) You'll see them listed under the headings that follow.

Trading securities. These are stock or bond holdings that a company intends to sell within a short period of time (usually less than one year) and are accounted for as current assets on the balance sheet.

The Microsoft Cash Machine

At business schools, professors teach the concept of the "cash cow." This is a company with a long history of success that is in an industry that has matured. Since there are no new entrants in the marketplace, the company does not have to spend much money on advertising or capital expenditures. In a sense, it essentially has a monopoly. The result is a nice, steady cash flow.

Although it's rare to find one, a fast-growing company can have monopoly characteristics and, as a result, be a cash cow. This is the case with Microsoft, which was able to wield its power to dominate the PC operating system and office productivity applications markets (see Figure 4.1).

By 2002, the company had $40 billion in the bank and was generating $1 billion a month in free cash flow. Although it's a problem any company would be glad to have to deal with, it turns out managing this amount of cash is no easy trick. Microsoft has used its software prowess to develop an ultra-sophisticated computer system called Catastrophe Hedging Program (it is in version 2.5). This software uses techniques to diversify across different types of investments and uses derivatives to maximize returns while lowering overall risk. From the middle of 2000 to 2001, the company generated an impressive 9.42 percent return on its money. Interestingly enough, this interest income became a significant part of the company's profits.

With its cash, Microsoft has been able to easily invest in R&D ($4.4 billion or 17.3 percent of sales), launch new products (such as the Xbox), buy companies (such as Great Plains Software for $1.1 billion), and buy back its own shares ($6.1 billion).

The value of trading securities is adjusted according to any unrealized gains or losses. The word *unrealized* means that the stock has not been sold, yet the value of the security has changed. For example, suppose Fast Co. buys 10 million shares of Fake.com at $5 per share, intending to hold it for less than a year. This would be a trading security of $50 million on the balance sheet. But say the stock value of Fake.com falls to $1 per share in the next quarter; the resulting current asset will be worth only $10 million. Moreover, there is an unrealized loss of $40 million, which is reflected on Fast Co.'s income statement.

Available-for-sale (AFS) securities. These are stock or bond holdings that a company does not intend to sell in the short term, but (in the case of bonds or other debt securities) does intend to sell eventually. As with trading

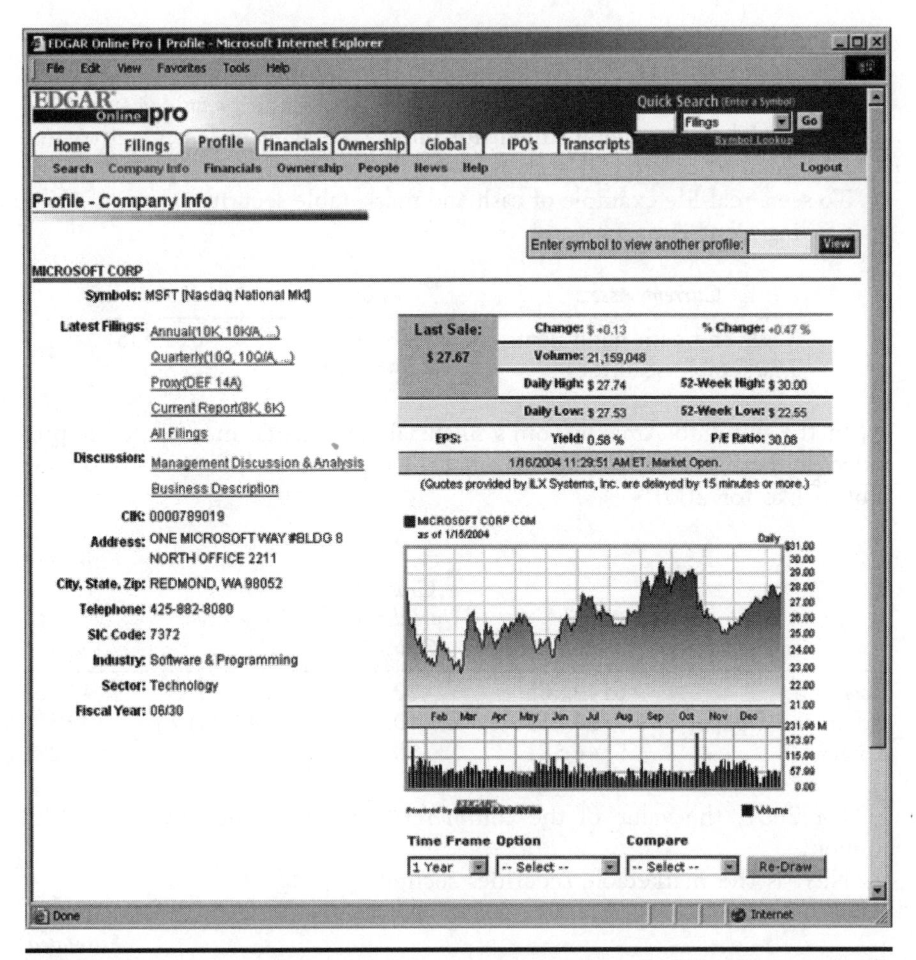

Figure 4.1 Microsoft is a cash machine and has an incredibly sophisticated software system to manage its cash flows. From EDGAR Online Pro (http://www.edgaronlinepro.com).

securities, the company must make adjustments for unrealized losses and gains. However, these are reported on the equity portion of the balance sheet, not the income statement.

In some cases, a company will own so much of another company's stock as to constitute an equity investment that will give it substantial control of the other company's managerial operations. If this is the case, the value of the investment is likely to be accounted for by the equity method. I'll go into this in much more detail in Chapter 5, when I get to the discussion of debt and other forms of financing on the other side of the balance sheet.

For bonds or other debt securities, GAAP sets up the following category.

Held-to-maturity (HTM) securities. As the name implies, the company intends to own the bonds until they mature (when the principal amount is paid back). There is no adjustment for unrealized gains or losses; rather, the value is booked at original cost on the balance sheet.

To see a real-life example of cash and marketable securities, here is a look at e-tailing giant Amazon.com:

Current Assets	*2001*	*2000*
Cash and cash equivalents	$540,282	$822,435
Marketable securities	$456,303	$278,087

In the notes to Amazon.com's financial statements, more detail is provided on these items. First, here is what the cash and cash equivalents section looked like for 2001:

Item	*Cost*	*Gross Unrealized Gains*	*Gross Unrealized Losses*	*Estimated Fair Market Value*
Cash	$149,968	$0	$0	$149,968
Commercial paper	394,613	0	(4,299)	390,314
Totals	$544,581	$0	$(4,299)	$540,282

For 2001, the value of the commercial paper declined by about $4.2 million.

Next is the marketable securities section:

Item	*Cost*	*Gross Unrealized Gains*	*Gross Unrealized Losses*	*Estimated Fair Market Value*
Certificates of deposit	$18,692	$0	$(533)	$18,159
Commercial paper and short-term obligations	28,614	8	0	28,622
Corporate notes and bonds	37,370	240	(8)	37,602
Asset-backed and agency securities	231,912	909	0	232,821
Treasury notes and bonds	125,687	260	0	125,947
Equity securities	12,395	832	(75)	13,152
Totals	$454,670	$2,249	$(616)	$456,303

For the most part, the value of Amazon.com's debt assets increased. The same was the case with its stock holdings. For those holdings that went up, the total value was $2.2 million; the losses on the rest of the holdings were $616,000.

Smart investors, though, should be conservative with the equity portion of the marketable securities. After all, what if these are upstart companies — such as Webvan or Pets.com? If so, it is a good idea to discount the value of the equity section (say by 25 percent or so).

Accounts Receivable

When a company makes a sale, the customer is likely not to pay immediately. Instead, the sale may have terms such as "2/10, net 30"; that is, the bill is due in 30 days, but a customer who pays within 10 days receives a 2 percent discount.

Suppose that Fast Co. sells a widget to XYZ for $10,000 and the terms are 2/10, net 30. XYZ winds up paying the $10,000 after 25 days. Up until this time, XYZ owes Fast Co. $10,000 and this represents an account receivable for Fast Co.

In other words, receivables are very liquid assets that are likely to be paid. As a consequence, some companies use them as a form of financing, that is, selling them off at a discount to raise cash. While this is not necessarily a bad thing (Harley Davidson and other top companies do it), it can be a sign that a company is having cash problems. Look to see if discounted receivables have been sold *with recourse,* which means the company is responsible for paying the purchaser the full amount if the receivables prove to be partially or completely uncollectable. The transaction is a contingent liability and must be disclosed in the notes to the financials.

The following are other types of receivables.

Short-term notes receivable. This is a more formal agreement between the company and the customer. For instance, a promissory note is often used, which is *negotiable* (that is, it can be sold to a third party). Moreover, a note receivable pays a certain amount of interest and has penalties for nonpayment. A promissory note may also have collateral backing it.

When are notes receivable used? One common use is to refinance existing accounts receivable because a customer is having problems making payments. Another use is for part of the payment of a divestiture. Here is an example from the year 2000 Northrop Grumman annual report:

> Included in the miscellaneous other assets at December 31, 2000, was a promissory note received as partial payment in the 2000 sale of the Aerostructures business. This note was collected in full in 2001. The note was recorded with an initial value of $125 million,

with the discount being amortized as interest income over the original life of the loan.

If a note receivable is expected to take longer than a year to be paid, then it is likely to be classified as a noncurrent asset. This is, in fact, the case with defense contractors like Northrop because their projects can take many years to complete and payments are made in installments over the life of the contract. (Chapter 6, the first income statement chapter, will provide more info on this.)

Nontrade receivables. These are the same as accounts receivable but are not from customers. Rather, they are from employees, officers, directors, and/or stockholders. The category also includes interest and dividends due from investments.

Analyzing the accounts receivable is a critical part of any investment strategy. I'll get back to this in much more depth in Chapter 6.

Allowance for Doubtful Accounts

A company that uses accrual accounting — basically, any publicly traded company — recognizes revenue at the time of sale but collects much of the money later. I'll discuss the details of how this works in Chapter 6, but one point bears on the balance sheet. The accounts receivable total is apt to be larger than the actual worth of the asset because some of the sales will turn

Terms of the Trade

For the most part, an account receivable will be in the form of a simple invoice. Depending on the industry practice and negotiation, there are a variety of forms of payment:

- *1/10, net 30.* Full payment required in 30 days, but the customer gets a 1 percent discount if paying within 10 days.
- *Net 30.* Payment is due within 30 days (which, by the way, is the most common approach).
- *Net due on receipt.* Pay now or else you do not get the product.

If a customer is late with a payment, a company has a variety of options. It may have its own collection department or may outsource this function. However, in some cases it may prove impossible to get payment and the item will need to be written off as an expense (this is analyzed in more detail in Chapter 7, the second income statement chapter).

into bad debts. So the company needs to estimate how much of a factor this will be and show it on the balance sheet as a deduction from accounts receivable.

It is important to understand that this is an estimate. Companies have different methods for coming up with the number; the most common approach is to look at past history. If in the last five years the unpaid accounts receivable written off amount to 10 percent of the total, a company may just stick with this number. Then again, if the economy is going into a recession, this percentage could be wide of the mark. If so, the company will eventually have to write off even more sales.

It is certainly tempting for a company to lower the amount. After all, this increases overall sales, which potential investors will regard as an indication that higher profits are on the way. Cutting the allowance from 10 to 5 percent means a substantial increase in apparent sales.

When analyzing the allowance, you need to look at least five years back. Some things to consider include:

- Has the percentage been declining while sales have been declining? Typically, if sales are falling, a company is having problems with its customer base and this may mean customers that eventually do not pay, so the conservative approach is to increase the allowance for bad debts — not reduce it — in the face of falling sales.
- Has the percentage been declining even though the rest of the industry has been keeping it stable or increasing it? If so, look for a good reason for the company to be bucking the trend. If you can't tell why it stands out from the crowd, chances are it's being unduly optimistic in an effort to improve the numbers.
- What is the composition of the customer base? If it tends to be small, upstart companies, then the percentage should be higher. Many telecom companies failed to do this and had massive write-offs from sales.
- Is the percentage declining while the accounts receivable total is increasing? This is a big red flag. A rise in accounts receivable could be masking deterioration in the customer base.

Inventory

For manufacturers and distributors, inventory is a major asset. If they don't have enough inventory to ship promptly, their customers may be alienated and go to competitors. On the other hand, if a company produces too much inventory, it will sit on shelves — racking up storage costs — and could mean a big loss if the inventory needs to be written off.

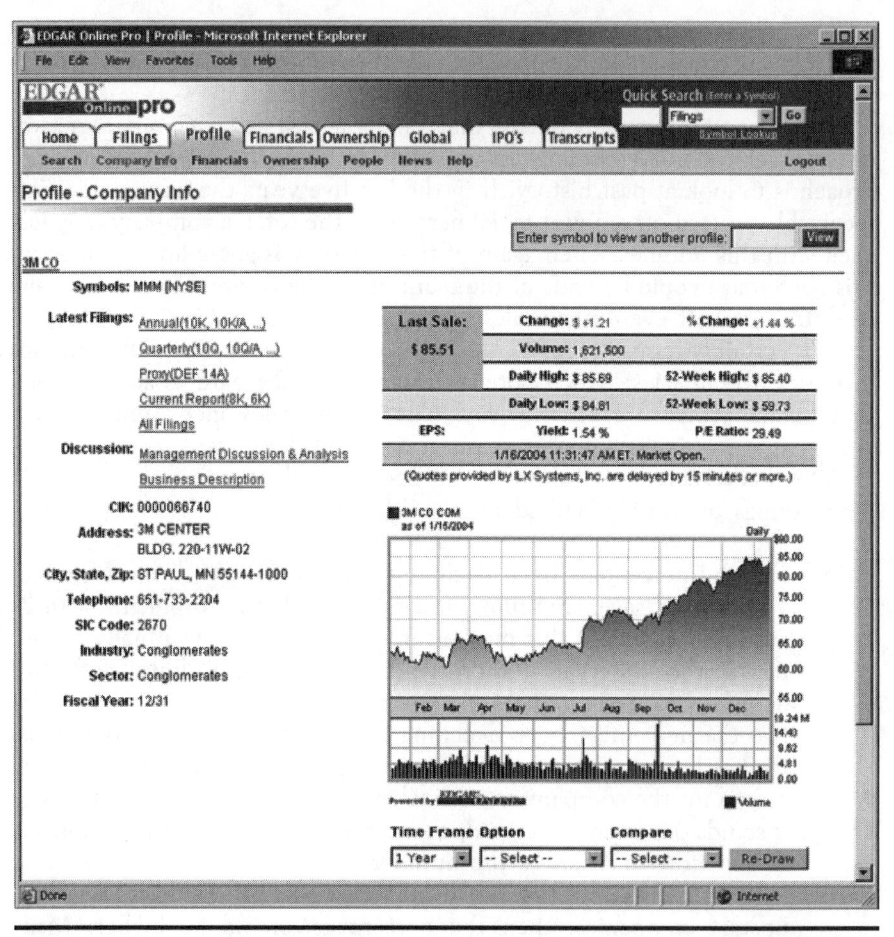

Figure 4.2 Inventory is critical for many companies. That is why the CEO of 3M has introduced a variety of strategies and systems, such as Six Sigma. From EDGAR Online Pro (http://www.edgaronlinepro.com).

It should be no surprise that legions of experts spend their time designing inventory management systems. A prime example is W. James McNerney, who became CEO of 3M in late 2000 (see Figure 4.2). Before this, he put in about 18 years as an executive at General Electric and learned firsthand the effective techniques of inventory management (he was one of the three finalists to succeed legendary GE CEO Jack Welch).

One of the first measures McNerney took when he came on board was to review inventory management techniques through an approach called Six Sigma. The results have meant consistent profitability during a difficult economic environment. Here is one example of the progress in inventory management that is mentioned in the 2001 annual report:

> The 3M ESPE Division — resulting from the combination of the Malcolm Baldrige award-winning 3M Dental Products Division and ESPE Dental AG — is using Six Sigma to take its performance to an even higher level. In 2000, the division introduced a differentiated new dental product used in tooth restorations. Using Six Sigma, a division team identified and implemented processes to improve manufacturing output and thereby satisfy the strong demand for the product. The result: 2001 manufacturing yields nearly tripled and unit costs were reduced significantly.

This is not to imply that Six Sigma is the only or even the best approach to inventory management. However, if you are thinking of investing in an inventory-intensive company, make sure it has thought through its approach to inventory management in some specific fashion. This can be a very useful differentiator against the competition.

For most manufacturing companies, inventory has three categories (shown here with 3M figures):

Taking Inventory

On the face of it, the process of "taking inventory" is quite simple. Just count how many products are sitting the shelves, right? Well, for small businesses, this is often the case — but not for most public companies.

A company may have different types of materials in its inventory. For instance, how do you inventory a chemical? Most likely a company will have a device to measure the weight.

A physical inventory can be performed, but this process is time consuming and not always foolproof. Besides, it can be disruptive to a factory (in some cases, it must be closed down to conduct the inventory).

Because of these problems, many companies are using automated systems that track products labeled with a coding system. This can be managed with hand-held devices that scan the information to a main computer system.

Take CVS as an example. The company is the largest retail drugstore chain in the United States, with more than 4,100 stores in 28 states and over 100,000 employees. Without a strong technology solution, it would be impossible to manage the inventory complications, so CVS used a wireless-based system from Symbol Technologies. Store employees use a hand-held device that has a bar scanner and can communicate via radio. In real time, employees can check inventory of any item, look at the order history, and place new orders.

Item	*2001*	*2000*
Finished goods	$1,103	$1,231
Work in process	611	663
Raw materials	377	418
Total inventories	$2,091	$2,312

What do all these mean?

- *Finished goods.* Products ready to be sold.
- *Work in process.* Partially finished products (that is, the process of being manufactured).
- *Raw materials.* Ingredients required to produce the product, such as outsourced parts and bulk chemicals.

Retailers, however, have a different inventory system because they buy existing products (which become their inventory) and then sell them to customers. There is no need to classify inventory into raw materials and work in process.

Chapters 6 and 7 will give you much more detail about inventory. For now, it's enough to know that it can have a significant impact on the profitability of a company.

Prepaid Expenses

Companies prepay certain types of expenses: insurance, rent, service fees. The amount of money paid out for services not yet consumed is considered an asset to the company. Example: Suppose Hot Corp. buys insurance for the next 12 months and makes the payment now for the coverage for $120,000. The company will list this $120,000 as an asset, calling it a prepaid expense.

Every month, the company will expense this asset by $10,000 (the expense is made to the income statement), and by the end of the year, the prepaid expense asset will fall to zero.

What if the company pays for two or three years of insurance? In this case, only the first year's premium would be a current asset. The rest would be classed as a noncurrent asset.

Interestingly enough, companies can play games with prepaid expenses. This is done by *capitalizing expenses* (more on this in Chapter 7).

Also, be wary if a company has a vague-sounding asset account, like "other current assets" or "other noncurrent assets" (these are known as "soft" asset accounts). This may be an attempt to capitalize expenses to help pump up profits.

Restricted Cash

Some balance sheets will show a "restricted cash" item. Basically, this records receipt of a significant amount of up-front cash, usually for a strategic agreement, that has yet to be spent. As the name implies, the cash is meant for the purposes of the contract and is not discretionary. So, when looking at the overall liquidity of a company — say, when you're calculating the current ratio — it is a good idea to exclude this item.

Noncurrent Assets

Noncurrent assets are those assets that a company is not expecting to turn over within one year or within an operating cycle. In fact, these are often called long-term assets. The main types of noncurrent assets include property, plant, and equipment and natural resources.

Prepaid Expenses Are a Big Deal for Williams-Sonoma

Williams-Sonoma, which started as a brick-and-mortar retailer of cookware, uses a unique category for prepaid expenses (see Figure 4.3). In the early 1970s, a customer of the company (and a copywriter) suggested that Williams-Sonoma start a mail-order catalog. The company thought the timing was right — and it certainly was.

The Williams-Sonoma catalogs became a critically important part of the business. According to *Catalog Age* (yes, there is actually a magazine on the subject), the company ranked number 25 on the list of catalog revenues ($735.8 million) in 2001.

The catalogs themselves are well crafted and aesthetically pleasing. This requires high production expenses — top-quality design and printing don't come cheap, and then there's postage and mailing. A lot of these expenses are up-front payments, but the benefits of a catalog can last a while. So the company has an item on the balance sheet called prepaid catalog expenses, which came to $191 million in 2001. The company expenses this asset over a six-month period to reflect the ongoing value of a catalog in a customer's hands — people place orders from a given catalog until they get hold of the next one, so it makes sense to spread out recognition of the cost over the period during which benefits can be expected.

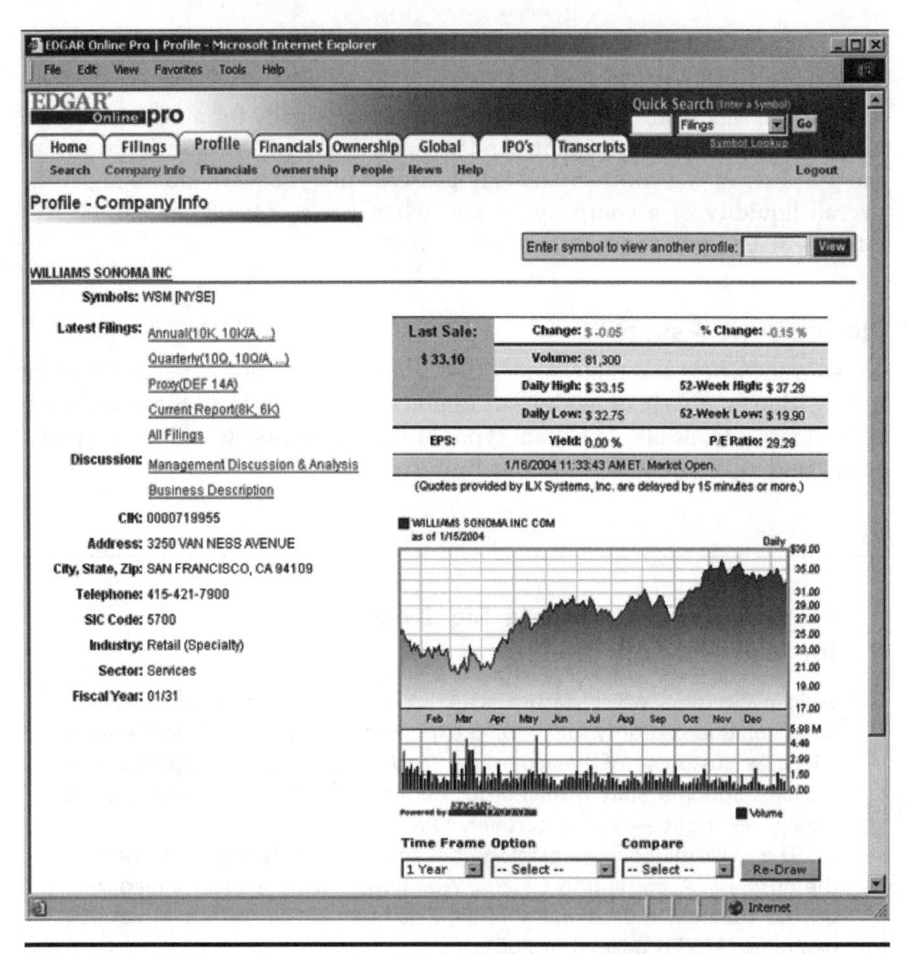

Figure 4.3 Williams-Sonoma has $191 million in prepaid expenses for its catalog. While the company is accounting for this legitimately, some companies may use prepaid expenses to pump up profits. From EDGAR Online Pro (http://www.edgaronlinepro.com).

Property, Plant, and Equipment

Property, plant, and equipment (PPE) is a catch-all phrase for the capital assets of a company that, over time, will provide profits (well, should provide profits). Before the emergence of high-tech business, the strength of a company was often measured in PPE. Companies like GM, Ford, and U.S. Steel had huge land holdings, factories, and machines that became a significant part of their balance sheets.

Brick-and-mortar companies seemed passé for a while during the late 1990s, but this is no longer the case. A company that has huge investments in PPE can represent a substantial barrier to entry and a lock on the market — generating nice cash flows. This appears to be the case with FedEx, an overnight delivery company with an extensive network of 647 aircraft and 68,450 motorized vehicles. The company generates revenues in excess of $21 billion and serves over 210 countries.

The following is how the company lists its PPE:

Item	*2001*	*2000*
Flight equipment	5,312,853	4,960,204
Package handling and ground support equipment and vehicles	4,620,894	4,203,927
Computer and electronic equipment	2,637,350	2,416,666
Other	3,840,899	3,161,746
Totals	16,411,996	14,724,543
Less accumulated depreciation and amortization	8,311,996	7,083,527
Net property and equipment	8,100,055	7,083,527

Notice that the net value of the PPE is reduced by an account that includes *depreciation and amortization.* What does this mean? Almost any new asset — say, a computer — will eventually wear out or become obsolete. It starts to lose value the moment it arrives on the premises, even before it comes out of the box. To track this reduction in value, accountants use a concept called *depreciation;* that is, a portion of the cost of the asset is expensed over its useful life. This is in accordance with the matching principle described in Chapter 2. If FedEx buys a computer for $2,000, it does not make sense to take the whole item as an expense for the current year. Instead, the expenses of owning the computer — which occur over time — must match the revenues it helps generate over time.

On the balance sheet, these depreciation expenses are accumulated over time and deducted from the PPE, giving the net value of the assets.

However, land is an exception; it is not depreciated. Land tends to increase in value over time unless it is damaged or poisoned. As a result, a company's accountants will try to determine the value of the land separately from the structures, such as buildings, fixtures, and improvements.

Here's an example of how the process of depreciation works. Suppose FedEx plans on building a distribution facility for $45 million (excluding the land value). Management will need to make a variety of estimates:

- *Useful life of the facility.* Based on history and internal studies, management believes the life of the facility is about 30 years.

- *Salvage value.* Even though the facility has a useful life of 30 years, the remaining structure will still be worth something at the end. This salvage value is expected to be $2 million.
- *Depreciation method.* This is the way in which expenses are deducted in terms of percentages per year. In this case, FedEx chooses *straight-line depreciation (SLD),* so it plans to expense an equal amount each year over the life of the asset.

The formula for calculating SLD is straightforward:

(Cost of asset – Estimated salvage value)/Useful life

If you plug the numbers from the example into the equation, you get:

($45 million facility – $2 million salvage value)/30 years
= $1.43 million depreciation per year

This is how FedEx handles its depreciation (residual value is the same as salvage value), which comes from the company's 2001 annual report:

> For financial purposes, depreciation and amortization of property and equipment is provided on a straight-line basis over the asset's service life or related lease term as follows:
>
> | | |
> |---|---|
> | Flight equipment | 5–20 years |
> | Package handling and ground support equipment and vehicles | 3–30 years |
> | Computer and electronic equipment | 3–10 years |
> | Other | 2–30 years |
>
> Aircraft airframes and engines are assigned residual values ranging up to 20 percent of the asset cost. All other property and equipment have no material residual values.

Straight-line depreciation is only one of three methods. The other two are units-of-production depreciation and accelerated depreciation.

Units-of-production (UOP) depreciation, also known as available to companies. This output method has the following formula:

(Cost of asset – Estimated salvage value)
/Units produced over asset's useful life

This is typically for a machine that outputs units of a good. Let's suppose Fast Co. purchases a machine for $1 million that has a useful life of 10 years and over this time is expected to produce 20 million widgets. The salvage value is $100,000. The UOP formula shows the following results:

($1 million – $100,000)/20 million = $0.045 per unit

Since Fast Co. expects to produce a million widgets per year (the 20 million widgets produced divided by the 20-year useful life), the annual depreciation value would be 1 million times $0.045 or $45,000.

The UOP method is best suited to those assets whose value is not based on time but on the benefits of an activity. Some examples:

- Machine hours
- Hours of use of an airplane
- Miles traveled by a cruise ship

Nuclear fuel from power plants also fits the UOP profile. For example, Duke Energy, which had $59 billion in revenues in 2001, had $788 million in nuclear fuel included in its PPE. The company depreciates it using the UOP method.

Using the third option, *accelerated depreciation*, a company will expense a larger proportion of an asset's value in the early years. This method is best suited for use in circumstances like these:

- The asset has a tendency to become obsolete.
- The asset needs heavy repairs after some time has elapsed.
- The asset's benefits trail off over time.

Companies have two main ways of using accelerated depreciation. The choices are known as double-declining-balance and sum-of-the-years'-digits.

Double-declining-balance (DDB) depreciation involves two steps. First, you estimate the value that would be applicable if using the straight-line method, assuming no salvage value. For example, say a hardware system has an estimated useful life of five years. You would then use the following formula:

100 percent/Estimated useful life = SLD amount

That is,

100 percent/5 = 20 percent

Then you multiply the result — called the DDB factor — by 2, which gives 40 percent (2 times 20 percent) in this case. The amount of the depreciation is then calculated with the following formula:

$$\text{(Cost of the asset} - \text{Accumulated depreciation)} \times \text{DDB factor} = \text{Current year's depreciation}$$

Suppose the asset has a cost of $100,000 and there is no accumulated depreciation yet. The formula would work out like this:

$$(\$100{,}000 - \$0) \times (40 \text{ percent}) = \$40{,}000$$

For the next year, it will be

$$(\$100{,}000 - \$40{,}000) \times (40 \text{ percent}) = \$24{,}000$$

And so on. As you can see, the value will get smaller and smaller. This is a real advantage with transitory assets, because the company gets the most mileage out of the depreciation expense early in the asset's life, when it is producing the most income.

With the *sum-of-the-years'-digits (SYD)* method, you start by estimating the useful life of the asset and then add up all the years. For instance, suppose an asset has a useful life of five years; you would then add up the years as follows:

$$1 + 2 + 3 + 4 + 5 = 15$$

Of course, you don't actually have to string out the numbers like this, which can be a real pain for long-lived assets. Instead, you can use this formula:

$$\text{Estimated years} \times (\text{Estimated years} + 1)/2 = \text{SYD}$$

or

$$5 \times (5 + 1)/2 = 15$$

Next, you can figure out the amount of the depreciation using this formula:

$$(\text{Remaining years left/SYD}) \times (\text{Cost of asset} - \text{Salvage value})$$

Suppose an asset has a cost of $200,000 and a salvage value of $20,000. The estimated life is five years. The formula would look like this:

$$(5 \text{ years}/15) \times (\$200{,}000 - \$20{,}000) = \$60{,}000$$

This is what it looks like for five years:

Year	Formula	Depreciation	Accumulated Depreciation	Book Value
1	5/15 × $180,000	$60,000	$60,000	$140,000
2	4/15 × $180,000	$48,000	$108,000	$92,000
3	3/15 × $180,000	$36,000	$144,000	$56,000
4	2/15 × $180,000	$24,000	$168,000	$32,000
5	1/15 × $180,000	$12,000	$180,000	$20,000

Because of management discretion, depreciation can be an effective method for companies to artificially boost profits. I'll get back to this intriguing point in Chapter 7.

Natural Resources

For companies in the business of extracting and processing natural resources, things like oil, timber, and coal, the supplies still in or on the ground represent a long-term asset just as surely as property, plant, and equipment does. And just as PPE declines in value over time, the same is true for natural resources — not because an unpumped barrel of oil will be worth less next year than it is now, but because the deposit will contain fewer barrels. Accountants call this type of value loss *depletion* instead of depreciation.

Example: Suppose Mineral Corp. spends $100 million for land that has major coal deposits. Initially, the coal deposits are classified as a long-term asset on the balance sheet, at cost. As the coal is extracted, the $100 million cost will be reduced. In a way, this depletion is similar to depreciation by the units-of-activity method. That is, depletion only occurs as a company exhausts the natural resources (that is, turns them into products).

To calculate depletion, a company must determine the salvage value and the amount of the resources that can be extracted, which may be expressed in a measure of weight (such as tonnage).

To continue the example, suppose that Mineral Corp. estimates that the salvage value is $5 million and the tonnage is 20 million. It can calculate the depletion rate by this formula:

(Cost of asset – Salvage value)/Amount of resource = Depletion rate

That is,

($100 million – $5 million)/20 million tons = $4.75 per ton

Keep in mind that depletion is recorded only when the natural resource is sold. Thus, suppose that in 2002 Mineral Corp. extracts 200,000 tons and sells 100,000 tons. The depletion is $475,000 (100,000 × $4.75). The remaining 100,000 tons of coal are recorded as inventory.

Weyerhaeuser, which is engaged in the growing and harvesting of timber, is a good example of a company that makes use of the depletion method. In 2001, the company listed $1.8 billion in "timber and timberlands" as a long-term asset. Here is how it determines depletion for the asset, according to the company's 2001 10-K:

> Timber and timberlands are carried at cost less fee stumpage charged to disposals. Fee stumpage is the cost of standing timber and is charged to fee timber disposals as fee timber is harvested, lost as the result of casualty or sold. Depletion rates used to relieve timber inventory are determined with reference to the net carrying value of timber and the related volume of timber estimated to be available over the growth cycle. Timber carrying costs are expensed as incurred. The cost of timber harvested is included in the carrying values of raw material and product inventories, and in the cost of products sold as these inventories are disposed of.

Intangibles

As the name implies, *intangible assets* are those that have no physical attributes; you can't touch them. But they certainly have value, both immediately and for the long term. These assets include copyrights, patents, goodwill, customer bases, and so on.

Intangible assets are rarely valued properly on the balance sheet. Why? The historical cost method, which works so well for physical assets, can't really cope with intangibles. For instance, suppose a company goes through the process of obtaining a patent on a new technology. Do the R&D expenses incurred for the work that led to the patent count as part of the cost base of the patent? Nope. They are classed as expenses and subtracted from current revenues as they're paid out.

Instead, the costs of a patent include legal registration and research, legal fees to defend the patent, and any models or drawings that were developed for inclusion in the patent application. In the context of business operations, this is usually a vanishingly small amount of money. Yet if the patent covers a significant technological breakthrough, its *value* could be huge — and the balance sheet will still show it as being "worth" peanuts.

You may say, "I'm not interested in buying high-tech so, I should not have to worry about things like patents." Be careful. Even seemingly low-tech firms have large patent portfolios. Just think of Gillette; the shaving-supplies business

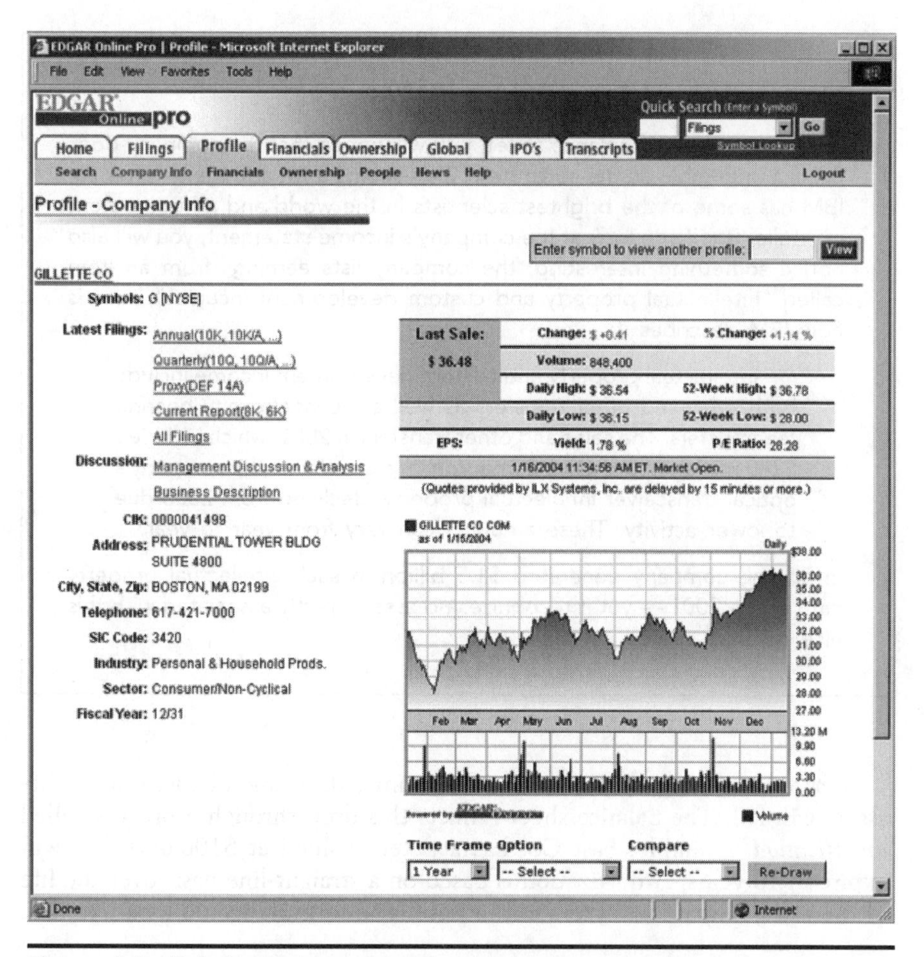

Figure 4.4 Only invest in traditional companies, so you do not have to worry about things like intellectual property? Well, this can be a mistake. Take Gillette, a traditional company, which uses patents to protect its razors. From EDGAR Online Pro (http://www.edgaronlinepro.com).

may seem as low-tech as it gets these days, but Gillette has many patents on its razors as well as on the manufacturing process to create the razors (see Figure 4.4).

Upcoming sections will discuss the main types of intangibles: goodwill, patents, franchises, copyrights, and trademarks. But most companies do not break out these categories on their balance sheet; rather, they lump them all in a catch-all category called "intangibles." It takes a fair amount of study to identify what goes into the total and assess how well it reflects the real value of the various elements that compose it.

No Intellectual Property at IBM?

If you look at IBM's balance sheet, you will notice that the company does not list intangible assets as an item. This seems a bit strange — after all, IBM has some of the brightest scientists in the world and a huge patent portfolio. But if you look at the company's income statement, you will also notice something interesting: the company lists earnings from an item called "Intellectual property and custom development income." Here is how IBM describes it:

> Intellectual property and custom development income include both sales and other transfers as well as license/royalty bearing fee transfers. The sales and other transfers in 2001, which included $280 million of pre-tax income from the transfer of the company's optical transceiver intellectual property, declined from 2000 due to lower activity. These amounts can vary from year to year.

In all, the company generated $1.5 billion in such intellectual property earnings in 2001 — yet it recognizes no asset directly associated with this nice revenue stream.

Furthermore, the theory is that, over time, the value of these intangible assets will fall. The balance sheet reflects this drop through a process called *amortization*. Example: Fast Co. has a patent valued at $100,000 that will expire in 10 years. Amortization is based on a straight-line basis over the life of the asset, which is 10 years in this case. The formula would look like this:

$100,000/10 years = $10,000 per year

So the patent, for a widget that may well have cost Fast Co. millions to develop and is helping it to rake in yet more millions per year, starts out with a value far below its actual importance to the company and then bleeds away to nothing. Other intangible values are similarly illusory on the balance sheet.

Goodwill

Goodwill is the value of a company that goes beyond its hard assets. These intangibles include:

- Reputation
- Customer loyalty

- Strong management
- Brand recognition
- Best practices

Goodwill is not automatically calculated and put on the balance sheet; rather, it results from the purchase of another company. Example: Big Corp. decides to purchase Dogood Corp. for $10 million in cash. Dogood Corp. has total assets of $10 million and debts of $5 million and thus has a book value of $5 million. So why is Big Corp. willing to fork out twice the book value? The main reason is that Big Corp. believes that Dogood has $5 million in goodwill assets. It is this amount that is booked as an intangible asset on the balance sheet of Big Corp.

This goodwill can change over time. If the acquisition goes smoothly and the combined company prospers, the value should increase. On the other hand, if the two companies don't mix well, the acquisition could mean a reduction in goodwill. In some cases, an acquisition could wind up amounting to a complete write-off of the purchase price.

In 2001, the FASB introduced new rules to account for changes in the value of goodwill. The new system is called the *impairment method*. Basically, a company must periodically test the value of its acquisitions and see if there is any reduction in the value of the goodwill it picked up with them. If so, it must reduce it on the balance sheet, which will also be an expense on the income statement. How often must the test be done? According to FASB rule 141 and 142, a company must perform the impairment test at least annually.

Sometimes a company will choose to take a huge write-off in one year (called a "big bath") and thus avoid write-offs for the foreseeable future. The amounts can be staggering, as seen by the $99 billion write-off that AOL Time Warner took for its megamerger with AOL. According to Jim Jubak of MSN Investor, the hit was about the same size as the gross national product of New Zealand (and even after the write-down, the company still had $80 billion in goodwill) — that is, when it was first only at $54 billion.

A big write-down can certainly rattle investors — especially if it comes as a surprise. If big enough, it could result in a negative book value. To help avoid the surprise, keep in mind that a goodwill write-down is likely for companies that are aggressive acquirers. Moreover, a smart calculation is the following:

$$\text{Goodwill/Market capitalization} = \text{Exposure}$$

If goodwill amounts to 30 percent or more, it could be a danger sign. In fact, as a general rule, you should be wary of companies that engage in aggressive mergers and acquisitions — it could be an attempt to mask faltering growth rates. (See the sidebar titled "The Dark Side of M&A.")

The Dark Side of M&A

Mergers and acquisitions (M&A) can be an effective strategy for companies that want to grow. A well-planned transaction can mean adding a new product line, entering a thriving market, gaining market share, or even adding talented employees. However, some companies forget that M&A is not the only way to grow; rather, it is merely one option among many.

M&A can turn into an addiction — "deal fever" — that is very dangerous. It has proved fatal for some companies. WorldCom fell victim to this corporate malady and imploded as a result. Other companies experienced trouble, such as Tyco and even Cisco. In fact, this is not a recent phenomenon. Companies like ITT, Litton, and LTV engaged in tremendous M&A activity in the 1960s and suffered tremendously during the 1970s as the acquisitions became too difficult to manage.

When analyzing a company, be cautious if you spot one that has engaged in lots of M&A deals. How many is too many? I can't give you a clear benchmark, but I would be concerned if a company has done more than 20 acquisitions in the past five years.

Why the problems with M&A? Following are some main concerns.

Due diligence. This is the necessary process whereby one party investigates the other to make sure everything is OK. After all, someone may be trying to hide massive environmental liabilities or accounting fraud. If a prospective buyer or merger partner does not spot this, it can be a disaster.

And yes, there are many examples of failed due diligence. Take the case study of Henry Silverman. No question, he was a whiz at M&A and knew just about everything about due diligence. He spent years at the

Patents

While the U.S. Constitution contemplated many lofty goals, it was also a practical document. The delegates to the Constitutional Convention believed that it was important to encourage innovations, and a great way to do this was to guarantee the inventor a monopoly on use of a new product.

They accomplished this end by creating the patent system. A patent is an exclusive right to use an innovation for a period of time (which can be up to 20 years). Three types of patents are available:

1. *Utility patent.* This is a new or useful process, article of manufacture, machine, or composition of matter.
2. *Design patent.* This is a new, original, and ornamental design for an article of manufacture.

elite M&A firm of Blackstone Group. In 1990, he formed his own company, HFS, by buying Ramada and Howard Johnson. He did not stop there and bought many other companies (see the sidebar titled "A Company May Have Many Entities" in Chapter 2 for a list).

The mega deal came in 1997 when he merged HFS with CUC International, a marketer of discount membership clubs. The new company became Cendant. It did not take long until massive fraud was discovered at the CUC unit and Cendant's stock value lost more than $14 billion in a day.

Accounting. Large amounts of M&A activity can muddy the financial statements. In fact, it is easy for companies to fudge the numbers to pump up the appearance of growth.

Integration. Corporations are persons in the eyes of the law, and M&A is how these corporate persons get married. Unfortunately, marriage has a high rate of failure — and so does M&A. Just like husband and wife, the two companies in an M&A transaction may not mesh well. That is why companies use strategies known as integration to make the M&A process as smooth as possible.

A typical integration problem is merging a traditional company with a tech company. This happened when Mattel purchased the Learning Company, an educational software maker. The CEO of Mattel, Jill Barad, had high hopes for the combination and thought there were many synergies. (When you hear companies mention the S word, watch out!) Mattel had an incredible portfolio of brands that could be transitioned into CD-ROM and the Net. But it proved too difficult to integrate the two companies. Within two years, Mattel lost $3.5 billion and Barad lost her job.

3. *Plant patent.* This is the invention or discovery of an new variety of plant that is asexually produced.

In many cases, a company will not want to exclude others from using its patents; instead, it will require that third parties pay a licensing fee to use the technology. For some companies, the licensing fees can be substantial, as has been the case with Qualcomm.

Qualcomm is the brainchild of a techie named Irwin Jacobs. He has a bachelor's degree in electrical engineering from Cornell, as well as master of science and doctoral degrees in the same subject from MIT. After this, he became a computer science and electrical engineering professor at the University of San Diego. But he decided to use his brain to make money — and proved very successful at it. In 1980, he sold a company to M/A-COM and made a bundle. Not wanting to retire, Jacobs founded Qualcomm, since he believed there was tremendous opportunity to develop new technologies for cellular communications. He called his innovation Code Division Multiple Access (CDMA), and his company didn't just get a patent for it — it has been granted almost *2,000* patents. Qualcomm has very successfully licensed this technology to third parties, which means that more than 100 million consumers use CDMA and that in 2001 the company generated sales of $2.8 billion and profits of $123 million.

Without question, for many tech companies, the patent portfolio is a critical success factor; some savvy investors spend much time analyzing the complex issues. One firm, called CHI Research, provides high-end patent analysis reports for professional investors (a report can easily fetch $15,000). The firm has developed a variety of indicators, but these are the top two:

1. *Academic references.* How often a patent is cited in academic journals.
2. *Citation impact.* How many times a patent has been cited in new patent applications. The idea is that if it is mentioned with frequency, it must somehow have validity.

CHI even has a patent on its own methodologies for researching the investment implications of patents!

As an individual investor, how can you analyze a patent portfolio without paying huge sums to a third-party researcher or becoming your own patent expert? You will definitely not have the resources to do the type of research that CHI does, but following are some tips to help out.

Database searching. The government agency that administers the patent system is the Patent and Trademark Office (PTO). It has a huge database of all patents issued and pending on its Web site at http://www.uspto.gov/ (see Figure 4.5). You should spend some time glancing at the patents your company has been granted. For example, when you search for Qualcomm, here are some of the patents you'll see:

Patent No.	*Description*
6,434,404	Detection of flip closure state of a flip phone
6,434,403	Personal digital assistant with wireless telephone
6,430,603	System for direct placement of commercial advertising, public service announcements, and other content on electronic billboard displays
6,418,328	Voice dialing method for mobile telephone terminal
6,411,926	Distributed voice recognition system
6,385,463	Wireless communication device with detachable flip keyboard

Patent documents are often long and complex, but you can glean some useful information from them. All patents must answer a variety of questions:

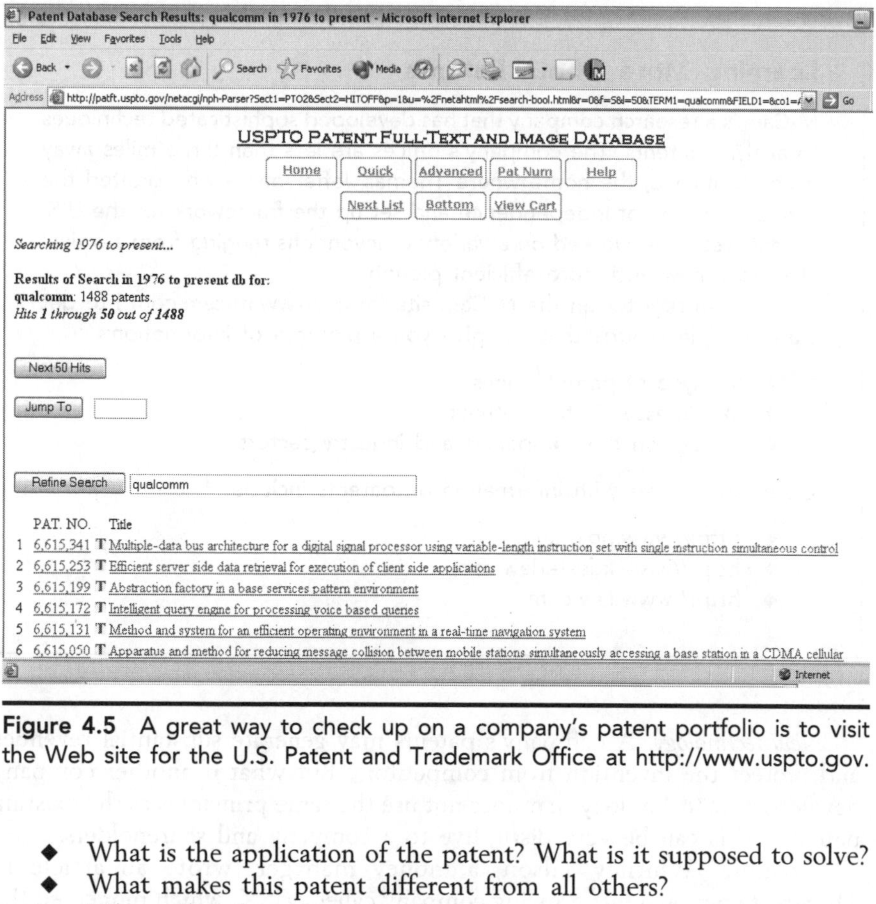

Figure 4.5 A great way to check up on a company's patent portfolio is to visit the Web site for the U.S. Patent and Trademark Office at http://www.uspto.gov.

- What is the application of the patent? What is it supposed to solve?
- What makes this patent different from all others?
- What value does the patent bring?

In fact, reading patents can be a great way to get a strong understanding of a company's underlying technology. Moreover, a patent will show you who the inventors are. If it was the company's two chief scientists and they just left, there could be trouble.

History of success. Look at the history of the company's patents from the PTO database and see if, over time, the company has been successful in commercializing its intellectual property.

Time frame. Make sure you know when a company's main patents expire. For instance, a big concern for investors in 2001–2002 was the fact that major pharmaceutical companies had many patents that were on their last legs — meaning that makers of generic equivalents could flood the market with low-cost substitutes, driving prices down. What's worse, there were not many drugs in the pipelines to make up for the revenue shortfall.

Learning More About Patents

M-Cam is a research company that has developed sophisticated techniques to analyze patents. The company's offices are less than three miles away from Monticello, the home where Thomas Jefferson — who drafted the U.S. Declaration of Independence and set up the framework for the U.S. patent system — worked on a variety of inventions ranging from a swivel chair to a new and more efficient plough.

You can register on the M-Cam site (http://www.m-cam.com) to get some sample reports that will give you a plethora of information:

- Analysis of patent claims
- Weaknesses in the patents
- Impact on the companies and industry sectors

Other useful sites with information on patents include:

- http://www.nolo.com
- http://www.kuesterlaw.com
- http://www.law.com

New technology. A company's patents may generate substantial revenues and protect the invention from competitors. But what if another company develops new technology that does not use the same principles as the existing patents? This can be very disruptive to a company and shareholders.

Example: Whitney Tilson, a money manager, wrote an article in TheStreet.com on a fast-growing company called VISX, which pioneered the technologies for laser eye surgery. The company was in healthy shape, with no debt and tons of cash. Moreover, the company had 140 patents granted and another 70 already filed. In the company's 10-K, it declared:

> Thus, the company's patents create a formidable barrier to any would-be competitors. In addition, the company earns revenue not only for laser systems sales, but also for each performed procedure through "VisionKey card" sales....Because a unique VisionKey card must be used with each procedure performed, the company earns guaranteed royalties for each operation.

Sounds great, huh? Tilson thought so; not only was he thinking of buying the stock, he was also going to have laser surgery. He talked to a variety of doctors and mentioned VISX. One of the doctors — who was currently using the VISX technology — told him about a newer and better system soon to be introduced, and it was cheaper. The doctor said he was likely to use it. Tilson went ahead with the surgery, but he did not buy the stock. He realized that VISX's patents were protecting an older technology, not a newer one.

Prior litigation. What has been the litigation history? Has the company prevailed on its patents or has it lost court cases?

Franchises

When one company gives (well, sells) another company the right to use a brand, what the purchaser has bought is called a *franchise.* Would-be businesspeople often find it attractive to purchase a franchise in the hope of skipping some of the problems that cause so many new businesses to fail within their first few years for lack of customers or entrepreneurial skills.

Example: If I buy a McDonald's franchise instead of opening "Tom's Tomato Paradise," I know that lots of potential customers will know just what I'm selling and be ready to buy. Moreover, McDonald's has a training system and a strong track record for helping people like me set up successful restaurants, so I won't be hanging out to dry on my own. Meanwhile, McDonald's also benefits — I pay them for the privilege of setting up a restaurant in a place they think will work out, rather than their having to pay someone to put a restaurant there.

A company that sells franchises can boost its overall growth rate, reduce its capital costs, and decentralize management. On the other hand, it risks its good name with every franchise it sells. Without solid quality control, a franchise system can quickly deteriorate.

Copyrights

A copyright is a federal protection for works of art, writing, photographs, design, and software. Like a patent, a copyright gives its holder standing to sue anyone who infringes on the intellectual property.

Major publishers, movie studios, record labels, and other content companies have extensive portfolios of copyrights. And their enforcement can be aggressive, as when the record industry sued the online music site MP3.com in the late 1990s.

Trademarks

A trademark is a federal protection for a symbol or a brand of a company. No doubt, the trademark value of some brands — such as Pepsi and Starbucks — is immense. Companies will spend heavily on advertising and PR to create brand awareness. Even such things as microchips can be branded, as seen with the successful "Intel Inside" campaign.

Going Beyond the Numbers

Clearly, the focus of this book is on reported financials. However, this does not imply that you should only look at financials. All great investors use just about everything they can to get an edge.

Craig Gordon founded a firm in 1983 called Off the Record Research, which has more than a hundred employees who try to determine the latest trends. The firm then sells this information to institutional investors such as Fidelity.

Gordon calls his method of research *marketplace checks.* Ultimately, it is about having each of his employees focus on a few industries, make many calls to people in these industries, and develop hypotheses about trends.

Gordon wrote a book on the subject called *Off the Record,* which is geared to individual investors. Some of his guerrilla research techniques include:

- *Talk to people.* A common trait for investors is an inquisitive mind. So talk to as many people as possible. If you are at a Levi's store, ask people what is selling or what is not. Perhaps you would have spotted the big trend toward women wearing jeans.
- *Trade publications.* Gordon believes that if you read about a trend in a national publication, such as *Forbes* or *BusinessWeek,* it is too late. Investors have already made their money. Rather, a better approach is to read industry journals and magazines. They tend to

Interestingly enough, it can prove difficult to protect a brand (see sidebar titled "Wrestling with a Name"). Or the name can be damaged, as when Martha Stewart's brand suffered when she was accused of alleged insider trading in the biotech stock ImClone.

To me, brand is a very important part of an investment. In the fiercely competitive economy, it is extremely difficult to differentiate a product offering to get more and more customers. One way to rise above the noise is to build a powerful brand that pulls in customers and keeps them. You will not find the full value of a brand listed anywhere. After all, the Starbucks brand doesn't even show up on the company's balance sheet! But it's worth your attention along with the assets that do show up there.

To build a brand, many companies spend a tremendous amount of money on advertising. But this is not foolproof — just think of the oceans of cash that dot-coms such as Pets.com dumped on Super Bowl ads. They were still out of business in an eyeblink.

be great predictors of new trends. And these publications are usually free, as well as posted on the Web.

- *Join an investment club.* Nobody can read everything, but a group of like-minded people can get through an amazing amount of material. You still have to make your own decisions, but an investment club can really enhance the reach of your attention.
- *New store.* Has a new store in your neighborhood started generating lots of business? Is the company public? If not, perhaps you should keep an eye on it anyway — it may go public in the future. Imagine if you lived in Atlanta and saw the first Home Depot open or visited the first Wal-Mart in rural Arkansas.
- *Learn to be curious.* Basically, observe your surroundings. On your last trip to the grocery store, did you notice a new product? How about a product that is no longer there? Also, try to hypothesize from the observations. For example, suppose you notice that wine is becoming more popular. Does that mean exotic cheeses will be popular too?
- *Trade shows.* If you have a chance, attend some trade shows. You are likely to spot some trends, as well as talk to knowledgeable people who may become contacts for your network.
- *Want ads.* Look at local newspapers sites and job sites, such as hotjobs.com and monster.com. Do you notice that some companies are advertising aggressively for new employees? If so, this could be a sign that these companies are experiencing substantial growth.

Meanwhile, some companies succeed with almost no advertising budget. Can you guess how much Starbucks has spent on advertising for its whole existence? Only $20 million. So how did the company build its incredible brand?

It certainly was not easy. For the most part, coffee is a commodity that has shown stagnant growth during the past 20 years. According to a study by the management consulting firm Booz-Allen Hamilton (in late 2001), Starbucks was able to develop an asset called "relationship capital." That is, the company was able to build very strong ties with employees, suppliers, partners, and customers.

For an investor, the best chance to catch on to this development before it became big news was to visit a store and talk to employees and customers. You'd have soon noticed that the employees were not only motivated but also knowledgeable. Starbucks pays employees higher wages than other small restaurants and even provides health benefits and stock options to part-time

Wrestling with a Name

For many years, the World Wrestling Federation (WWF) made millions from such shows as *Raw* and *Smackdown.* At the same time, the company spent millions branding the term WWF. However, the World Wildlife Fund was not pleased and sued for trademark infringement, citing its use of the acronym along with its panda logo for more than 30 years, as opposed to the mere 20 years since formation of the World Wrestling Federation.

In fact, the World Wildlife Fund won a preliminary judgment against the wrestling company, and by 2002 the latter had changed its name to World Wrestling Entertainment or WWE. Of course, the WWE said the name change was not a response to the lawsuit; rather, it was based on the contention that the company was a much broader *entertainment* company, with books, video games, music, and even movies (one of the WWE wrestlers, The Rock, was in the popular movie *The Scorpion King*).

The fact remains that WWE will need to spend lots of cash to rebrand itself. Some estimates cite $50 million as the cost of making up the ground lost by changing one letter.

employees. The company also has extensive training. No wonder it gets the best.

If you'd asked customers why they like Starbucks, they certainly wouldn't have talked about the price, which is a premium. Rather, customers would have talked about the quality of the coffee as well as the convenience and community atmosphere of a store.

Starbucks believes its branding is about having its stores themselves become advertisements. They are clean, well designed, and welcoming, and they are clustered in small geographic areas, making it convenient for customers to find a Starbucks outlet whenever they want a cup.

I highly recommend experiencing investments: use the products, visit the stores, talk to the employees and customers. You will learn invaluable information to make more informed investment decisions. The sidebar titled "Going Beyond the Numbers" gives you more of a look at some of these techniques.

Environmental Policies as Assets

In 1989, the oil tanker *Exxon Valdez* ran aground. It spilled about 11 million gallons of crude oil in Prince William Sound, off Alaska, causing tremendous environmental destruction and economic hardship for local fishermen. As for

Exxon, the company became a pariah and faced massive lawsuits and clean-up costs.

More and more, companies are becoming mindful of their environmental responsibilities, and some have even placed environmental policies in their annual reports. While such environmental policies are not tangible assets, they are nonetheless valuable. Besides avoiding a disaster like the *Valdez* incident, they can also help a company get favorable tax treatment for using certain types of environmentally sound techniques in manufacturing processes, obtain lower premiums on insurance, and build stronger relationships with foreign nations.

Starbucks has a particularly strong environmental policy. Interestingly enough, in 2001, the company published an annual report for social responsibility. Here are some of the elements it included:

- "Starbucks is committed to sourcing coffees of the highest quality that support a sustainable social, ecological and economic model for production and trade. In April 2000, Starbucks formed an alliance with TransFair USA that provides an additional opportunity for us and our customers to have a meaningful impact on the working and living conditions faced by many who grow, harvest and process coffee throughout the world."
- "Starbucks is strongly committed to preserving and protecting our environment....[By] taking steps to reduce, reuse and recycle, we can preserve the earth's natural resources and enhance the quality of lives around the globe."
- "Our many community building programs help us to be a good neighbor and active contributor in the communities where our partners and customers live, work and play. We encourage and reward volunteerism and participation in neighborhood clean-ups, walk-a-thons, and leadership activities."

Conclusion

What makes financial statements convenient is the standardization. Most balance sheets list cash, accounts receivable, PPE, and so on. This certainly helps with quick analysis. Then again, the standardization can hide significant assets, such as patents, customer lists, brand, and reputation. It is important to always keep in mind that financial statement analysis is much more than reading numbers; it is also about going beyond the numbers and trying to get a sense of the real company.

In the next chapter, I give you a look at the right-hand side of the balance sheet, which includes the debts and equity, the essential ingredients that finance the assets of a company.

Sources

1. Tilson, Whitney, VISX: a hard look found the flaws, TheStreet.com, January 25, 2000.
2. Jubak, Jim, First-quarter earnings are impossible to parse, MSN Investor, April 10, 2002.

5

Balance Sheet, Part Two

How Is the Company Financed?

You'll often hear professional investors talk about "cap structure," which is short for *capital structure*. In essence, the capital structure is how the company has financed its assets — that is, how much it borrowed (called *debt*) or applied from resources it owned (called *equity*) to get to its current position. In some cases, the cap structure can be quite bleak — with negative equity and huge debt that could plunge a company into bankruptcy.

A company's cap structure appears on the right-hand side of the balance sheet, with liabilities on top and the equity portion on the bottom. As with Jane's business in Chapter 2, the asset side must equal the financing side (that is, the debt and equity).

Investors are often grouped based on the style of investing. For example, growth investors are looking for sales and profit strength and so focus on a company's income statement. Value investors, on the other hand, look mostly at a company's balance sheet.

I'm not promoting any one approach to investing; value, growth, and even technical analysis can all get good results, but the fact is some of the investors with the best long-term records have pursued a value strategy. Peter Lynch, Bill Miller, Warren Buffett, John Neff — that's a good group to follow.

Debt

For public companies, debt is absolutely necessary. Even a company like Microsoft — with over $40 billion in its bank account — still has liabilities.

Value All the Way

One of the all-time value investors is John Neff, who launched his career as portfolio manager of the Windsor Fund in 1964. If you had started investing with him then and stuck until he retired in 1995, every dollar you put into the fund would have brought you $56. That's more than double the $22 return for the S&P 500.

Neff describes his brand of value investing in his book *John Neff on Investing,* in which he sets forth the following criteria:

- *Low P/E ratios.* He looks at companies' historical price/earnings ratios. When these ratios dip to the lows, Neff will consider buying the stock, as long as the company has growth potential. When the P/E ratio is low, expectations are low as well. Thus a company is subject to much less fluctuation caused by disappointment.
- *Fundamental growth in excess of 7 percent.* Neff likes moderate growth, between 7 and 20 percent. Anything above this range is too risky for Neff.
- *Dividends.* Neff believes that a dividend provides good downside protection for a stock. See Chapter 7 for more information on dividends.
- *Superior relationship of total return to P/E paid.* Neff developed something he calls the *total-return ratio,* which is calculated as follows:

  Total return/P/E ratio = Total-return ratio

  The total return is equal to the growth in the company's earnings plus its dividend yield. For example, say Fast Co. has a growth rate of 10 percent, a dividend of 5 percent, and a P/E ratio of 5. The total-return ratio will be

  (10 percent + 5 percent)/5 = 3.0

  As a general rule, Neff would look for companies with a total-return ratio of 0.7 or greater.
- *Solid company in a growing field.* Neff would look at companies with strong brands, market share, and product lines, but would not buy these stocks until they were out of favor.
- *Strong fundamental support.* Neff would perform extensive analysis on a company's financial statements, looking at such things as return on investment (ROI) and cash flow growth.

After all, at any given time, Microsoft owes money to suppliers or partners or employees or governmental tax authorities — and probably to all of them at once.

Just as with assets, debt has two classifications: (1) *current liabilities* (which must be paid off in one year or one operating cycle) and (2) *noncurrent liabilities* (which last longer than current liabilities).

Current Liabilities

Current liabilities are subdivided into several categories. Following are the ones you're most likely to see.

Accounts payable. If Fast Co. purchases $10,000 in components to build microchips but has not sent the check, then the amount it owes to the supplier is called an *accounts payable.* Or perhaps an attorney has provided $1,000 in services to Fast Co. but hasn't been paid yet; again, this is an accounts payable. Accounts payable are really the opposite of accounts receivable. Just as with its customers and its own accounts receivable, a company that owes money expects to have some time, usually 30 days, to pay the bill.

Short-term notes payable. This is a debt that is owed within one year that is part of a company's financing. For example, Fast Co. may have borrowed $1 million on a loan that it needs to pay back this year. Or Fast Co. may need to pay back $500,000 on a credit line, as specified in the bank contract.

Unearned revenues. In some cases, a customer will pay for a product before the product is shipped — or sometimes even built. The company has the money in the bank but has not officially earned it, so the amount is considered a liability. That reflects the product owed to the customer. On the asset side of the balance sheet, the cash balance increases by the amount of the unearned revenue. As the revenue is earned, it is reported on the income statement, as well as the costs that were incurred in the development of the revenue.

Income tax payable. These are taxes based on a company's earnings that have yet to be paid to the federal and state government.

Vacation wages payable. This is vacation pay earned by employees. When an employee takes a vacation, part of this liability is reduced, balancing the cash payout.

Dividend payable. When a company declares a dividend, it becomes a liability until it is paid to shareholders. See Chapter 7 for a more in-depth discussion of dividends.

Interest payable. These are interest payments owed for outstanding short-term or long-term debt.

Microsoft's Steady Growth by Using Unearned Revenues

High growth in revenues and profits. High margins. Seemingly unlimited opportunities. These are the keys to any great investment, and from the late 1980s to the 1990s, they meant incredible returns for Microsoft shareholders. But all great companies eventually slow down, and this has been the case with Microsoft. True to form, however, Microsoft is not giving up — it's still trying to find ways to keep the growth going.

One approach is to change its business model and some of its accounting. For years, Microsoft has made the bulk of its revenues by licensing its software to customers on a perpetual basis. That is, a customer will pay a lump sum up front and get to use the software forever — or until the customer pays a few bucks to upgrade to a newer version.

This results in early revenue growth that quickly tails off. However, Microsoft would prefer to have steadier revenue growth, so it's looking at a recurring model (also known as a subscription-fee model). It would like its customers to basically pay a monthly or quarterly rental fee for the software.

From an accounting standpoint, current revenues will fall. But, because of the licensing agreements, Microsoft will receive future revenues that it will put into the "unearned revenues" account. According to the 2001 annual report:

> At June 30, 2000 and 2001, Desktop Applications unearned revenue was $1.84 billion and $2.19 billion. Desktop Platforms unearned revenue was $2.34 billion and $2.59 billion. Enterprise Software and Services unearned revenue was $433 million and $413 million. Unearned revenue associated with Consumer Software, Services, and Devices and Other was $200 million and $427 million at June 30, 2000 and 2001.

Thus, for stock analysts, the unearned revenues account is extremely important. In theory, it essentially means that Microsoft will have steady growth for the foreseeable future.

Spontaneous Financing

You can classify financing in many ways — equity and debt financing, for example, or long-term or short-term financing. Something else you may hear about is the difference between issued financing and spontaneous financing. *Issued financing* is when a company takes a formal approach to raising money, such as by drawing up a promissory note or even going to Wall Street to file a registration statement to sell bonds or stock to the public.

Spontaneous financing is a natural or automatic system. Here's an example to show how it works. Say Fast Co. is definitely growing nicely. In the next quarter, the company expects to see a 20 percent increase in sales or $20,000. The company's current assets and liabilities look like this:

Current Assets	*Amount*	*Current Liabilities*	*Amount*
Cash	$100,000	Salaries payable	$30,000
Accounts receivable	$200,000	Accounts payable	$100,000
Inventory	$100,000		
Total	$400,000	Total	$130,000

The 20 percent increase in sales isn't pure profit. For one thing, the company will not receive all $20,000 immediately in cash. Instead, about $14,000 will be in accounts receivable (this was calculated by applying 20 percent growth to the current accounts receivable total) and the balance, or $6,000, will go into cash.

And the company will see an immediate increase in costs. First, it needs more hands on the job. For this, it adds $5,000 to salaries payable. The company will also need to invest in inventory, say $10,000. This amount also shows up in accounts payable, since the purchases for inventory will not need to be paid for a month. The new totals look like this:

Current Assets	*Amount*	*Current Liabilities*	*Amount*
Cash	$106,000	Salaries payable	$35,000
Accounts receivable	$214,000	Accounts payable	$110,000
Inventory	$110,000		
Total	$430,000	Total	$145,000

The 20 percent increase in sales has translated into a $30,000 increase in current assets. Current liabilities increased by $15,000 at the same time, and that increase is the spontaneous financing that helped allow for the sales and increases in current assets. This just happened, with no planning required; it was purely automatic.

Noncurrent Liabilities

Noncurrent liabilities are also known as long-term debts. Generally, these types of liabilities must be paid off within 5 to 30 years. The structures can be quite complex and creative, but some rules of thumb do apply in long-term debt financing.

Matching the term. The term of the loan (the time until the date it must be paid back) is typically matched against the use of the asset. For example, if Fast Co. builds a factory that is expected to last 10 years, it is likely to use a loan with a term of 10 years. The theory is that the asset will be producing revenues during this period, and those revenues will ultimately be used to pay off the loan.

Interest. This is the cost of borrowing money and is usually based on a base rate plus a premium. The base rate may be the *prime rate,* which is what banks charge their best customers. Then the premium is based on the quality of the borrower. The more solid the borrower, the lower the premium. So, if Fast Co. takes out a loan for $1 million and its bank thinks the company is a good credit risk, the bank may agree to a premium of 3 percent above the prime rate. If the prime rate is 5 percent, then the annual interest rate is 8 percent or $80,000 per year. In most cases, the interest is paid on a quarterly basis, which would be $20,000 each quarter.

Principal (also known as face value). This is the amount a company has borrowed. At the end of the term of the loan (also known as its maturity), the company needs to repay the principal amount.

Secured or unsecured. A *secured loan* is backed by certain assets that guarantee repayment. For example, suppose Fast Co. borrows $1 million to build a facility. In the loan, the facility can be used as security (this is also known as a mortgage). In this transaction, the asset that backs the loan is called collateral. What if the company decides to sell the facility? It can't do it without repaying the loan, because the lender will have filed a *lien,* a public disclosure indicating that the property is subject to a secured loan. (Lien documents are filed at the county registrar's office.)

As the name implies, an *unsecured loan* is not backed by any collateral. However, this does not necessarily mean the lender is in trouble. The only worry is that in the event of bankruptcy the unsecured lenders will be next in line after all the secured lenders are paid off. Lenders that do without collateral usually get higher interest rates to counterbalance their less favorable position.

Loan agreement. This is the contract between the borrower and the creditors. Material loans are disclosed in a company's 8-K filings, as well as its 10-Q and 10-K filings. Unfortunately, 8-K documents can be hundreds of pages long and involve complex legal verbiage. But if you look at a company's 10-Q or 10-K, the material terms should be described.

Each material term of a loan agreement is called a *covenant.* Examples:

- Maintaining certain levels of cash.
- Requiring minimum financial ratios, such as the current ratio or the time interest earned ratio (the rule of thumb is that the ratio should be 8.0 or greater).

- Restrictions on what areas a company can spend its capital on.
- Putting a cap on the amount of dividends that can be paid.

As with any contract, if there is a breach, then the consequences can be severe. Perhaps the most serious breach is when a company fails to make an interest payment. In this case, the creditors have a right to force the company into bankruptcy. (See the sidebar titled "What Is Bankruptcy?" for more on this.)

Long-Term Debt

On the balance sheet, you will see certain types of long-term debt. The main ones include the following.

Credit lines. This is when a bank allows a company to borrow a certain amount of money for a set term, say two or three years. The company usually is not required to borrow the money; rather, the credit line is a flexible option providing ready access to quick capital. In fact, it is normal for companies to use credit lines to handle periodic shortfalls and restore the money when conditions improve — rather like having legitimate access to a checking account with somebody else's money in it. For example, in anticipation of the Christmas season, a retailer may need to spend heavily to buy inventory and have every expectation of being able to cover the withdrawals after the holiday.

Notes payable. These are also known as promissory notes. The company pays no interest until such a note comes due.

Bonds. A bond is a note that is issued to the public in an offering similar to an IPO (except an IPO is an offering of stock). The owner of a bond gets a certificate indicating ownership in the security. According to the certificate, the bondholder gets periodic interest payments and repayment of the principal (usually after 10 years or more).

Here's an example of a bond: Suppose Fast Co. raises $5 million by issuing 5,000 bonds at $1,000 a pop. The bond has a *coupon rate* — an annual interest payout — of 10 percent, or $100 per year per bond. The payment interval can vary, but most bonds pay out quarterly, semi-annually, or annually. The bond has a *term* — or maturity — of 10 years.

It also has a "call feature." This gives Fast Co. the right to buy back the bonds after three years if it pays a premium on the face value; in this case, it can buy them back for $1,100 per bond. Why does Fast Co. want this feature? Suppose interest rates fall to 5 percent. If it could reissue the bonds, instead of paying $500,000 per year in interest, Fast Co. could pay $250,000 per year — cutting its outlay in half. In this case, it would make sense to buy back the whole set and issue new bonds at a 5 percent coupon rate. This is called *refunding* a corporate bond.

What Is Bankruptcy?

Simply put, bankruptcy is a process that is managed by a federal judge to restructure a company's operations. In fact, the goal of bankruptcy is to provide a company a fresh start. It is not meant to be punitive. In the crash of 2000–2002, even huge companies were filing for bankruptcy — and many of them planned to survive the experience (see Figure 5.1). However, for shareholders, bankruptcy can be fatal. Why? The shareholders are legally the last in line to receive any proceeds from a bankruptcy. After all, if a company had enough money to pay off shareholders, why would it need to file for bankruptcy?

Rather, it is the company's creditors that are paid off first. The priority is as follows:

- Secured creditors
- Unsecured creditors
- Preferred shareholders
- Common shareholders

Bankruptcies come in two flavors:

- *Chapter 11.* This is called a *reorganization*; it gives the company a breather to attempt to turn things around. In the filing, all lawsuits are stopped and a company can get easier financing for its short-term needs. That sounds hopeful, but even if the company is ultimately successful in emerging from bankruptcy as a going concern, its shareholders may not benefit. In fact, the creditors may eventually wind up with the whole company, rendering existing shareholders' stock worthless.
- *Chapter 7.* This has the grim and accurate name of *liquidation.* A court-appointed monitor steps in and runs the business with a view to minimizing loss and maximizing return to the creditors, and it's highly unlikely that its owners will get it back or that it will stay in operation for any length of time. And it's even less likely than with Chapter 11 to have any scraps left over for the shareholders. It was not uncommon for dot-com companies to file for Chapter 7, as eToys and Pets.com did. These companies had very little value at the end, and none of it went to the shareholders who had gleefully run their stock values up and up.

The price of the Fast Co. bonds will not stay at $1,000. Rather, since the bonds are traded on an open market, the price will fluctuate according to demand. Several factors can affect the price of a bond.

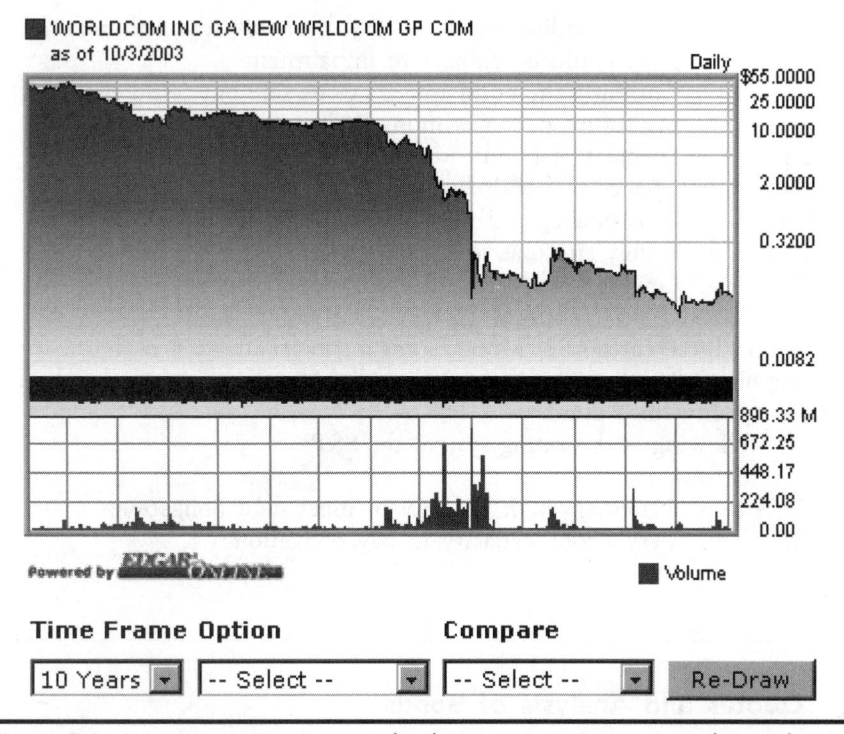

Figure 5.1 It is tempting to invest in bankrupt companies — since the stock price is so low. Keep in mind that, in many cases, the shareholders wind up with worthless stock, as was the case with the WorldCom bankruptcy. From EDGAR Online Pro (http://www.edgaronlinepro.com).

Prospects of the company. No doubt, if a company is starting to lose money and its competitive edge, bond investors will become edgy. Will the company be able to pay its interest payments? Will it have principal amount on hand when the bond matures? Maybe not. This uncertainty will put downward pressure on the price of a bond. On the other hand, if the company is strong and growing, this will encourage investors to pay somewhat extra for the bonds.

Bondholders should make sure they track the bond ratings of their investments. As noted in Chapter 1, several third-party companies, such as S&P and Moody's, analyze the probabilities of a company paying the interest and principal on its bonds. Both services use a letter system to rate bonds.

The Moody's system looks like this:

Aaa	Highest-quality bonds, often referred to as "gilt edge"
Aa	High quality, known as "high-grade bonds"

A	Upper medium-grade quality; probably sound though the bond could be subject to impairment
Baa	Currently the bond appears to be safe but could change if the future becomes more challenging
Ba	Speculative bond
B	Chance of bonds being paid off is small
Caa	Poor quality and may already be in default
Ca	Highly speculative
C	Lowest quality and the prospects are poor

Within these categories, Moody's has a subclassification of 1 to 3 (with 1 being highest). A bond rated Aaa1 has what Moody's views as the absolute highest quality for a bond.

The following is the rating system for S&P:

AAA	Extremely high capacity to meet debt obligations
AA	Very strong capacity to pay obligations

Quotes and Analysis of Bonds

Investors often overlook bonds, but this can be a big mistake. In fact, you should make it a habit to periodically check not only the stock price of companies you own but also the prices and yields of their bonds. To do this, you can go to http://bonds.yahoo.com (see Figure 5.2).

Here's an example of a quote for one of the sets of bonds issued by WorldCom:

Price	43.875
Yield to maturity	16.187
Current yield	15.84
Maturity	08–15–2028
Credit rating	Ba2/BB

Here's how to read the quote:

Price. The price of a bond is expressed as a percentage of the face value. For this WorldCom bond, this is:

$1,000 face value × 43.875 percent = $438.75

In fact, looking at the price of a company's bonds can be a way to see what institutional investors feel about the company's prospects

A	Strong capacity to meet obligations but can be subject to adverse effects
BBB	Adequate capacity to pay obligations (everything below this level is speculative or "junk bond" status)
BB	Ongoing uncertainties
B	Uncertainty remains and there could be more problems on the horizon
CCC	Vulnerable to being unable to pay obligations
CC	Highly vulnerable to being unable to pay obligations

Again, S&P has a subclassification system but uses plus (+) or minus (–) to indicate differences. So AAA+ would be the absolute highest rating.

Interest Rates

Overall interest rates fluctuate in the U.S. economy. If the economy is slowing down, interest rates tend to fall. The Federal Reserve Board manipulates

---

(after all, it is mostly institutional investors that purchase these types of bonds).

The vice chairman of Dresdner Kleinwort Wasserstein, Henry Miller, has a great way to analyze these prices.

Price as Percentage of Face Value	*Interpretation*
80–90	This may be an indication the company is having problems, but there probably isn't an emergency.
60–80	Investors are getting very worried. The company may suffer from serious problems in the future.
40–60	Investors believe bankruptcy is likely.
40 or below	Bankruptcy could come at any moment.

Investors were right about that WorldCom bond!

Yield to maturity and current yield. These values are explained in the text of the "Interest Rates" section.

Maturity. When WorldCom must pay off the principal of the bond — the amount it borrowed.

Credit rating. This is in the order of Moody's and then S&P.

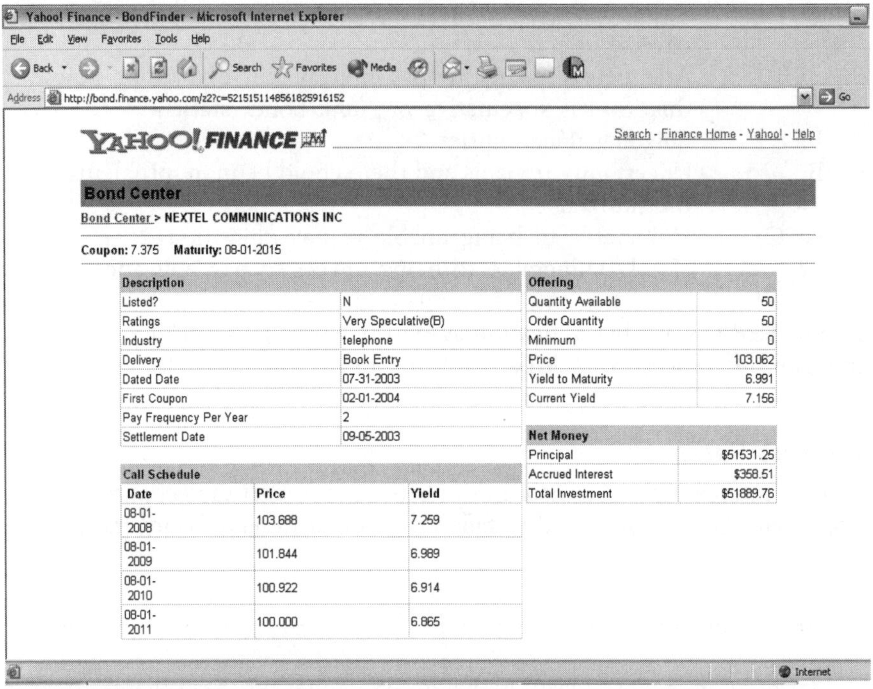

Yahoo! Finance - BondFinder - Microsoft Internet Explorer

File Edit View Favorites Tools Help

Address http://bond.finance.yahoo.com/z2?c=52151511485618259161 52

YAHOO! FINANCE

Search - Finance Home - Yahoo! - Help

Bond Center

Bond Center > NEXTEL COMMUNICATIONS INC

Coupon: 7.375 **Maturity:** 08-01-2015

Description	
Listed?	N
Ratings	Very Speculative(B)
Industry	telephone
Delivery	Book Entry
Dated Date	07-31-2003
First Coupon	02-01-2004
Pay Frequency Per Year	2
Settlement Date	09-05-2003

Offering	
Quantity Available	50
Order Quantity	50
Minimum	0
Price	103.062
Yield to Maturity	6.991
Current Yield	7.156

Net Money	
Principal	$51531.25
Accrued Interest	$358.51
Total Investment	$51889.76

Call Schedule

Date	Price	Yield
08-01-2008	103.688	7.259
08-01-2009	101.844	6.989
08-01-2010	100.922	6.914
08-01-2011	100.000	6.865

Internet

Figure 5.2 Looking at the bonds of a company can be a smart way to see how the pros view its prospects.

them via the discount rate in an effort to stimulate companies to borrow and help them return to profitability and growth. If the economy is overheating, interest rates will tend to rise. Again, the Federal Reserve Board uses them to put a brake on growth in an effort to help moderate inflation.

These fluctuations in overall interest rates have a big impact on the prices of corporate bonds. The rule of thumb is simple:

- If overall interest rates increase, corporate bond prices should fall.
- If overall interest rates decrease, corporate bond prices should rise.

Why? Take another look at the Fast Co. example. Currently, the bonds trade at $1,000 each and have an interest payment of 10 percent or $100 per year. Say the Federal Reserve Board announces that it has increased the discount rate. That ripples through the market, and now companies like Fast Co. need to offer 12 percent — $120 per year on a $1,000 bond — to attract new bond money.

Should You Buy Bonds?

This book focuses mostly on assessing stock, but investors can participate in the fortunes of a company by buying its bonds. Should you do so?

Actually, buying company bonds is something all investors should consider. Here are the advantages:

- Bonds guarantee a fixed amount of interest plus repayment of principal at the end of the term of the bond, as long as the company survives. Because of this, bonds are known as *fixed income instruments* — and many investors like knowing what the future income stream will be.
- Company bonds tend to pay higher interest rates than government bonds. Even top-notch companies can go bust, creating significant losses for bondholders, whereas it's widely assumed that the federal government will never fail to pay its obligations. As a result, to compensate for the risks, companies generally have to offer more than investors could get from the government.
- You can make truly astonishing profits if a distressed company manages to make a turnaround. If your assessment of a company's financials suggests that it will manage to resolve its difficulties, you can snap up the company's bonds, which will usually be selling at a big discount because investors are adjusting the price for the risk of default. If the company does engineer a turnaround, you're in fat city. You get the elevated interest plus the full face value of the bonds if you hold them to maturity, and you may even have a chance to resell the bonds at a premium if their prices soar past face value, as they may well do in the general euphoria following restoration of the company's fortunes. And if the company does go bust despite your assessment, you are likely to get at least some of your money back; unlike a stockholder, you have creditor protection in bankruptcy.
- You sometimes have the opportunity to buy *convertible* bonds, which you can trade for a set number of shares at will. This gives you the protection of bondholding if the company is in difficulty while allowing you to switch horses and take your profit if the stock price soars.

Of course, there are disadvantages:

- The corporate bond market tends to be *illiquid.* In other words, if you want to buy a few bonds, it is hard to find a seller. As a result, you may have to pay a higher price to get the bonds you want.

Also, commissions on bonds can be high, so it is a good idea to shop around.

- The interest rate on the bond is usually fixed, which limits the upside. Also, if inflation increases, this will erode the return from the interest payment.
- Many bonds have call features. This means that, after a certain period of time, the company can buy back its bonds. So you may have a high-interest-rate bond that you'd love to keep to maturity, but you have no choice; you must sell it if the company decides to buy it back from you by activating the call feature.

As an investor, would you pay $1,000 for a Fast Co. bond that gives you $100 when you could get another similar bond that gives you $120 for the same price? No doubt, you would select the latter. Consequently, to keep the Fast Co. bonds attractive, the price will need to fall to about $833. Bond investors would say that the Fast Co. bonds are selling at a *discount*. On the other hand, if interest rates fell, the Fast Co. bonds would almost instantly be selling at a *premium* — that is, for more than $1,000 apiece.

An important calculation for bonds is the current yield:

Coupon rate/Bond price = Yield

In the Fast Co. example, the current yield was originally 10 percent:

$100/$1,000 = 0.10

But after the fall in the bond price, the current yield is in line with the new market level:

$100/$833 = 0.12

Another important calculation is the yield-to-maturity (YTM). This is a quite complex calculation, well beyond the scope of the book, but you can generate the figure at http://www.fool.com, which has an online calculator.

Essentially, the YTM is a more inclusive calculation because it accounts for the premium or discount in the bond. For example, in the Fast Co. example, an investor who buys the discounted bonds will get $100 per year, which is a yield of 12 percent. At the end of the term, assuming Fast Co. is still there to redeem the bond, the return of principal will cover both the $833 discounted price and an extra $266 — it's still a $1,000 bond as far as Fast Co. is concerned, and the difference is a profit to the investor and is included in the YTM. Now, if the bond were purchased at a premium, the

YTM would have accounted for this — lowering the overall return on the bond.

Leases

Basically, a lease is quite easy to understand; it is a method to acquire the use of property at a set rate for a set term. For companies, leases can be used for many things other than land and buildings; airplanes and other big-ticket items are often leased rather than bought.

A company can have two types of leases:

1. *Capital lease.* After the lease term expires, the company may get ownership in the underlying property if it meets a variety of criteria (although this is beyond the scope of the book).
2. *Operating lease.* The company has no ownership rights in the underlying property.

Capital leases must be recorded in the liabilities section of the balance sheet. As noted in Chapter 3, operating leases show up only in the footnotes of the 10-Q and 10-K filings, but they're still important to consider.

Equity Financing

A company that owns 20 percent or more of another company must report the financials of that company on its own balance sheet and income statement. This sounds like a major protection for investors, but it actually makes it relatively easy for companies to hide debt incurred by subsidiaries or investments.

Companies can choose between two approaches to this required reporting, one that provides easily accessible information and one that does not:

1. *Consolidation method.* This is the conservative approach. Say Fast Co. buys 80 percent of the stock of Small Co. for $4 million. Small Co. has debts of $1 million and assets of $4 million. On a consolidated report, Fast Co. will add the $1 million in liabilities to its own balance sheet liabilities and the $4 million in assets to its assets.
2. *Equity method.* This is a much more aggressive approach, and investors should be wary when they see it. If Fast Co. chooses this method, it will start by netting the assets and liabilities of Small Co., resulting in a positive total of $3 million ($4 million in assets minus $1 million in liabilities). It then adds $3 million to its own reported assets. In other words, the $1 million in liabilities does not show up on the balance sheet of Fast Co.

Investors Can Take on Debt, Too

Margin can be a very dangerous thing, especially for investors who do not understand the risks. This does not necessarily mean you should avoid a margin account; working on margin can be quite useful — but you do need to pay attention.

Basically, a margin account allows you to borrow against the assets in the account. This is known as *leverage* and can be very powerful. It has made some people rich and lots of people poor.

Typically, you can borrow up to 50 percent of the value of your margin account. So, if your account has $10,000 in Cisco stock, you can then borrow $10,000 to buy another $10,000 in Cisco stock.

But this is not free money. You have to pay interest on this loan, at a rate based on how much you have in your account (the more money, the lower the rate).

Getting back to the Cisco purchase, which is now $20,000 in value, suppose that Cisco goes gangbusters and surges 50 percent, bumping your overall portfolio to $30,000. If you sell everything, you must pay back the $10,000 loan (as well as any interest due). On a $10,000 investment, you made a hefty profit, somewhere near $20,000 or 200 percent. If you hadn't used margin — and instead invested all $20,000 to buy the stock — your return would have been 50 percent. In other words, margin supercharges your portfolio on the upside.

It also supercharges it on the downside; a falling market can wipe out your account in almost no time. Remember that 50 percent rule: You must own securities in the account worth at least as much money as you've borrowed, or the broker is required to *call* the loan. If you don't have enough money to pay into the account to make up the difference, you can lose everything and wind up in debt besides.

In the footnotes of the 10-Q and 10-K, you will see which method is being used.

Equity

Equity represents the ownership structure of the company. On a very simple basis, suppose you buy 100,000 shares of Fast Co. and the company has five million shares outstanding. Your ownership position in the company would be 2 percent. Of course, chances are you will not have this much equity in a company — but other kinds of shareholders are likely to do so, such as pension funds, insurance companies, hedge funds, and mutual funds. In fact, it is a smart idea to identify the major institutional shareholders of a company; you can find this information using EDGAR Online Pro (http://www.edgaronlinepro.com). EDGAR Online Pro provides real-time access to the equity holdings information filed by over 2,200 institutional investors in their quarterly 13F filings (see Figure 5.3). With intra-day updates and multiple search methods for researching and analyzing over 17,500 securities to see how these holdings change throughout the year, EDGAR Online Pro provides views of New, Sold Out, Decreased, and Increased positions to help users determine institutional buy/sell momentum.

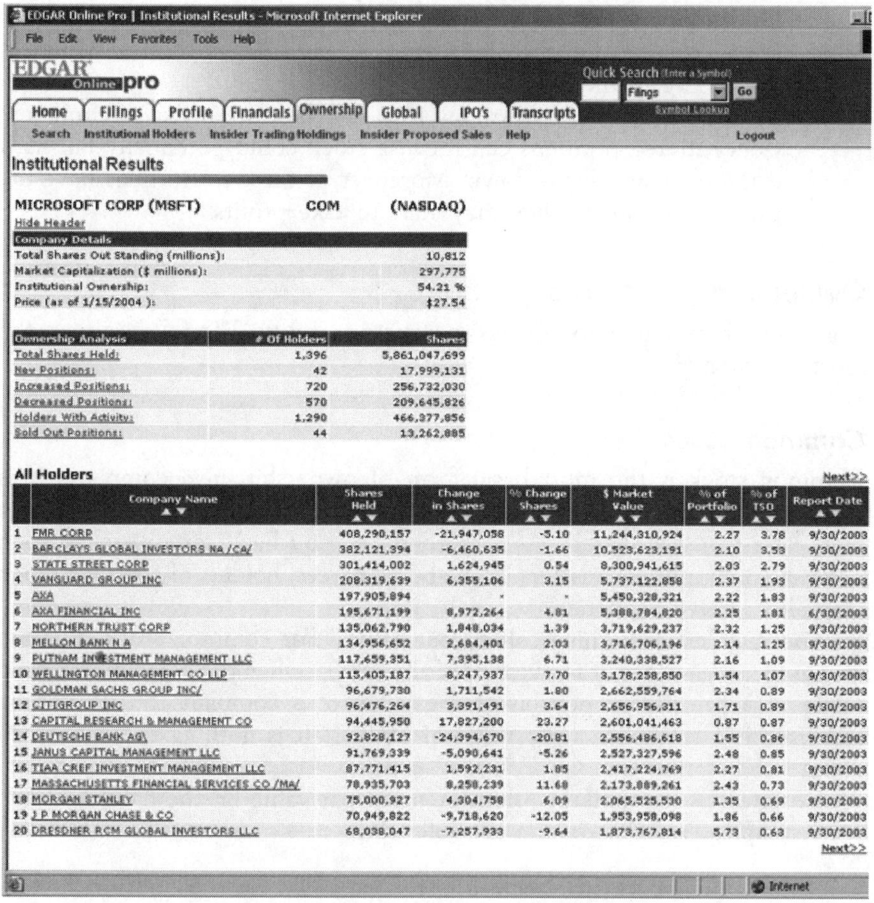

EDGAR Online Pro | Institutional Results - Microsoft Internet Explorer

File Edit View Favorites Tools Help

EDGAR Online pro

Quick Search (Enter a Symbol) Filings Go Symbol Lookup

Home | Filings | Profile | Financials | Ownership | Global | IPO's | Transcripts

Search Institutional Holders Insider Trading Holdings Insider Proposed Sales Help Logout

Institutional Results

MICROSOFT CORP (MSFT) COM (NASDAQ)

Hide Header

Company Details	
Total Shares Out Standing (millions):	10,812
Market Capitalization ($ millions):	297,775
Institutional Ownership:	54.21 %
Price (as of 1/15/2004):	$27.54

Ownership Analysis	# Of Holders	Shares
Total Shares Held:	1,396	5,861,047,699
New Positions:	42	17,999,131
Increased Positions:	720	256,732,030
Decreased Positions:	570	209,645,826
Holders With Activity:	1,290	466,377,856
Sold Out Positions:	44	13,262,885

All Holders Next>>

	Company Name	Shares Held	Change in Shares	% Change Shares	$ Market Value	% of Portfolio	% of TSO	Report Date
1	FMR CORP	408,290,157	-21,947,058	-5.10	11,244,310,924	2.27	3.78	9/30/2003
2	BARCLAYS GLOBAL INVESTORS NA /CA/	382,121,394	-6,460,635	-1.66	10,523,623,191	2.10	3.53	9/30/2003
3	STATE STREET CORP	301,414,002	1,624,945	0.54	8,300,941,615	2.03	2.79	9/30/2003
4	VANGUARD GROUP INC	208,319,639	6,355,106	3.15	5,737,122,858	2.37	1.93	9/30/2003
5	AXA	197,905,894	-	-	5,450,328,321	2.22	1.83	9/30/2003
6	AXA FINANCIAL INC	195,671,199	8,972,264	4.81	5,388,784,820	2.25	1.81	6/30/2003
7	NORTHERN TRUST CORP	135,062,790	1,848,034	1.39	3,719,629,237	2.32	1.25	9/30/2003
8	MELLON BANK N A	134,956,652	2,684,401	2.03	3,716,706,196	2.14	1.25	9/30/2003
9	PUTNAM INVESTMENT MANAGEMENT LLC	117,659,351	7,395,138	6.71	3,240,338,527	2.16	1.09	9/30/2003
10	WELLINGTON MANAGEMENT CO LLP	115,405,187	8,247,937	7.70	3,178,258,850	1.54	1.07	9/30/2003
11	GOLDMAN SACHS GROUP INC/	96,679,730	1,711,542	1.80	2,662,559,764	2.34	0.89	9/30/2003
12	CITIGROUP INC	96,476,264	3,391,491	3.64	2,656,956,311	1.71	0.89	9/30/2003
13	CAPITAL RESEARCH & MANAGEMENT CO	94,445,950	17,827,200	23.27	2,601,041,463	0.87	0.87	9/30/2003
14	DEUTSCHE BANK AG\	92,828,127	-24,394,670	-20.81	2,556,486,618	1.55	0.86	9/30/2003
15	JANUS CAPITAL MANAGEMENT LLC	91,769,339	-5,090,641	-5.26	2,527,327,596	2.48	0.85	9/30/2003
16	TIAA CREF INVESTMENT MANAGEMENT LLC	87,771,415	1,592,231	1.85	2,417,224,769	2.27	0.81	9/30/2003
17	MASSACHUSETTS FINANCIAL SERVICES CO /MA/	78,935,703	8,258,239	11.68	2,173,889,261	2.43	0.73	9/30/2003
18	MORGAN STANLEY	75,000,927	4,304,758	6.09	2,065,525,530	1.35	0.69	9/30/2003
19	J P MORGAN CHASE & CO	70,949,822	-9,718,620	-12.05	1,953,958,098	1.86	0.66	9/30/2003
20	DRESDNER RCM GLOBAL INVESTORS LLC	68,038,047	-7,257,933	-9.64	1,873,767,814	5.73	0.63	9/30/2003

Next>>

Internet

Figure 5.3 Who are the big holders of the company stock? You can find out by reading Form 13Fs. From EDGAR Online Pro (http://www.edgaronlinepro.com).

The following shows the top five owners of Wal-Mart:

Shareholder	*Number of Shares*	*Ownership*
Barclays Bank Plc	131,509,128	2.95
Fidelity	101,219,314	2.27
Vanguard	78,757,449	1.77
Taunus	49,253,346	1.11
Mellon Bank	47,927,781	1.08

Factors to consider when analyzing this type of information:

- Look for top-notch institutions, such as Fidelity and Franklin.
- Keep track of these numbers every quarter. Are the top institutions lowering their percentages? This could be a sign that the institutions are bailing out. On the other hand, be encouraged if the institutions are adding to their positions.
- Be wary if a few institutions own big percentages of a company. Concentrated positions can mean a stock could potentially fall hard if the company slows down. Moreover, if these institutions have big gains in the stock, they may start to take profits.

Ownership Structures

Companies have a myriad of ways to structure equity. The following are the most common.

Common Stock

Common stock is the most basic form of ownership in a company. It is represented in an actual certificate (see the sidebar titled "In Street Name or Not" later in this chapter). As a shareholder, you have certain rights, such as voting on important matters. If the board agrees, holders of common stock may also receive dividends.

You may see something called "par value." For common stock, this has no significance; rather, it is a vestige of the 1800s, when par value did actually relate to a specific proportion of the value of a company. So do not be surprised if a stock has a par value of $0.001. It is nothing to be alarmed about.

Despite this, accountants often mention par value on the balance sheet. For example, Fast Co. reports the following:

Common stock (par value $1 per share)	$1 million
Additional paid-in capital	$10 million
Total capital	$11 million

The "total capital" line shows what Fast Co. has raised by issuing shares to investors — $11 million. The par value was $1 per share, but this is not what investors paid. Rather, they paid $11 per share. The additional $10 million above the par value is known as paid-in capital.

A company may decide to divide its common shares into different classes. An example is Martha Stewart Living Omnimedia (MSO). Martha Stewart took her company public in October 1999 but only sold Class A common stock, which amounted to 14.3 million shares. But the company also had Class B common shares, of which there were 34.1 million. According to the company's bylaws, Class A shares had one vote per share whereas Class B shares had 10 votes per share. In the end, Martha Stewart owned 100 percent of the Class B shares, giving her 96 percent voting control of the company. In other words, it was very clear that she essentially had absolute control of the company.

Preferred Stock

Preferred stock is called a *hybrid security*, because it shares aspects of both a bond and a stock. By definition, this type of security gives preferences to certain investors. Thus companies that encounter difficulty raising capital may be tempted to use preferred stock to entice investors. Here are the chief features of preferred stock:

- *Par value*. Unlike common stock, preferred stock actually does sell for its par value — so the amount is more than trivial. If the par value is $100 per share, then this is what investors will pay initially.
- *Dividends*. The dividend of a preferred stock is expressed as a percentage of the par value. If the dividend is 10 percent of the $100 par value, it would be $10 per year. It's not quite predictable, though, because the board of directors of a company has the right to terminate the dividend payment on preferred stock without triggering a default. That makes it a particularly useful long-term device, as it gives the company a way to staunch its cash outflow without falling into bankruptcy. But, to protect investors, preferred stock usually has a *cumulative* feature. This means that preferred shareholders must be paid all current and past dividends before common shareholders get any dividends.
- *Priority*. In bankruptcy, the claims of secured and unsecured debt holders come before preferred shareholders. However, preferred shareholders will get proceeds before common shareholders do.
- *Call*. As with bonds, the company can call preferred stock. If it does, it typically pays a premium to the par value.

Preferred Stock — Getting the VIP Treatment

It is rare for a company to have preferred stock traded on stock exchanges. In many cases, preferred stock is issued to strategic investors, major institutions, or venture capitalists that want to protect their investment.

For example, in August 2001, Lucent raised $1.75 billion from a convertible stock offering. The par value was $1,000 per share and the annual dividend was 8 percent. If the common stock price were to increase to more than $7.48, the holders could convert their preferred stock into common stock. In August 2006, Lucent could call the preferred stock.

In some deals, you may also see warrants issued to a preferred stock holder. A *warrant* gives a person the right to buy a certain number of shares of the company if the stock price rises above a fixed price. Warrants can be particularly attractive to preferred investors, who can benefit from the upside of future stock movements. On the other hand, as these warrants are exercised, this will dilute the ownership of existing shareholders.

- *Redemption.* Preferred stock may also have a redemption feature, which requires the company to purchase it back after a certain amount of time (this could, for example, be 10 or 20 years after the offering).
- *Voting.* Another enticement is special voting privileges. For example, a holder of preferred stock may get five votes for every share instead of only one.
- *Convertible.* In some cases, a preferred stock may be convertible into a fixed number of common shares. This is known as an *equity kicker* and could be a nice attraction to help raise capital.

Treasury Stock

Treasury stock is stock that a company has repurchased on the open market. On the surface, this is good news and companies are wont to publicize any buybacks. When the news breaks, it is not uncommon to see the stock price pop.

A company could have a variety of reasons to buy back its own shares:

- To fulfill the requirements of an employee stock option plan.
- To make the best use of excess cash. For instance, a company may not have many growth prospects. Instead of plowing the money back into the company to, say, refurbish the offices, the company can invest in its own stock to reduce the burden of future dividends.

- To invest in itself. If the company believes the stock is undervalued and will eventually increase in price, buying it back now will provide the same benefits other investors enjoy.

Bill Miller Knows Financial Statements

Consider Bill Miller a New Age value investor. His philosophy is that he will try just about anything to get an edge when picking stocks. And, yes, he will even attend New Age seminars (he pursued a doctorate in philosophy). Although he recognizes that reading the numbers is vitally important, Miller thinks great investors must also go beyond the numbers.

Miller is the top portfolio manager for the Legg Mason Funds, with over $11 billion in assets. What is very impressive is that he has beaten the S&P 500 index for 13 straight years — the only person who has done this.

Even though Miller is open-minded, he still has one guiding principle: He looks for companies that trade at substantial discounts to their intrinsic value. For many value investors, this means looking at companies in mundane businesses and also usually means avoiding tech stocks. But Miller believes that investors can determine intrinsic values for tech stocks.

For instance, in 1996, Miller analyzed AOL. At the time, the company was in turmoil as customers frequently got busy signals when trying to log on. Miller went against conventional wisdom and thought AOL was in a great situation: it had lots and lots of customers. He also understood that once these customers signed on, they were likely to stay customers (simply put, it is a big hassle to change online services). With its lead, AOL would be able to generate substantial amounts of cash, and Miller thought that the stock price came nowhere near reflecting this fact. So Miller bought the stock aggressively.

Another stock that captivated Miller was Dell. Again, it was a controversial decision because many investors thought that Dell would suffer from a business that was rapidly turning into a commodity. And commodity businesses always have low margins.

Miller looked beyond this and delved into the inner workings of Dell. He saw that the company was able to turn over its inventory at a much higher clip than its competitors (see Chapter 9 for more information on this metric). Basically, Dell was the low-cost leader and was able to enjoy substantial cash flows and profits.

For more information on Miller, you can read *The Man Who Beats the S&P* by Janet Lowe.

- To improve its appearance. By buying back stock, the number of shares outstanding will fall. This should help boost the company's earnings per share (EPS) numbers. I discuss EPS in more detail in Chapter 7 and Chapter 13.

Remember that even though a company announces a stock buyback, this does not necessarily mean it will carry it out. A company has the right to cancel such a plan — because management may consider the business environment to be too adverse or see new opportunities to invest in. Consequently, you should track treasury stock totals over time and see if a company is really buying back its stock.

Death Spiral Equity

Death spiral? Shouldn't a phrase like this be in a Stephen King horror novel, not a book on financial statement analysis? It is hard to believe, but *death spiral* is a technical term in finance; it really exists, and investors do need to be aware of the consequences. Ironically enough, even some CFOs do not know about the death spiral phenomenon and as a result lead their companies into terrible financing arrangements.

Of course, when reading financial statements, you will not see "death spiral" written out. It's not something anyone wants to announce. Rather, the language will be convoluted and harmless. If anything, it will look hopeful. After all, the company will have raised a lot of money.

Unfortunately, some investment funds provide financing of last resort. Some call it dirty money, yet it is not illegal. The form of financing I'm talking about is often referred to as PIPE, which stands for private investment in public entities. This is a fancy description for a private placement. So what is a private placement? Basically, this is when a company sells shares to a small group of institutional investors and wealthy investors.

PIPEs have many attractions. First, a company does not have to undergo the expense and time of making filings with the SEC. The reason is that the investors are all institutions and are savvy enough to not need extensive disclosures. Second, the paperwork tends to be quicker and a company can raise lots of money fast.

The problem is that PIPE investors tend to be more sophisticated than the managements of the companies they deal with. Besides, when a company is desperate, it is likely to do just about anything to get money. The upshot is a financing arrangement that mostly benefits PIPE investors and leaves individual owners of the company's stock holding the bag.

In most cases, the PIPE investors will structure securities that provide them with many benefits (which, of course, individual investors do not get).

Suppose Fast Co. goes for a PIPE deal. During the past few years, its industry has been terrible and Fast Co. has been losing substantial amounts of money. Within six months, the company will run out of cash. Currently, the stock price is $2 per share.

Fast Co. structures a deal with two PIPE funds to raise $20 million. For this, the PIPE funds get a convertible preferred stock on the following terms:

- *Dividend of 10 percent.* This is paid before any money goes to common shareholders.
- *Convertible feature.* The PIPE investors can convert their preferred shares into common stock at $1.75 or lower.
- *Preferred feature.* In the event of bankruptcy, the PIPE investors get the proceeds of a liquidation before the common shareholders do.
- *Participating.* This is a feature that gives the PIPE investors considerable upside if the company is sold. For instance, say the PIPE investors own 40 percent of Fast Co. Suppose the company is eventually sold for $500 million. The PIPE investors would get their $20 million back, plus any dividends. They will also get 40 percent of the purchase price, or $200 million.
- *Supercharged.* This is another nice feature for PIPE investors. It means that the company will be required to pay back the initial investment at a certain multiple, say two or three times the investment. In the current example, if the supercharge factor were 2, then the PIPE investors would get $400 million on the sale, not $200 million.
- *Warrants.* PIPE investors usually get millions of dollars worth of warrants, which means future dilution for existing shareholders.

OK, so where's the death spiral? Remember that the PIPE investment has a convertible feature. As the stock price goes down, the PIPE investors get more and more shares. In theory, this makes sense, as the PIPE investors are looking for some downside protection. But it can be — and often is — abused.

The keyword to look for in a PIPE financing is a convertible security that is *floorless* or has a "reset" provision. Looking again at the Fast Co. deal, a floorless convertible may have the following provisions: If the stock falls to $1.75, the PIPE investors get 500,000 more shares; if the stock falls to $1.50, the PIPE investors get 1,000,000 more shares, and so on.

The temptation is for the PIPE investors to short the stock. Short selling allows investors to make money as the stock price falls. See the sidebar titled "Going on the Short Side" in Chapter 6 for more information on this kind of investment.

If the PIPE investors short the stock at $2 and the stock falls to $1.75, then they would have made 25 cents per share for every stock shorted.

In Street Name or Not?
It's an Important Question

When you buy shares, the evidence of ownership takes the form of a certificate. Stock certificates can be quite ornate (with fancy designs and calligraphy), and some people actually spend lots of time and money collecting old certificates. This hobby even has a name: *scripophily*. In fact, certificates have been in existence for more than 400 years. You can find more information at http://www.stocksearchintl.com/collectibles.html.

As a shareholder, you have a choice in the way you hold your shares — in your possession or in "street name."

To get possession of the certificates, you merely ask your broker to have them delivered. This may give you some comfort, but there are problems. If you want to sell the stock, you need to send the certificates back to your broker, which may prolong the process of the sale. If you lose the certificates, you will not only have to pay a replacement fee but probably wait a few weeks to get new certificates. And if you move to another residence, you need to notify the company that sold the stock. (Otherwise company correspondence and even dividends may not reach you!)

Because of these problems, most investors prefer to have their shares put in *street name*. In other words, the broker will housekeep the shares and handle all the administrative work, such as correspondence and dividends or new residence. However, you are still the absolute owner of the shares (in legal terms, you are the "beneficial owner"). Another benefit is that your broker will send you periodic account statements and year-end information to help with your taxes.

Because the stock hit the $1.75 trigger, the PIPE investors will get 500,000 shares, which they can use to cover the short. Then the PIPE investors will short the stock at $1.75, wait until the price falls to $1.50, and then cover the short again. This process goes into a spiral — that is, a death spiral.

True, a PIPE investment document will have a "no short" clause. But this is useless, because PIPE investors can use offshore funds to engage in the shorting in secret.

A classic case of a death spiral was eToys. In June 2000, the company raised $100 million in a PIPE and then saw its stock plunge to zero by March 2001. Such stunning collapses are not uncommon. According to a study from UCLA, of the 500 PIPEs issued from 1995 through 1998, approximately 85 percent of them saw the stock price fall about one-third over the next year.

In fact, perception can be a negative for a company. It is not uncommon for a company's stock to plunge when it announces a PIPE deal. Investors are wondering: Is the company in dire straits? Is the financing deadly?

As with most arrangements, PIPEs are not completely negative. PIPE financing was instrumental for the biotech industry in the early 1990s and

Making Sense of Market Cap

The *market capitalization* (market cap for short) is the total value of the company based on the current stock price and number of shares outstanding:

Market cap = Shares outstanding × Price

For some companies, the market cap can be staggering. (GE's market cap is approximately $300 billion.) Founders of companies certainly like high market caps, which means their rankings on the Forbes 400 go higher and higher. Look at Bill Gates at Microsoft — that company's market cap is also $300 billion, and his own net worth is $61 billion.

Some investors look at the market cap as an indication of whether a company is undervalued or overvalued. For example, if a company is profitable and has $50 million in cash but the market cap is $25 million, a value investor would be intrigued. Then again, if a company has zero sales — and the prospect of sales is in the distant future — but the market cap is $10 billion, you should probably be concerned.

Market cap is also an important way to differentiate stocks. Research firm Morningstar uses the following classification:

Small cap	Up to $1 billion
Mid cap	$1 billion to $5 billion
Large cap	$5 billion to $100 billion
Giant cap	Over $100 billion

Interestingly enough, as markets change, the classification system has changed. There was a time when Morningstar, for example, classified a small cap stock as having a market cap of $250 million or below.

The classification is important because it is how mutual funds are differentiated. Investors might want to diversify their holdings into a cross-section of small, mid, and large cap stocks. As a result, these different types of stocks go through cycles. During the late 1990s, it was the large cap stocks that performed very well. This changed in 2000–2002 when small and mid cap stock performed better.

also helped some good-quality Internet companies in 2000–2001. One was the online travel service Expedia, which did a PIPE in June 2000 for $60 million when the stock was at $16.60.

However, it is important to note that the investors were not interested in making a quick buck on a death spiral. The main investor was Microsoft, and Expedia was its first spin-off. Certainly, Microsoft wanted to make sure it was a success. The other investor was Crossover Ventures, which did not want to disappoint a big client, Microsoft.

By the middle of 2002, Expedia's stock was about $80 per share.

Conclusion

The equation, on its face, is very simple: assets equal liabilities plus capital. But, as this chapter and its predecessor show, you can glean much useful information from assets, liabilities, and capital.

The next chapter will turn to the second of the Big Three: the income statement. That's where you can see if a company is making money or not.

6

Income Statement, Part One

Analyzing the Top Line

As the old saying goes, "Figures don't lie, but liars figure." And the figures on the income statement are the ones would-be liars play with most often and most enthusiastically. The income statement attracts manipulators for the same reasons it attracts investors: It seems to offer the most detailed and revealing information about what's really happening in a company, so it offers the biggest payoff both to those who want to twist it and to those who want to be able to rely on it.

Even though financial statement preparation rules are changing in an effort to try to prevent future scandals like the crop of 2002, the fact remains that income statements will still be tempting to manipulate. Why? Here's a look behind the scenes:

- Even strong companies have problems and all companies are under the intense scrutiny of investors. It is very tempting for senior management to make choices that dress up the figures. At first, it will be harmless. The theory is things will get better. But they don't, and management continues to get more and more aggressive. It is a common trap.
- Employee options have value if the stock price increases, and this usually happens if earnings increase. Senior managers will continue to get nice options packages and thus will be encouraged to ramp up earnings, even if it takes accounting that is on the aggressive side.
- GAAP requirements are fairly flexible and will continue to be so. For example, certain things are at the discretion of management, such as

the length of depreciation or the probable expense for doubtful accounts, and these choices have an immediate and direct effect on the income statement.

Like the balance sheet, the income statement comes in two parts: revenues and expenses. The picture of a company's health can be improved by enhancing its revenues or reducing its expenses, so both parts offer fertile ground to artists in figuring. This chapter focuses on the revenues, and the next turns to the reported expenses and profits.

Revenues

Revenues (that is, sales and other income) represent the cash and promises to pay from customers for either services provided or goods delivered. You will always find this figure at the top of the income statement — which is why you will often hear the phrase "top line."

Many companies provide rebates and discounts to encourage sales. These may be automatically deducted from sales, in which case the income statement will call the item "net sales." If not, the revenues are "gross revenues" and there will be a separate item that makes the necessary deduction.

Another adjustment to revenues is returns. This is no doubt a commonplace thing, especially in the retail industry. But sometimes returns reflect the recall of a defective product, and this can have a very negative effect on the company's finances and stock price. For example, for a while the news was full of stories about Ford's troubles with its Explorer line and a series of accidents apparently related to the Firestone tires used on the vehicle. Ford took quick action and had a massive recall. But the damage was done: Ford saw its brand tarnished, profits fall, and litigation rise. In situations like this, things only tend to get worse — and this was the case for Ford shareholders.

Sales Growth

Without question, you want a company with good sales growth. But what does this mean? After all, a new company will often have a substantial growth rate because it has lots of opportunity to grab market share. And the company can typically charge high prices as well. This was the case with many high-flying Internet companies, such as Amazon.com, Priceline.com, and Yahoo!.

So when analyzing a company's sales growth, you should account for the following factors:

- *Where is the company in its life cycle?* If it is a young company — 10 years or younger — then expect a relatively higher growth rate (say

Don't Be Fooled by the Seasons

Suppose that a company saw a 100 percent increase in sales in the fourth quarter compared to the third quarter. Sounds good, huh? Not if the company is a retailer. Of course, much of the sales and profits of a retailer come during the critical Christmas quarter. In other words, an investor should compare the current fourth quarter to the prior fourth quarter to see if there has been improvement. This is known as an apples-to-apples comparison.

Not all sales bump up during the fourth quarter. For example, consumers tend to buy more gasoline during the summer months because of vacations. In fact, as mentioned in Chapter 3, a company's 10-Q or 10-K will often describe seasonal factors, called *seasonality.*

This is from the filings of 1-800-FLOWERS.com:

> Sales of the Company's products are seasonal, concentrated in the second quarter, due to Mother's Day, Administrative and Professionals' Week and Easter, and the fourth calendar quarter, due to the Thanksgiving and Christmas holidays. In anticipation of increased sales activity during these periods, the Company hires a significant number of temporary employees to supplement its permanent staff and the company increases its inventory levels. If revenues during these periods do not meet the Company's expectations, it may not generate sufficient revenue to offset these increased costs and its operating results may suffer.

Also, a company's sales may be affected by the weather. An unusually warm winter, for instance, may mean lower sales for utility companies.

25 percent per year or more). In fact, if a young company's growth rate has been anemic, this is a sign that the company is likely to be a loser.

- *Is the industry maturing?* This is a hard question to answer. Microsoft is in the midst of a huge growth market that has lasted more than 20 years. But this is rare. Besides, even the mighty Microsoft has seen its sales growth rate fall over time.
- *What is the quality of the sales?* Companies get more mileage out of sales to strong, ongoing customers than to one-time users or shaky customers who may not pay their bills, and many other choices and events can influence the worth of any given sale. See the "Quality of Sales" section later in this chapter for more detail on this point.

Connecting the Dots

Investors suffered tremendous losses in the telecom sector from 2000 to 2002. Despite the carnage, some companies fared relatively well. Amdocs, for example, prospered through much of the worst of the plunge. Why the divergence? A big reason is that, in an effort to cut costs, the big telcecom companies began to outsource more of their operations — including billing, which was an Amdocs specialty.

Did that make Amdocs a good long-term choice? Unfortunately, when a huge sector, like telecom, is experiencing a major shakeout, just about all firms will do badly. Despite the appearance that Amdocs might weather the storm, it turned out to be a poor risk. In June 2002, the company warned about its prospects, and the stock plunged 39 percent in a single day.

Were there any warning signs besides the fall-off in the telecom market? Had you analyzed the company's prior quarterly report, you would have noticed that sales were starting to slow down (especially after factoring in the sales boost from the acquisition of Clarify). Also, the company's backlog fell $123 million — more than 8 percent — which was another indication of slowing sales.

- *How does the sales total compare to the rest of the industry?* Even though PC sales have slowed, a company like Dell has still been able to garner relatively stronger growth rates than many of its competitors.
- *Are both sales and losses growing at a rapid pace?* If a company is unable to turn a profit in good times, how will it do during bad times? This was the trouble with many tech companies in 2000–2002.
- *Is the company engaging in lots of acquisitions?* If so, then the sales may be somewhat questionable. If a company stumbles on a bad deal, it could mean disaster. See the sidebar titled "The Dark Side of M&A" in Chapter 4.
- *Is the growth somewhat suspect because the last year was a bad year?* For example, suppose a telecom company saw its sales fall 50 percent last year to $200 million. Then, this year, sales grew to $300 million. That's a 50 percent increase over the past year, which looks good, but it is still $100 million down from the level reached two years ago.

Segmented Sales

Some companies have various business segments and may break down the revenues accordingly. For example, perhaps Fast Co. gets 60 percent of its

The Beauty of Pricing Power

Pricing power is the ability for a company to increase its prices without losing many customers. Economists have a fancy way of expressing this idea; they call it *price elasticity.* If you can find a company with strong pricing power (or price elasticity), you might have a winner. It is an indication that the company has a strong brand and customer loyalty. With this, a company can potentially grow for many years.

Pricing power was a big advantage for Starbucks. Even though coffee is a commodity, Starbucks was able to build a tremendous brand that allowed it to charge premium prices without scaring away customers. Then again, this is definitely not the case with many other food service companies, especially fast-food operators like McDonald's and Wendy's.

revenues from chip sales but also has a thriving software business. If Fast Co.'s software business surged 50 percent in the last quarter, the company may be tempted to emphasize this in its earnings release and conference call — especially if chip revenues grew only 5 percent, which may indicate that the company's main business is deteriorating. In other words, fast-growing business segments can mask underlying problems with a company. In some cases, a company may try to trick investors by focusing on certain segments.

Nonoperating Revenues

Companies get money from sources other than their main business, just as individuals do. Assuming you're not a professional investor, you probably have a regular paycheck from some other business, and you also have your investment income, the interest on your bank account, the quarter you found on the sink in the company restroom, etc. The money that comes in from activities that aren't your regular business is *nonoperating revenue;* it's nice to have, but it's not the same as your primary business.

The same applies to companies. When you read an income statement, you need to keep an eye on the difference between operating and nonoperating revenues. For Fast Co., it's clear that its chip and software businesses are both integral parts of the business and should be classified as operating revenues. But what if the company also made a variety of venture investments that have done well, boosting its income in a very satisfactory manner? These would be considered nonoperating revenues, because Fast Co. is really not a venture fund, it is a chip company. Again, a company can use nonoperating revenues to mask underlying deterioration.

No less a company than Intel has used exactly that ploy to maintain its position with Wall Street. Intel is the premier chip company. Besides developing world-class technology, the company has been very savvy in creating strong brands. Its "Intel Inside" campaign was a critical part of the company's success in becoming a world leader.

Like most other tech companies, Intel was experiencing growth problems by the end of the 1990s. However, Wall Street wanted and expected the company to continue to report glowing numbers.

For its second quarter 2000 earnings report, it appeared that Intel was having no problem meeting the strenuous expectations. The press release announced:

> Intel Corporation today announced second quarter revenue of $8.3 billion, a new quarterly record, up 23 percent from the second quarter of 1999 and 4 percent sequentially. The company also had record unit shipments of microprocessors and flash memory in the second quarter.

Sounds great, right? Not really. The bulk of the reported revenues did not come from Intel's chip business; rather, they were from gains in its venture investment portfolio. If you factored out these gains, Intel's profits grew a mere 8 percent. Basically, Intel was experiencing problems with its core business — which became evident in subsequent earnings reports.

Revenue Recognition Policies

As noted in Chapter 2, the timing of revenues differs depending on the kind of accounting a company uses. It's simple with cash-basis accounting — revenues are generated when the cash comes in from a customer.

But this is not what public companies do; instead, they use accrual accounting and recognize revenues when they are *earned*. On the surface, this seems fairly straightforward, but it turns out to be quite flexible, giving companies many opportunities to manipulate the level of sales. Basically, if a company can recognize sales faster, the sales totals will be higher (at least in the short term) — and this should help the stock price.

For accrual accounting, revenue is generated if two requirements are met: (1) the earnings process is complete and (2) there is a reliable measure of the value of the goods or services provided to the customer. Here's an example. This time Fast Co. is a maker of tables. Obviously, if it is only half finished building a table when a customer commits to the purchase, the company cannot recognize it as a sale.

Assume Fast Co. finishes the table, which satisfies the first requirement. Next, the company sells the product — for $200 — to a retailer, who promises to pay within 30 days. Is this a reliable measure of value of the goods? Not entirely. True, the stated price of $200 is specific, but what if the customer returns the table? Or what if the customer does not pay for it? Then the sale is zero. To account for this, the company will attempt to estimate the likelihood of customers' not paying their debts and subtract this from sales — which is an item called *allowance for doubtful accounts*. I'll return to this point in more detail later, but for now it's enough to know that the reported sales totals are more or less optimistic depending on the company's allowance policies.

Once the two requirements are met, a company can recognize the revenues at the point of sale, regardless of whether it collects cash at that point or not. Companies that recognize sales before receipt of cash must disclose their revenue recognition policies in the notes to the financials. In particular, look for policies that address consignment sales, installment sales, or revenue recognized either during production or on completion of production.

Consignment Sales

Suppose that Fast Co. (switching businesses again) develops a popular book that it sends to several independent bookstores. These bookstores do not pay for the book but instead take supplies on consignment. As the books are sold, the bookstore gets a commission and Fast Co. recognizes the sale. Until a sale is made, Fast Co. retains the title to the merchandise.

If a company has a policy that recognizes sales on shipment of products on consignment, be wary. It is likely that the company is being too aggressive.

Installment Sales

In some cases, a company may sell products to customers that have poor credit ratings. To recognize the sale of an item when it is shipped would probably be too aggressive, so a company will use an installment method. For example, Fast Co. (which isn't called Fast Co. for nothing!) sells a refrigerator for $1,000 to a customer who has low income and bad credit. The customer makes a deposit of $100 and promises to make three quarterly payments to complete the purchase.

The company could maintain that it's likely that the total amount will be collected, so it can recognize the whole purchase price as revenue right now. But this would be a mistake. Instead, the company should recognize the revenue only when payments are made — which is the more conservative approach.

Revenue Recognized During Production

Some companies — in the defense industry, for example — engage in multiyear contracts because they're building things that take longer than a year to complete. As a result, many of these companies use methods to recognize revenues even though a completed product is not provided to the customer. Rather, it is assumed that revenue is generated as the product is being developed.

This does make sense. For example, suppose a construction company wins a contract to build a $1 billion dam that will take three years to complete. During construction, the company that recognizes revenue only when fully earned will show substantial losses as it pays for all the people, equipment, and materials the dam requires. Then, in the fourth year, when the company receives payment, it will have a huge windfall. Some companies do use this approach, which is called the *completed contract method.*

However, the completed contract method seems to ignore the matching principle, the key principle of accounting that calls for revenue and expense to be recognized in the same period. So many companies use the *percentage of completion method* to record revenue in the initial years of a contract. Under this approach, the profit from the contract is recognized as a percentage of the project that has been completed so far.

Using the construction example, suppose that the company expects to generate a $20 million profit from the contract. In the first year, the company finishes 30 percent of the project, so it will recognize $6 million in profit (30 percent times $20 million).

The percentage completed method tends to be on the aggressive side. For example, suppose a defense contractor wins a contract for $2 billion. For several years, the company meets its requirements and recognizes the profits on the deal. Then, suddenly, political fortunes shift and Congress decides to cancel the project. The company will now have to take a big charge against earnings. The percentage completed method is appropriate in the following circumstances:

- The company is likely to finish the contract on time. (Cost overruns or delays could result in much lower profits or even losses.)
- The likelihood of the customer keeping its commitment is high. (During the telecom boom, major projects seemed like a sure thing — then the market came undone and many projects were canceled.)

Revenue Recognized on Completion of Production

Some commodities have a definite value, such as gold or silver or agricultural crops. Since there is little need for marketing or distribution, a company can recognize the revenue when the commodity is mined or harvested.

But this is not a widely used method, even in the commodities industry. The main reason is that prices can vary widely in short periods of time.

Special Case of Software

The software industry has been very controversial in regard to revenue recognition. In fact, this industry has been notorious for such accounting scandals, as with Informix and even Oracle.

The big problem has been the evolution of software. Originally, it resembled a product. That is, you install it and it works. But as software became more complicated, its product characteristics began to blur. Software may include extensive installation and ongoing support. It may need (or at least get) periodic updates as well.

To help clear up the uncertainties, the new revenue recognition standard, called SOP 97–2, was instituted in 1998. A software transaction must meet many requirements before it can be classified as a sale:

- The code has been delivered.
- The price is fixed.
- It is expected the fee will be collected.
- There is persuasive evidence that there is a real agreement between the buyer and seller.

If there are upgrades and ongoing support, this revenue needs to be estimated and recognized over the period it is provided. Furthermore, if the transaction is a comprehensive customized software project, then revenue is recognized using either the percentage of completion or completed contract method.

Quality of Sales

Not all sales are created equal. For example, if you sell products to a company that is about to go bankrupt, it would certainly be a questionable transaction. Smart investors will look into the quality of sales.

As noted earlier, a company can potentially inflate sales by its choice of revenue recognition (say, using the percentage completed method instead of the completed contract method). But companies may take actions other than changing recognition policies to pump up revenues. One approach is to create fictitious revenues, which is clearly illegal. (See the sidebar titled "The Fine Art of Creating Revenue" later in this chapter.)

But there are more subtle ways to accomplish the same goal. One is called "stuffing the channel." Here is how it works: Suppose Fast Co. has $10 million in sales for the current quarter. Unfortunately, Wall Street is expecting $12 million, and the stock price will inevitably plunge when investors find out the bad news.

The Miscategorized Company

When Wall Street is negative, it can be *very* negative. When the dot-com bubble popped, for instance, investors dumped anything that had a hint of a dot-com regardless of how well a company was doing. It is in such times — when investors are throwing out the baby with the bathwater — that famed investor John Neff finds great bargains. (See the sidebar titled "Value All the Way" in Chapter 5 for more information about John Neff.)

Neff looks for what he calls the "miscategorized company" — a company that is one of the babies the market threw out. In 1990, Neff found such a company, Bayer AG. At that time, investors hated chemical companies and they all seemed to believe that Bayer AG was a chemical company. However, Neff delved into the financials and realized that the company was not a pure chemical plan. It had substantial presence in growth areas: about a third in pharmaceuticals, 8 percent from agricultural chemicals, and 13 percent from photographic or specialty chemicals. When Neff bought the company, it was selling for a lowly six times earnings. In a few years, it turned out to be a strong investment for his portfolio, as the company's earnings experienced strong growth and the multiple more than doubled.

To remedy the situation, Fast Co. ships $2 million in product to existing customers; that is, it stuffs the channel. Since the company recognizes sales on shipment, Fast Co. will meet its $12 million revenue benchmark and the stock will be saved.

True, there is nothing illegal about this — but that does not mean it is problem-free. Basically, Fast Co. is jeopardizing future sales to get a short-term pop. After all, why will customers want to place new orders if they already have enough on hand?

It can be tough to spot when a company is stuffing a channel. One of the simplest approaches is to keep an eye on the dates of a company's press releases. If you see a major deal signed within a week at the end of the quarter, this may indicate that the company is trying to stuff the channel.

Declines in the backlog — the amount of sales that have not been fulfilled — may indicate that sales are being accelerated or starting to fall for other reasons. One major red flag is when you see slower growth in net income than in cash flow; someone is pumping something somewhere when that happens. I'll get back to this point in more detail in Chapter 8. And keep an eye on the days sales outstanding (DSO) figure; if this ratio is increasing over time, it is an indication of degrading quality of sales (see Chapter 9).

Following are some other indirect ways of detecting this or other practices that cast doubt on the quality of sales.

Related-Party Customers

When a company has senior management or major shareholders with personal financial or family relationships with a customer, the company may not necessarily be getting a good deal from that customer. Such deals may be no more than "family discounts" and trivial in the overall business picture, but watch out if the exposure seems to amount to a substantial part of the company's operations. More on these transactions in Chapter 10.

Immediate Jump in Revenue After a Merger

M&A activity provides fertile ground for a company to engage in creative accounting. One technique can even help boost the acquirer's revenue. How is this possible?

Example: Fast Co. decides to purchase Small Co. In the current quarter, Small Co. is expected to produce $20 million in revenues. But Fast Co. encourages Small Co. to delay the recognition of, say, $15 million of these sales into the next quarter, when the merger is closed. Thus, Fast Co. will be able to add a nice $15 million to its revenue base.

If you see a sudden increase in revenues after a merger, be cautious. The company may be playing fast and loose with its accounting.

Vendor Financing

Vendor financing refers to the practice of extending credit to cover customers' purchases, something that is typically done with big-ticket items. Basically, when customers do not have the resources to pay up front but still have great growth opportunities, the seller of the product makes a loan to cover the price with a view to making money in the long run.

Vendor financing has many advantages for the seller:

- Helps clinch a sale
- Develops long-term relationships
- Produces interest income on the sale
- Allows the sale to be booked as revenue
- Tends to boost the price of the purchase

So what's the problem? The main one is the risk any lender has: the chance of default. If an upstart company experiences problems, it may not be able to pay off the loan and a write-down will need to be taken. This is precisely what happened to many telecom equipment manufacturers, includ-

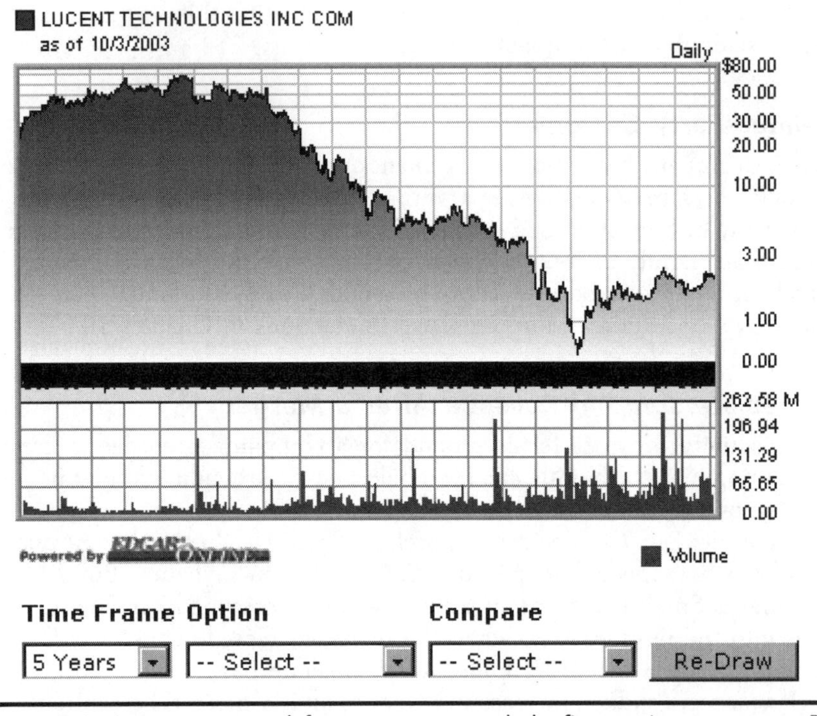

Figure 6.1 It is not unusual for a company to help finance its customers. But sometimes it can get too excessive, as was the case with companies like Lucent and Nortel during the telecom boom. From EDGAR Online Pro (http://www.edgaronlinepro.com).

ing Nortel and Lucent (see Figure 6.1). They provided massive amounts of vendor financing to new companies that quickly hit hard times and could not pay the bills.

Growth in Long-Term Receivables

Long-term receivables are amounts owed by customers and collected over a period of more than a year. If you see a surge in this and it becomes a large part of sales (say, over 10 percent of sales), it could be a sign that the company is becoming very aggressive in booking sales.

Both Buyer and Seller Transactions

Sometimes a transaction can be so complicated that it is not easy to determine who is the buyer and seller. For example, an online portal may strike a deal

The Fine Art of Creating Revenue

Despite a tough market, Miniscribe was able to buck the trend, becoming a very successful manufacturer of hard drives. Like clockwork, the company would — quarter after quarter — report improving sales and profits. Wall Street loved it and the stock price soared.

However, Wall Street was shocked when the company reported a $14.6 million loss for the fourth quarter of 1988. The board was concerned and conducted an investigation. The results were not pretty. No, Miniscribe was not an example of a great company. It was, instead, a company that knew how to manufacture fake revenues. Here are some of the techniques it used:

- Count defective disk drives as inventory.
- Break into the files of the auditors and change inventory valuations.
- Create side agreements with customers, allowing them to avoid being responsible for making any payments for the products.
- Falsify invoices.
- Understate bad debts.
- Send bricks to customers and count them as sales.

Another classic case is ZZZZ Best Carpet Cleaning, founded by a 16-year-old fast-talker named Barry Minkow. Although he was good at getting customers, he was bad at making profits. But that did not stop him from faking them, and he was even able to convince top Wall Street bankers to take his company public.

The scheme to create fictitious sales was quite intricate, involving expertly concocted invoices — that fooled auditors — and an elaborate check-kiting ring. Not long after the IPO, the fraud was uncovered and the firm went bust. Minkow also served time in federal prison, where he wrote a book called *Faking It in America.*

to sell advertising to an enterprise software maker. The enterprise software maker, in the same deal, sells a long-term license to the portal for its software. Such transactions often turn into *washes,* trades in which little real revenue is generated for either side.

Sudden Changes in Revenues

If you see a big surge in revenues, this could be a warning sign, especially if the rest of the industry is not showing strength. Of course, this test is not foolproof, as a company may have introduced a new product line that has been met with insatiable demand.

Nevertheless, an investor needs to be comfortable with the reasons behind the revenue surge. If there is no obvious good reason, it is probably a good idea to avoid the stock.

A classic example is Lernout & Hauspie, a leader in software for voice recognition. In 1998, the company had sales of $97,000 in Korea, which was mostly immaterial for the company. But by 2000, the company had $58.9 million in the first quarter from Korea. Moreover, this amount was higher than combined sales in Europe and the United States.

Was Korea a huge market? Or was something else happening? Well, Lernout & Hauspie had created many companies in Korea that bought lots of product. It was not long until the company went bust and the CEO was arrested for fraud.

While it would have been impossible to detect these Korean shell companies, a savvy investor would have nonetheless been very wary of the surge in sales in such a short time from such a small country.

Growing Gap Between Sales and Accounts Receivable

It is natural for a company's accounts receivable to grow with sales. It is to be expected. However, watch out if the accounts receivable are growing much faster than sales. A rule of thumb would be that a 50 percent gap in terms of growth rates is a danger sign. Here are some reasons to be concerned about the gap:

- It may indicate that the company is having difficulty in collecting from its customers. If this is the case, the company will eventually be required to write off these sales.
- The company may have terrible practices for collecting from customers.
- The company may be extending easy credit terms to customers to enhance sales growth. For example, a company may be giving generous rebates or discounts.

Inventory Pileup

Be wary if you see inventory increasing substantially more than sales. Again, a rule of thumb would be 50 percent or more. If inventory is piling up, it is an indication that a company is having trouble selling its products. Moreover, inventory can be very expensive — as it needs to be manufactured and stored in warehouses. If inventory cannot be sold, it will be written off against sales.

One ratio to keep an eye on is the inventory turnover, a number I'll look at in more depth in Chapter 9.

The Power of the Pen

It is the SEC's role to uncover corporate fraud and sue the offenders. But often, the SEC will get tips from investors, employees, or even journalists.

In fact, some of the biggest accounting scandals have been brought to light by hard-hitting journalism. One case was from *BusinessWeek*'s six-month investigation of Bausch & Lomb. Over a 12-year period, until late 1994, the company had a sterling growth rate, making the stock a hot commodity on Wall Street.

In the investigation, *BusinessWeek* learned what happens to be the characteristic of most corporate frauds: a culture that demands impossible goals. According to the report: "By the early 1990s, when the company's markets slowed at the same time that several acquisitions soured, B&L's culture was a train wreck waiting to happen."

Managers constantly feared losing their jobs if they did not hit their numbers. They dreaded the so-called Red Ball day — the last day of the quarter, which was marked by a red dot on employees' calendars. A manager who was unable to make a sale as the deadline approached would offer rebates or lengthen the time to pay for customers. Of course, customers would expect this and wait until the last few days so as to get lucrative terms. As a result, B&L had an overloaded distribution system that required lots of scrambling and overtime to meet the last-minute orders.

Moreover, managers would simply ship items to customers and book them as sales, even though there was no order. In some cases, a distributor would have two years worth of inventory on hand.

In the Hong Kong division, managers would even fake invoices and place the inventory in rented warehouses.

By 1995, the problems resulted in a huge earnings hit and the stock price plunged. Ultimately, the company admitted that it overstated revenues by $17.6 million and paid a $42 million shareholder lawsuit.

Word Clues for Aggressive Sales Practices

EDGAR Online Pro allows you to search lengthy documents electronically, which can be invaluable in spotting phrases that may indicate questionable company practices (see Figure 6.2). Following are two of the phrases to watch out for.

Unbilled revenues. These are long-term contracts in which the percentage of completion method is used. When a company records unbilled revenues, it is indicating that part of the services are complete and payment is expected. But there is no cash yet and it could take several years to get the cash. And

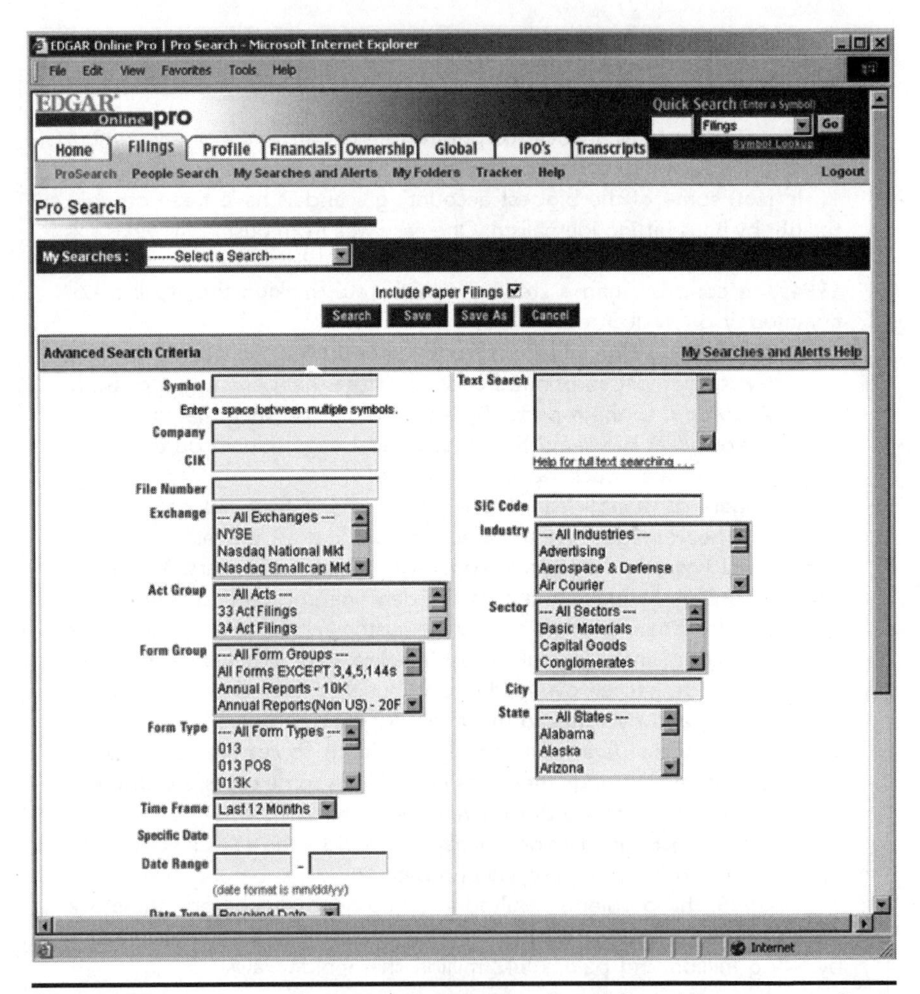

Figure 6.2 You can conduct extensive text searches of financial statements. Some red flags to look for include "unbilled revenues" and "bill and hold." From EDGAR Online Pro (http://www.edgaronlinepro.com).

if the customer has troubles, it may not be able to pay the cash. In other words, unbilled revenues are far from solid.

Bill and hold. In this arrangement, the seller agrees to sell a product to the customer. However, the seller will hold the product in its warehouse until delivery is requested, and the buyer doesn't have to pay until the product is shipped. That sounds remarkably like not buying the product, but with "bill and hold" accounting a company can call this transaction a sale.

Going on the Short Side

What if you spot problems in the financial statements? Can you make money if a stock falls? Yes, you can. The process is called ***short selling.***

Take Robert Sanborn, who practices a strong value-investing approach, which worked quite well when he was the portfolio manager at the Oakmark fund from 1991 to 1999. But when tech skyrocketed, he stayed away and his performance lagged many other tech-laden funds. By March 2000 — when tech peaked — he was fired.

Undeterred, he started a hedge fund. Why? He thought the big problem with mutual funds is that they find it too difficult to short stocks. Sanborn believed that if he could have shorted the stocks he wanted, he would have had a much better performance at Oakmark.

Basically, a *hedge fund* is geared for wealthy investors who are presumed to understand the essentials of investing. Lately, because of the success of hedge funds, Wall Street is finding ways for individual investors to jump aboard — mainly through an investment vehicle called a ***hedge fund of funds.*** This is a hedge fund that invests in a variety of other hedge funds so as to lower the minimum investment while preserving diversification.

Since starting his hedge fund, Sanborn has done well. He still invests in prosaic but valued-oriented companies, such as Maytag and American Greetings. He also engages in lots of short selling.

Keep in mind, though, that the fee structures for hedge funds can be high. A typical structure is 2–20. That is, the portfolio manager gets 2 percent of assets under management plus 20 percent of the profits. Then again, if the portfolio manager does well, investors are not likely to complain about the fees. In fact, because of this incentive structure, many of the top mutual fund portfolio managers have left to start their own hedge funds.

This is a very aggressive practice, and it's best to avoid companies that use it. A classic example was Sunbeam, whose high-flying CEO Al Dunlap engaged in many "bill and hold" transactions. Eventually, the company had to reverse about $29 million in misplaced revenues. These transactions, by the way, were described in the notes to the financials.

Sales Flameout?

When sales surge, the stock price usually follows. A big question you must ask is whether the product sales are mostly the result of a fad or real, long-term growth. It is far from an easy question to answer. Many investors thought Starbucks was a pure fad. Who would, over the long term, keep buying such expensive coffee? Well, people do keep buying it, and the company has been able to show strong growth for years. Nonetheless, it is important to realize that certain industries are prone to fads.

Toys

Kids are fickle. Today, they may want a Cabbage Patch doll; tomorrow, they may want a Britney Spears doll. It is rare for a toy to remain popular for

Pure Plays and the $20 Billion Curse

There is something called the $20 billion curse. In other words, when a company achieves this level, it becomes much harder to continue its growth rate. After all, if a company is growing 30 percent per year, this means it will need to go from $20 billion to $26 billion in 12 months. Adding $6 billion to the top line is no easy feat. Yet it is common for Wall Street to grow lax and expect the growth rate to continue, ignoring the physical reality that high-percentage growth rates are impossible to maintain forever — the growing company would eventually own the universe, and no other businesses could exist. That is simply not going to happen, but nonetheless, once a company shows several quarters of disappointing sales growth, its stock begins to slide.

This is not to imply that you should avoid companies with $20 billion in sales. Far from it. These can be great investments. However, if Wall Street analysts are expecting continued growth rates, then it is a good idea to stay away from the stock until valuations come down to earth.

Another problem with mega companies is that even if they introduce a popular product, it is unlikely to have a major impact on revenues. A wildly successful new product release would be one that results in $1 billion in revenues for 12 months (which does happen, for example, in the healthcare industry). But for a $20 billion company that means only a 5 percent increase in sales. In other words, it takes a lot to move the needle.

Thus, to find growth, investors will look at small- to medium-sized companies that have sales of $500 million to $1 billion. A $1 billion product can have a tremendous impact on their top line — and of course their stock price. This was the case with Amgen in the early 1990s, which introduced two $1 billion drugs. The stock price soared.

Moreover, it is easier to analyze a company that is smaller, because it will typically have only a handful of products you need to learn about.

Rogues' Bookshelf

Earlier in the chapter, I talked about Barry Minkow's ZZZZ Best scheme, mentioning that he eventually wrote a book about the experience. Actually, you can find a lot of good books on big scams or just plain financial meltdowns. In case you're interested, here are some ideas:

- *Rogue Trader: How I Brought Down Barings Bank and Shook the Financial World* (by Nick Leeson and Edward Whitley): A smart, high-profile trader, Nick Leeson was an inveterate gambler. His risky trades brought down one of the world's oldest investment banks.
- *Bre-X: The Inside Story* (Diane Francis): It was the biggest gold strike ever. Or was it?
- *Den of Thieves* (James Stewart): The 1980s were full of hostile takeovers, surging stock prices, and insider information. This book goes into the fascinating stories of the main characters, Michael Milken, Ivan Boesky, Dennis Levine, and Martin Siegel.
- *The Pretender: How Martin Frankel Fooled the Financial World and Led the Feds on One of the Most Publicized Manhunts in History* (Ellen Joan Pollock): Martin Frankel created a house of cards with sham portfolio trades, asset skimming, and money laundering to bilk insurance companies out of $200 million.
- *Metal Men: How Marc Rich Defrauded the Country, Evaded the Law, and Became the World's Most Sought-After Corporate Criminal* (A. Craig Copetas): Marc Rich made his multibillion-dollar fortune by high-risk commodities trading. When his firm pled guilty to tax evasion, Rich fled the country and found refuge in Switzerland.

many years (the best example of a long-term winner is Mattel's flagship toy, Barbie).

A classic case of a toy company caught up in a fad was Happiness Express, which had about 80 percent of its sales from the extremely popular Mighty Morphin Power Rangers. By 1996, the company was bust. Interestingly enough, even though the company saw a big surge in sales, it still could not turn a profit.

Restaurants

The failure rate for restaurants is very high. And, even when successful, a restaurant can quickly flame out as consumers look for something else to

Life After Prison?

What happens after someone serves time for a corporate crime? In some cases, the felon will continue being a felon — going to the next scam. Or the felon may make some cash from the ordeal. The "Rogues' Bookshelf" sidebar mentions books by two notable frauds, Nick Leeson and Barry Minkow.

Barry Minkow seems to have turned his life around. After serving seven years in prison, he became a pastor. Then there is Leona Helmsley, who was convicted of tax fraud. She spends her time on philanthropy now.

Another interesting case is Hartley Bernstein, who was a top New York attorney. One of his clients pulled off a stock scheme that ripped off investors for about $150 million. Bernstein cooperated with authorities and stayed out of jail. Since then, he has been operating a great Web site at http://www.stockpatrol.com, attempting to uncover stock schemes.

tantalize them. True, in some cases, a restaurant will not be a fad — McDonald's is still going strong, though even its results aren't as bright as they once were. But in many cases, *fad* is the operative word. Look at Planet Hollywood, which had big money and celebrity backers including Demi Moore, Bruce Willis, and Arnold Schwarzenegger. Despite the big names behind it, the food was not that good; the company fell into bankruptcy in 1999.

Technology

It is all too common for a tech company to have one red-hot product and then be unable to find an encore. Lotus minted money when it released its spreadsheet, but its other products lagged. Palm was very successful with its handheld device, but had problems with newer editions. Whenever a tech company is in the midst of a transition in its main product line, be careful. History is not comforting.

Conclusion

Revenue is only one part of the income statement. But, as seen from this chapter, it is a critical part. Can you trust it? This is a tough question to answer and there are no foolproof methods for finding the answer. However, by using the techniques in this chapter, you can gauge the quality of the company's revenues. If the red flags start to pop up, it is probably a good idea to skip the stock and look for another one.

Sources

1. Maremont, Mark, Blind ambition, *BusinessWeek*, October 23, 1995.
2. Zaslow, Jeffrey, Life after Lompoc: post-prison, *Wall Street Journal*, September 17, 2002.

7

Income Statement, Part Two

The Bottom Line

The income statement gives a company lots of ways to look good by inflating its revenues and, as a result, inflating its profits. But there is another approach: reduce expenses. Although this ploy isn't as common as inflating revenues, many companies do play fast and loose with the expense lines on the income statement. WorldCom, for example, basically cooked its expense items to lower costs and boost profits.

On the other hand, well-run companies try to find ways to improve their efficiency and lower the cost structure for real. Dell has proved expert at this, and it has meant above-average rates of return for investors.

This chapter will give you a look at the main cost items — and provide the analytical techniques to spot both the manipulations and the signs of a well-run organization.

For the most part, growth investors focus on the income statement. The belief is that, as long as companies are growing profits, stock prices should increase. (See the sidebar titled "Growth Versus Value Investing.")

Two Types of Income Statements

Companies take one of two approaches to the income statement: single step or multiple step. By far, the single step is the most common and the easiest to set up and use. Basically, it presents the following equation:

Revenues – Expenses = Net income

Growth Versus Value Investing

Growth investing did extremely well in the middle to late 1990s, then performed miserably in 2000–2001. But some growth portfolio managers were able to deal with the downfall, and Tom Marsico was notable among them. He had managed the Janus Twenty Fund (since 1988) and then started his own funds (Marsico Focus and Marsico Growth). From 2000 through 2002, his funds were down only 1 percent per year. During this time, the Janus Twenty Fund sustained average losses of 16 percent per year.

Somehow the market has adopted the belief that growth stocks are mostly in the tech area. As for Marsico, he thinks this is a big mistake. True, he made lots of money from tech stocks in the 1990s, but he also took profits from these positions.

Marsico knows that investors can find growth outside tech, so he started to invest in such companies as GM, Wal-Mart, and Lennar.

Moreover, Marsico believes that growth investors need to look for *secular trends* (that is, long-term trends, running 10 to 50 years). One that he spotted was the surge in home ownership, which was fueled by three main factors: historically low interest rates, baby boomers buying second homes, and the children of the baby boomers buying their first homes.

He also looks for negative secular trends. For example, he stayed away from pharmaceutical stocks because of thinning pipelines of new drugs and competition from generic drugmakers.

Expenses are expressed in two ways:

1. *Natural classification.* Expenses that share similarities are grouped together (such as salaries and wages).
2. *Functional classification.* Expenses are grouped based on function, such as manufacturing, administration, selling, and so on.

As for the multiple-step approach, the income statement follows these equations:

Revenues (which might be divided into segments)
– Cost of goods sold (what it costs to manufacture the goods) = Gross profit

Gross profit – Operating expenses (selling, general, and administrative expenses)
= Operating net income

Operating net income + Other revenues or gains (one-time gains and so on) – Other expenses or losses = Pretax income from continuing operations

Pretax income – Tax expense
= Income from continuing operations (the company's actual profits)

Although the single-step approach is easier to work with, analyzing the multiple-step form makes it easier to follow what's really happening. All the categories of expenses that it reports must be tracked for both approaches. As a result, I'll be following the multiple-step structure in the rest of this chapter; when you understand what it's doing, the single-step variety will be a snap to follow.

Cost of Goods Sold and Inventory

Before inventory is sold, it is booked on the balance sheet as a current asset. Of course, when the inventory is sold, it turns into an expense and is part of the income statement. The expense is part of a company's cost of goods sold or COGS.

On the income statement, COGS is the first expense subtracted from a manufacturing or distribution company's sales. (If a company is in the services industry, it has no COGS because it isn't selling anything physical.)

Figuring Cost of Goods Sold

Different types of companies use different ways to determine COGS (see the following).

Retail Merchandise Company

In most cases, a retailer does not manufacture a product; rather, it buys products in high volume and then resells them in its distribution channels. This is how the calculation works:

Beginning merchandise inventory + Net purchases of inventory
= Cost of goods available for sale

Cost of goods available for sale – Ending merchandise inventory = COGS

Filling in the numbers, it might look like this:

$1,000,000 in inventory + $200,000 in purchases
= $1,200,000 in goods available for sale

$1,200,000 – $500,000 in ending merchandise = $700,000 in COGS

In other words, the inventory that is no longer within the company must have been sold, and this becomes the COGS. This is a fairly straightforward process. However, it's tougher for manufacturing companies.

Manufacturing Company

For a manufacturer, two elements normally combine to create a finished product — raw materials and work in process. But the final value of the finished product is not the only cost that is part of COGS. A company must also calculate the overhead (utilities, equipment, depreciation) and labor that were directly related to the creation of the product. This is what the formula looks like:

Beginning finished goods inventory + Direct material costs (raw materials and work in process) + Direct labor costs + Overhead = Cost of goods available for sale

Cost of goods available for sale – Ending finished goods inventory = COGS

Inventory Valuation

As you can see in both methods, you need to determine the value of either "merchandise inventory" or "finished goods inventory." In an ideal world, this is no problem. For example, if inventory costs a retailer $10 per widget, then this is the value for any widget sold.

But in practice, this inventory valuation is far from easy. There may be a shortage of a key ingredient; it gets unusually expensive and the resulting widgets may cost $15 apiece. Or there may be a glut and widgets fall to $5 each. In other words, the market value can be fickle and companies need to account for its variations.

Companies can choose among four main ways to do this, as illustrated in the following sections (all based on the same generic example). Suppose Fast Co., now a retailer of stereos, has the following inventory purchases:

July	100 units for $100
August	50 units for $110
September	400 units for $120

In October, Fast Co. sold 300 stereos for an average price of $300. Its choices are known as *FIFO, LIFO, weighted average,* and *specific identification.*

FIFO (First In, First Out)

It's often useful to presume that the company is always selling older inventory first. That means Fast Co. would first draw on July and then go from there.

Month	*Units*	*Unit Cost*	*Total*
July	100	$100	$10,000
August	50	$110	$5,500
September	150	$120	$18,000
COGS			$33,500

You can also determine the total sales and gross profit:

Sales	300	$300	$90,000
COGS			$33,500
Gross Profit			$56,500

LIFO (Last In, First Out)

Companies can take the opposite approach to FIFO and presume that they're always selling most recent inventory. The example works out like this:

Month	*Units*	*Unit Cost*	*Total*
September	300	$120	$36,000
COGS			$36,000

That is, the most recent month's purchases cover the whole sales figure. The gross profit is:

Sales	300	$300	$90,000
COGS			$36,000
Gross profit			$54,000

Interesting, huh? It's still our old friend Fast Co., but — just by using different inventory valuation methods — it can show a higher profit with the FIFO method than the LIFO method. Is this coincidence? Not necessarily. In fact, FIFO is the most common method for inventory valuation, and perhaps the reason is that it helps boost profits. Generally, prices of inventory increase over time, so a company will see better gross profit margins if it uses older prices for the COGS.

Is this deceptive? Not really. However, if an industry primarily uses LIFO and one company chooses FIFO, you should be wary. It could be an attempt to give a kick to gross margins.

Weighted Average Cost

Some companies value inventory by emphasizing larger unit amounts and then taking the average. Applying this approach to the example, you first determine the total amounts:

Month	*Units*	*Unit Cost*	*Total*
July	100	$100	$10,000
August	50	$110	$5,500
September	400	$120	$48,000
Total	550		$63,500

Next, you find the average cost, according to this formula:

Total dollar amount/Total units = Average cost

or

$63,500/550 = $115.45

Since 300 items were sold, the COGS is

300 × $115.45 = $34,635

The gross profit margin thus looks like this:

Sales	$90,000
COGS	$34,635
Gross profit	$55,365

By and large, this method is the least likely to be subject to manipulation; it always reflects the total value of the whole inventory rather than focusing on either the most or the least expensive parts of it. But it's complex and therefore rarely used — especially since the other methods allow companies to skew their profits in whichever direction they desire without crossing the line into shady practice.

Specific Identification

As the name implies, this approach allows a company to determine the value of each item separately and then match it to what is sold. No need for formulas here; in the example, the company would simply list out the serial numbers of the 300 units sold, tot up their individual cost, and use that for the COGS figure. But a dealer in low-cost video machines would never bother with specific identification. The few companies that use this approach tend to have few — and costly — items for sale, each with a unique serial number, individual appraisal, or other clear identification.

Manipulating Inventory

Simply put, overvalued inventory results in higher gross margins. The choice between the FIFO and LIFO methods gives companies a legitimate way to use inventory values to influence margin, but some companies don't stop there. They go on to fraudulently inflate the value of inventory. Here are some of the most common schemes:

- Inflating the physical count of inventory on hand
- Counting the value of inventory that has become worthless
- Artificially increasing the alleged value of inventory on hand

In fact, the overvalued inventory will boost a company's current assets and make it look more solvent than it really is. Some companies have done this, for instance, to help get loans or other financing, which were backed by the false liquid assets. (Sometimes literally liquid assets, as with the guy in the 1960s who had several huge tanks he claimed were full of salad oil, but actually had only a thin layer of oil floating on plain water. This was the handiwork of Anthony De Angelis, whose scheme crashed in late 1963 and the losses in fake inventory were about $175 million.)

It's clearly fraudulent to produce false inventory counts or place arbitrarily high values on inventory, but delaying worthless inventory is a subtler issue. The rule is that inventory must be booked at its cost, or if the replacement cost of the inventory is lower, then the latter value must be used.

It is not uncommon for inventory to decline in value. It may become obsolete, suffer from sagging demand, or experience price declines. If any of these conditions occur, a company is required to write down the value of its inventory. But this is subject to the discretion of management. Management will look at a variety of factors: current demand, forecast demand, industry trends, and so on. It's always tempting to delay a write-down if a company believes that things will eventually get better — and it's always tempting to believe that things will get better.

When a company does announce a write-down, though, it typically jolts Wall Street. Investors realize that the company is not growing nicely but instead showing weakness. For me, this is a time to avoid or sell a company's stock. It can take quite a while for a company to regain its footing.

Boom and Bust and Inventory Corrections

During the late 1990s, many investors fondly believed that the business cycle had ended. In hindsight, this sounds outlandish, but the proponents of this theory made what seemed like some very good points. The economy was showing nice productivity gains during the 1990s, which meant both low inflation and strong growth. Even dour Federal Reserve Chairman Alan Greenspan agreed with this assessment and believed that companies were effectively using software technologies to better manage their inventory and forecast demand.

But even the best software is not immune to mistakes, and this was certainly the case when the booming economy slowed down and many tech companies plunged. John Chambers, CEO of dominant networking giant Cisco, said the new sobering environment was like a hundred-year flood.

With interest rates increasing, the demand for tech products fell. However, tech companies were predicting surging demand and inventories were piling up at an alarming rate. As a result, most tech companies had to take huge inventory write-downs. Cisco alone wrote down over $2 billion in inventory. But it survived. Quite a few companies — especially in the telecom space — did not have the financial resources to absorb the write-downs and had to file for bankruptcy.

Such inventory corrections can be very damaging for tech companies. Besides the huge costs, tech companies must also deal with the fact that their wares grow obsolete very quickly. In other words, inventory is often a very perishable good.

Investors do not realize that this is not new with high-tech. Industry has seen several major inventory corrections, and in all cases it has meant substantial loss in shareholder value.

What is an investor to do? Watch industry trends very closely. If you see surging demand and talk of shortages (Cisco mentioned shortages several times), yet the Federal Reserve is tightening monetary policy, then it is probably a good idea to reduce your exposure to tech.

Gross Profits

Turn on CNBC, and you will hear about *margins* within at most five minutes. Hype? Not really. Margins are very critical to a business. Calculating a company's margin is simplicity itself:

$$\text{Revenues} - \text{COGS} = \text{Margin}$$

You need to be careful, though. This calculation is known as the *gross profit margin*. You also have to watch the net operating margin, a figure I'll deal with later in the chapter.

As described in the "Figuring Cost of Goods Sold" section, COGS is directly related to the revenues generated. So if it costs about $4 to make each product and a company can sell these products for $10 each, this translates into a healthy profit margin of 60 percent. In fact, some companies can have incredibly high profit margins — eBay, for example, revels in a margin of 82 percent or so. It costs very little to post an auction on the Web, and eBay has persuaded hosts of potential sellers and buyers that it's the place to be.

Investors lucky enough to have gotten in on the stock early in its life span love looking at eBay's margins (the numbers are in millions):

	1999	*2000*	*2001*
Net revenues	$224,724	$431,424	$748,821
Cost of net revenues	$57,588	$95,453	$134,816
Gross profit	$167,136	$335,971	$614,005

A high-margin business may not necessarily have a low cost structure; rather, it may instead have tremendous pricing power. For instance, a company like Coca-Cola can charge premium prices for its soft drinks.

This does not imply that low-margin businesses are bad investments. Far from it. A grocery store, for instance, has very low gross margins, but it also has a huge volume of business. And commodity-type companies — with little pricing power — rarely need to spend much on marketing, advertising, or R&D, so their net profit can look very appealing indeed.

Operating Expenses

Operating expenses typically include the following items:

- Salaries, wages, and payroll taxes for employees in areas such as sales, marketing, technical support, and business development, whose work is not directly part of producing goods for sale
- General and administrative expenses for rent, professional services (legal, consulting, accounting, and so on), postage, supplies, employee travel, and repairs and maintenance
- Commissions for sales personnel
- Advertising
- Marketing

- Product development or R&D
- Depreciation and amortization

Administaff, a provider of employee placement services, reported the following operating expenses:

	2001	*2000*	*1999*
Salaries, wages, and payroll taxes	$67,661	$54,477	$36,690
General and administrative	$44,549	$35,426	$23,219
Commissions	$11,173	$9,278	$6,429
Advertising	$6,092	$5,117	$4,090
Depreciation and amortization	$16,881	$12,002	$7,103
Write-off of software development costs	$0	$0	$1,438
Total	$146,356	$116,300	$78,969

Often, when a company attempts to cut costs, it will chop at the operating expense line items. At first, these measures will bear fruit, but if the pinch continues for too long, it can eventually be detrimental to a company. So keep an eye on the trends in operating expenses and also compare them to industry peers.

Then again, a company may be getting too lazy, allowing operating expenses to bloat. The best gauge, again, is to compare the item's growth to that of the company's industry peers.

Moreover, when looking at the income statement, it is important to note that costs come in two types: variable and fixed. Variable costs change as sales volume changes. Thus variable costs tend to be in the COGS. Fixed costs, on the other hand, remain mostly unchanged even if sales increase or decrease. Fixed costs are usually operating expenses.

If sales are increasing, having large fixed costs can be a big advantage as it allows for operating leverage. But if sales fall, the fixed costs can be a tremendous problem.

Here's an example: Say Fast Co. has sales of $100 million and COGS of $60 million. In fact, COGS tends to be about 60 percent of sales on average. The company also has operating expenses that are fixed at about $20 million, giving it a $20 million profit. If sales increase to $200 million, then the COGS will be $120 million (or 60 percent of sales) and operating expenses will remain at $20 million. This means that profits will be $60 million ($200 million in sales minus $20 million in operating expenses and $120 million in COGS) — triple the profit for double the sales.

But what if sales fall to $80 million, which is a 20 percent drop? COGS falls to $48 million but SG&A is still $20 million. Profits are only $12 million — a drop of $8 million, or 40 percent.

The fixed costs of operating expenses can eventually be cut, but it takes some time for this to happen. Simply put, a company must pay for some things regardless of sales (such as offices, administration, and so on). To cut the expense for office space, for example, the company will almost certainly have to move, a costly and inconvenient operation that may well take a long time to pay for itself in reduced outlays.

R&D Expenses

Even for seemingly nontech companies, R&D expenses can be quite high — and valuable. But, of course, tech companies rely heavily on R&D. If a tech company is not continually providing new products to the marketplace, it will likely disappear and so will its stock value.

To boost profits, it is tempting for companies to cut R&D. Yet it can be a huge mistake; be especially careful if you see this. A company could be mortgaging its future to its competitors. A cut of 25 percent or more is definitely troubling.

What is the right amount for R&D? There is no magic number, but I like to see tech companies spend anywhere from 10 to 15 percent of sales on R&D. Also, what do these percentages translate into in absolute dollar amounts? For example, Intel has much larger sales than Advanced Micro Devices. So if Intel spends 10 percent of sales on R&D, then it will be pouring far more money into research than AMD will with 20 percent of sales (see Figure 7.1).

From an academic standpoint, there is support for the relationship between stock returns and R&D spending. This was the finding from a study Louis Chan, Joseph Lakonishok, and Theodore Sougiannis (professors at the University of Illinois) performed in 1999. They found that companies that spend more on R&D in terms of sales tend to perform 2.5 percent better than companies with lower expenditures.

EBITDA

EBITDA means earnings before interest, taxes, depreciation, and amortization. It is quite common for companies to focus on this number when publishing their earnings releases. Obviously, by excluding such things as interest and taxes, they can make the numbers look much better.

In some cases, the EBITDA total can be extremely misleading. Take the example of the high-flying telecom company Winstar. In February 2001, a company press release said:

> The combination of strong revenue growth and margin improvement enabled Winstar to narrow its EBITDA loss for the

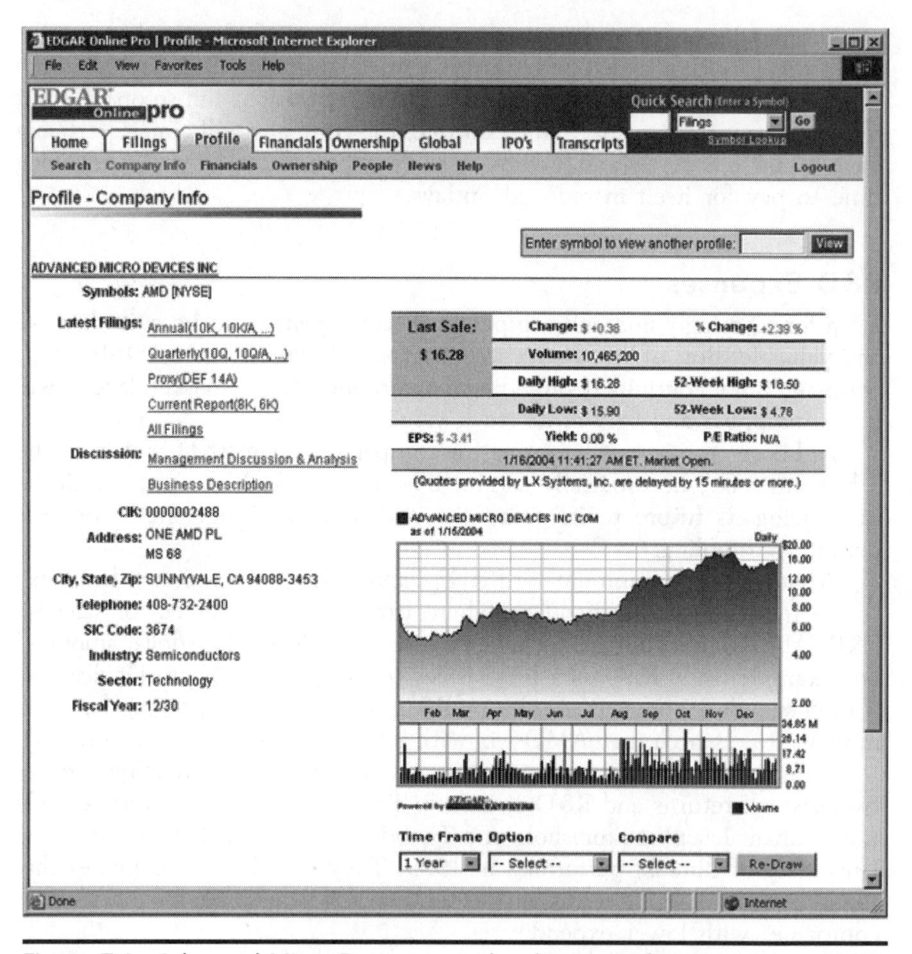

Figure 7.1 Advanced Micro Devices spends a big part of its revenues on R&D. However, since Intel has significantly more revenues, its R&D expenditures dwarf AMD's. From EDGAR Online Pro (http://www.edgaronlinepro.com).

> quarter to $19.9 million, a $41.9 million improvement from the year-ago quarter, and a $12.0 million, or 37.7 percent, improvement from the prior quarter.

Sounds like things were getting better and better, right? In two months, the company filed for bankruptcy and shareholders were eventually wiped out. Basically, investors mistake EBITDA for cash flow. It is not. I'll return to EBITDA in Chapter 9 to give you more detail on how the figure should be used.

Taxes and Interest Payments

If a company does not pay its taxes, it will no doubt be in trouble. The same goes for interest payments. Kind of common sense, right? Yet investors often fail to look at these key obligations — that's one of the ill effects of focusing on EBITDA.

As for taxes, look at the amounts and compare them to the company's profits. If the company is showing strong profits but tax payments are low, the company may not really be making much money.

Look at what a company pays in interest and compare this to the cash flow (the topic of Chapter 8). If interest is 80 percent or more of the cash flow, a company could be in jeopardy of missing a payment and possibly being thrown into default and bankruptcy.

An interesting case in point is Polaroid, a leader in photography (see Figure 7.2). By the end of 1999, the company was very profitable and pros-

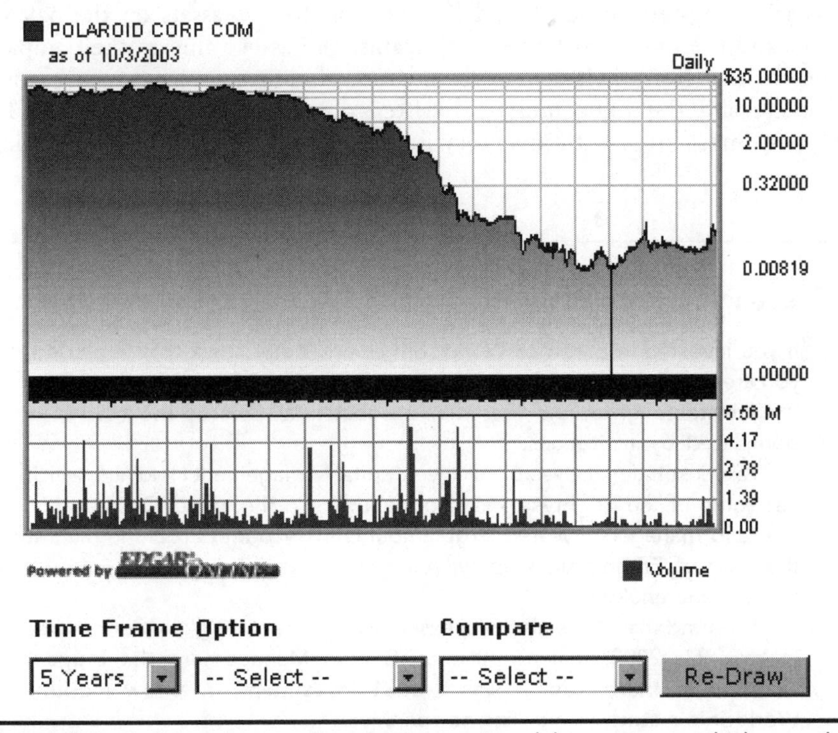

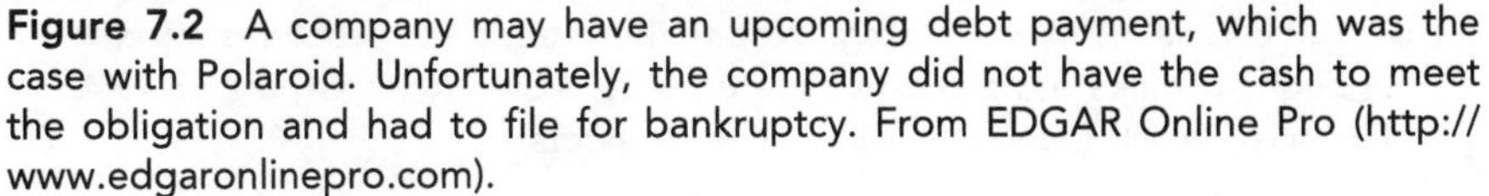

Figure 7.2 A company may have an upcoming debt payment, which was the case with Polaroid. Unfortunately, the company did not have the cash to meet the obligation and had to file for bankruptcy. From EDGAR Online Pro (http://www.edgaronlinepro.com).

pects looked bright. But the company was feeling competitive pressures and had a large debt load. By the summer of 2000, the company needed to make a $77 million interest payment. While it had EBITDA of $107 million, the company was running at what amounted to zero cash flow and eventually had to declare bankruptcy.

Capitalizing Expenses

One of the fundamentals of accounting is matching revenues with expenses. If not done properly, the results will be skewed and profits can be inflated or understated (although, of course, companies focus on the inflation side of the equation).

Like so much else in accounting, costs can be viewed in various ways. Besides the fixed/variable split, costs are divided into short-term (salaries, taxes, advertising, and so on) and long-term (investments in plant and equipment and inventory — basically, anything with benefits that last more than a year). Long-term costs should first be classified as assets on the balance sheet and then reduced (expensed) against the asset value as the company gains benefit from their use. In some cases, of course, an asset may become obsolete and the value must be written down to zero all at once. That happens most often with inventory items, but machines and even buildings

Even the Pros Blow It

If you invested in Enron or WorldCom or any other stock that imploded, you are not alone. Even the pros have had these bombs in their portfolios. It's inevitable given the fact that a substantial part of the market is dominated by institutions.

Take institutional investor Alliance Capital Management Holdings, which has some of the brightest portfolio managers in the world. Despite this, the fund managers invested large amounts in Tyco and Enron. In fact, at the time of Enron's bankruptcy, Alliance Capital Management was the biggest shareholder.

The fund managers also purchased 10.9 percent of WorldCom shares in May 31, 2002, making Alliance Capital Management the biggest shareholder there, too. It was a $531 investment. In a few months, WorldCom's stock was selling for pennies.

Of course, it helps to be big. Despite their size, these problems weren't enough to make a significant difference to ACM. ACM is part of AXA Financial, which manages $433 billion in assets.

can become obsolete if technology changes so much that they become unusable.

Changing an item from short-term expense to long-term expense results in higher profits. Example: Say Fast Co. spends $10 million on advertising. If advertising is classified as a short-term expense, all $10 million must be expensed in the current year. If it is a long-term expense, only a portion of it is expensed every year, say $2 million, providing an $8 million boost in the first year.

No doubt, it is tempting for companies to reclassify expenses so as to get better results on the bottom line. This process is called *capitalizing expenses.* Here are the main danger signs:

- *Recent change.* In the footnotes, see if the company has made a change and is now capitalizing certain items it used to class as expenses. (It is especially worrisome if the change occurs a couple of weeks before the end of the quarter.) Common items to be wary of: advertising, marketing, landfill costs, subscriber acquisition costs, membership costs, and interest costs.
- *Prepaid expenses.* A boost in this may be a sign of increased capitalization of questionable expenses.

Depreciation and Amortization

Has a company recently changed its depreciation or amortization policy? Or does a company have a more aggressive policy than most of its peers?

Lengthening the time on depreciation and amortization is another easy way to make profits look bigger. Example: Suppose Fast Co. builds a factory for $10 million and depreciates this asset equally over 10 years, at $1 million per year. If the company decides to increase the period to 20 years, the annual expense falls to $500,000, and profits will improve correspondingly.

Furthermore, be wary if you see aggressive — that is, unusually slow — depreciation or amortization in tech companies. High-tech assets have a tendency to become obsolete and thus basically worthless much sooner than their counterparts in heavy industry. If depreciation or amortization is slow, the company will have assets lingering on its balance sheet long after they have vanished from day-to-day use.

One-Time Gains or Restructuring Charges

Chapter 6 discussed nonoperating revenues and the way companies use them to make current results look better than they really are. A similar technique is for a company to rely on one-time events that have a significant impact on the bottom line by reducing expense items. What are such events? Following is a look at some of the main culprits.

Gains from the pension fund. The pension fund should be for retirees and not a method to inflate a company's earnings.

Sell-off of assets. A company may have real estate or a division whose value is understated on the balance sheet. When the asset is sold off, the company makes a nice gain. The problem is twofold: a company has only so many assets it can sell off and these transactions are not part of the core of the company. In fact, keep in mind that if a company sells off a division, it will be forgoing its future income streams.

Write-off of tax-deferred tax assets. A company gets value for this type of asset if it makes a profit. But if the likelihood of making a profit is remote, a company will need to write it off. Thus, if you see a write-off of this type of asset, you should be very concerned. The company could be in big trouble. In fact, this was very common in the steel industry, and it should be no surprise that many steelmakers went bust. When looking at a company's income figures, subtract out these asset sales. Would the income be substantially lower?

One-time gains offset against one-time losses. Suppose a company has several one-time gains that add up to $20 million. It also takes one-time losses of $15 million. On a net basis, the company has gained $5 million. But be skeptical when you see this. It is often a way for a company to try to smooth out earnings results, as well as hide underlying problems with the operations.

When a new CEO comes into a company, you will often see swift action and a big restructuring charge. For example, the company may post a huge loss and the CEO will say something like, "We made the hard decisions but it will pay off. This should set us on track for a better future."

True, these actions were probably necessary — but it is also likely that the CEO will take as many losses as possible all at once. There is nothing wrong with this; even Jack Welch did it when he became CEO of General Electric.

But it can be misleading. How? Let's say a new hotshot CEO comes into Fast Co. and takes a $200 million charge. Then, a year later, the company posts a profit of $10 million. This sounds somewhat small — but not in comparison to last year's big losses. If anything, it looks like the company had a surge in growth. As an investor, you need to make adjustments for such things and realize that the following year is not likely to look as strong.

The problem is: What if next year is just as bad? It is definitely a sign to bail out of the stock. In fact, this was the case with the telecom equipment providers, such as Lucent and Nortel. For several years, the companies continued to have restructuring charges because of the massive deterioration of the overall industry.

Finally, a company will set up a reserve on its balance sheet to estimate the costs of a restructuring. Continuing our example, the $200 million charge will be classified as a liability on the balance sheet. But what if the costs of

Legitimately Making Money from Crime?

If a company inflates its profits, it means that it is likely to pay more in taxes than required. So when a company restates its financials, will it get some of the taxes paid returned? The answer is yes.

Here's another wrinkle: If a company must pay a civil settlement with the SEC or pay off a lawsuit, is this a legitimate expense for IRS purposes? Yes it is. And such companies as WorldCom and Adelphia have made efforts to take advantage of these deductions. Sound unfair? It may be — but the IRS considers these to be expenses regardless of how they came about. In fact, this is what the IRS said in a recent case:

> From the facts before us, it appears that the proximate cause of the litigation was the dissemination of false and misleading statements and press releases. Such dissemination of financial information is a routine business activity...and therefore the expense of settling allegations regarding disseminating inaccurate information may be considered ordinary...The amounts paid by Taxpayer pursuant to the settlement are currently deductible.

Look at Merrill Lynch, which paid a $100 million civil settlement in regard to practices of its research department. It looks like it will be deductible. With an effective tax rate of 30 percent, Merrill Lynch could save $30 million in taxes. By the same reasoning, Exxon was able to deduct its $1 billion in cleanup costs for the *Valdez* oil spill.

the restructuring are, say, $150 million? The reserve is reduced and profits increase. In other words, a company may try to overestimate the reserve and, over time, release these reserves to boost profits.

The former CEO of software company Network Associates, Bill Larson, was a frequent user of this technique and had a name for it: "honey pot accounting." Whenever he was falling short on a quarter, he would reach into the pot and get some profits to satisfy Wall Street. It worked for a while — that is, until the SEC investigated the company's practices.

Pro Forma Earnings

Besides focusing on EBITDA, a company may also want to direct investors' attention to pro forma earnings, that is, earnings adjusted for unusual events and charges (see Chapter 3 for more info on this point). Essentially, any time a company wants to redirect your attention away from GAAP earnings, you need to be leery. There are probably underlying problems.

While GAAP earnings are not perfect, pro forma earnings have many more problems and are almost impossible to use effectively from an analytical standpoint.

Earnings Per Share

Earnings per share (EPS) is something you will constantly hear analysts discuss. Since earnings are a key driver for stock values, analysts will spend much time trying to accurately forecast EPS numbers for a company.

Before the Fair Disclosure rule (Regulation FD), top analysts with enough clout with companies could have private meetings with management to get a sense of where earnings would be next quarter. But this changed with Regulation FD, which outlawed this practice and now requires that a company must provide wide disclosure of any material information it chooses to share. Many companies simply don't provide the information at all now; they didn't mind sharing it with a few select individuals, but they don't want to tell the world. That means analysts have to work harder to estimate earnings — but shouldn't they do some hard work to earn their high salaries?

As for EPS, it is reported at the bottom of a company's income statement and is calculated as follows:

Net income/(Weighted average) Outstanding shares = EPS

If the income includes totals from extraordinary circumstances or one-time gains, then there will be separate EPS figures for these. Also, it can be tricky to determine what number to use as the shares outstanding total. What if a company has options outstanding whose exercise would increase the number of shares? And what about warrants, which are long-term options that also increase the number of shares outstanding when they're exercised? Or convertible bonds that can be exchanged for a number of shares?

To account for the possible increase in number of shares outstanding, companies make two EPS calculations:

1. *Primary earnings per share*. This divides income by the number of shares that are outstanding at the present time (weighted average of shares outstanding during the quarter/period).
2. *Fully diluted earnings per share*. This divides income by the total possible shares, including all warrants, convertible bonds, and options capable of being converted (again, the weighted average of shares outstanding plus the weighted average of dilutive shares the company maintains that is calculated under the treasury method and tax effected for nonqualified options, etc.).

Dividends

Dividends also come in two types: cash and stock. For example, here's how Fast Co. deals with the question. First, the company's board of directors must vote in favor of a dividend. Suppose management decides to pay the dividend in stock. It is usually expressed as a percentage, say a 10 percent dividend. That is, for every 10 shares owned, you will get an extra share. Stock dividends, though, are usually one-time events.

By contrast, cash dividends are usually paid on a quarterly basis. Fast Co., for instance, may decide to pay a 10-cent dividend. This means that each quarter you will get 10 cents per share in dividends. If you own a thousand shares, this amounts to $100 per quarter or $400 per year.

Until the 1960s, it was common for companies to pay cash dividends. Perhaps this was a throwback to the Great Depression, when skeptical investors wanted some type of cash payment to make them feel secure. However, as the Depression became a memory and the markets underwent a bull phase, many growth companies enticed investors with thoughts of huge run-ups in the stock price. If a company had many growth opportunities, why give money back to investors? Wouldn't a better approach be to reinvest all the company's profits into operations and continue the growth?

Over time, this became an accepted philosophy. Fast-growing companies like Oracle and Microsoft, for example, would not pay dividends — and shareholders did not seem to mind. After all, the stock prices increased substantially every year.

So is it appropriate for growth companies to pay dividends? This question has no easy answer. It is inevitable that surviving growth companies will eventually became mature companies; growth always stabilizes, if only because it's physically impossible for a company to keep growing at double-digit rates until it becomes larger than the economy of which it is a part. True, a company may diversify into other industries — but this poses risks. When a company reaches this stage, investors tend to expect to receive dividends.

But companies are often reluctant to start paying dividends for any of several reasons. First, a company may still believe that its core business will again see strong growth. Next, paying a dividend signals to investors that the company is slowing down, and that in itself makes it likely that the stock price will start to fall. (That drop should be temporary. Chances are, Wall Street has already factored in the fact that the company and the overall industry are moderating. Nonetheless, few companies want to be the first on the block to declare that the growth boom is winding down.)

Although starting to pay dividends often triggers overreaction and dropping prices, *cutting dividends* is much more dangerous. Individual investors are well advised to be wary when this happens, and the stock tends to plunge

Dividends: A New Trend?

In 2002, some growth companies started to pay dividends, and it may be a trend. The payments seem to be an effort to engender confidence in the companies — especially in light of the many scandals of 2002. After all, a company would not pay dividends unless it had *real* earnings.

Also, if the markets continue to stagnate, companies may be encouraged to increase dividend payments. This should help increase *total return* (the growth in the stock price plus the dividend payout). In fact, if the market falls, a dividend can act as a cushion, helping to reduce the magnitude of a stock price decline.

So definitely do not ignore dividends. They could be a critical part of the performance of your portfolio. Besides, dividends could represent a degree of steady income. If, like many investors, you're retired or in the group that will be retiring soon, you'll find that anything that augments your pension and Social Security payments will come in very handy.

after such an announcement. The reason is simple: The company is deeply concerned about its current and future cash flow and is taking immediate and drastic steps to prevent further problems.

You should also be aware of dividend terminology and procedures:

- *Declaration date*. This is the date that the board sets the amount of the next quarterly dividend.
- *Record date*. The board also announces the record date, which is the day on which you need to be a shareholder of record in order to receive the dividend.
- *Ex-dividend date*. This means that if you buy the stock on this date, you will not receive the next quarterly dividend (*ex* means "without"). Because of this, the stock price will fall by the amount of the dividend. Interestingly enough, some investors mistakenly believe that the actual value of their stock has declined and may panic somewhat. Well, do not worry. The ex-dividend date is three days before the record date. Why? The reason is that it takes three days for a stock trade to clear, that is, for the buyer to become a shareholder of record. As long as you purchase the stock before the ex-dividend date, you will receive the next quarterly payment.
- *Payable date*. This is when the company sends payments to its shareholders.

Employee Stock Options: An Expense?

One asset that does not show up on the balance sheet is a talented workforce. Offering good salaries helps attract talent, but it is often not enough. Top people want to be rewarded for their hard work and intelligence, and companies have found that stock options provide an effective inducement. Stock options give employees the potential for considerable upside if a company's stock surges. In some cases, the riches can be enormous. For example, stock options have produced more than 2,000 millionaires at Microsoft.

True, investors certainly like to see incentives that result in higher stock prices, but there are costs. The more shares handed out to employees, the smaller the part of the company each share held by existing shareholders represents. Example: Suppose John, a hotshot CEO, has an option to purchase a million shares per year at $20 each. His efforts prove very successful, the company is wildly profitable, and the stock price skyrockets to $80 per share.

John exercises this year's stock option and buys his million shares at $20 each, that is, for $20 million. Instantly, his holdings are worth $80 million. To cover the option, the company had to issue one million new shares to John. If it originally had 10 million shares outstanding, it now has 11 million. Essentially, the ownership percentages of existing shareholders have declined (that is, have been *diluted*) by 10 percent across the board (of course, except for John).

The transaction has clearly cost the stockholders something, yet it is not required to appear as an expense on the income statement. Why is that? In fact, there have been attempts to change this — but many influential CEOs (especially from the tech industry) have thus far successfully resisted. The belief is that if options are expensed, companies will not provide as many to employees and productivity will suffer.

However, companies are required to have a footnote in their financials that calculates the impact of option exercises on earnings. Continuing with John, when he exercises the option at $20 per share, the company receives the $20 million into its bank account. Next, the gain on the transaction, which is $60 per share ($80 minus $20), is treated as if the company paid a $60 million bonus to John; that is, the company can deduct this for tax purposes (but not on the income statement). The footnote shows how the expense would have affected the company's net income. A couple of thoughts: First, the pro forma expense recorded in the footnotes has nothing to do with the exercise. The expense is actually calculated at the time of the grant using a pricing model to determine the fair value of the options at the time of grant (there are many variables, including life of the options, attrition rates of the company, historical volatility in the company's stock price, etc.; ultimately

Bizarre Results of Employee Stock Options

On many occasions, Warren Buffett has expressed his deep displeasure with employee stock options (see Figure 7.3). For example, in his 1998 annual report to his shareholders, he said options were "often wildly capricious in their distribution of rewards, inefficient as motivators, and inordinately expensive for shareholders...Whatever the merits of options may be, their accounting treatment is outrageous."

He has a point; employee stock options can produce some bizarre results. This is especially the case with options that are *deeply underwater,* that is, the stock price is currently far below the exercise price. For such options to have any value, the stock will need to surge.

Take the following scenario: John, the hotshot CEO, has an option to buy 10 million shares at $50 each, yet the stock price is $20. Big Corp. calls him up and offers to buy the company for $35 per share. No question, shareholders would love this. But would John? Probably not. If he sells at this price, his options are worthless. Why sell?

this becomes the present value of future exercised options). The fair value is then multiplied by the expected number of options to be exercised. This gives you the total future compensation cost of the granted options. Then it is spread out over the number of periods the options will vest. This amount is the reported pro forma expense, or reduction of profits, that is disclosed (there is actually much more to this, but that is the basics). Second, stock options come in two forms as outlined in IRS codes: Statutory (ISO, qualified, incentive, etc.) and Nonstatutory (nonqualified). ISOs are those given to employees, such as John, as an incentive to perform. Nonqualified options are those given to directors and other outsiders. Incentive options bear no tax benefit to the company when exercised, except when sold within one year of the exercise (disqualifying disposition), which then would revert back to the same treatment as nonqualified options (this would be the case in the cashless exercise noted below). Nonqualified options, when exercised, create a tax benefit. The recording of the benefit is just as described in the paragraph, the $60. The transaction is recorded by increasing common stock by $60 and decreasing taxes payable by $60.

It's definitely confusing and seemingly unfair. So it is no surprise that with the scandals of 2002, the calls for option reform reached fever pitch. Eventually, all companies may be required to expense options. In the meantime,

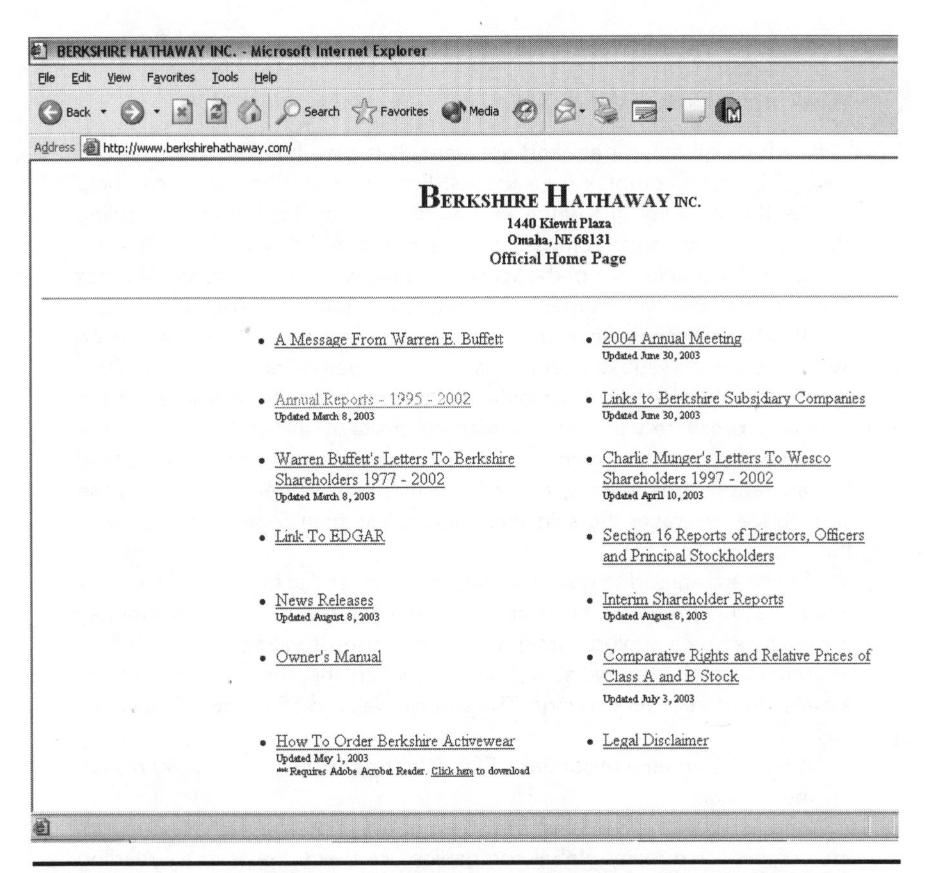

Figure 7.3 Warren Buffett is one of the most respected and outspoken investors. You can read up on his thoughts on his Web site at www.berkshirehathaway.com.

some companies (such as Coca-Cola) have decided not to wait for the rules to change; they have started showing options as an expense item. But, for the most part, the tech industry is still resistant.

I believe that options represent a true expense to a company. The problem is, though, that it is very difficult to calculate the true expense because it basically requires predicting the future. And, as the history of the stock market has shown, even the best investors have a difficult time making correct predictions.

To continue with our example, suppose that John is not successful and the stock price plunges to $1 per share. For his options to have any value, the stock price must go up past $20. Well, five years go by and the stock does well, rising to $18 per share. But this is not enough, and John lets his

Walking on the Wild Side

With advanced computers and software, it is possible for companies to engage in quite complex transactions. For instance, companies can help reduce the volatility in foreign exchange by using sophisticated trading strategies. To do this, companies will run models that look at different scenarios. Of course, one of the scenarios is the worst-case variety. Chances are slim that this will happen, but companies must consider it.

So what happens when the worst-case scenario hits? Well, it can be awful, resulting in substantial losses for a company. Take Electronic Data Systems (EDS), the huge computer consulting firm. The treasurer of the company presented a complex plan to make it easier to pay for the employee stock option plan. It was based on the stock price of EDS, and he ran various possibilities, one of which was a 50 percent drop in the stock price. However, he said there was a less than 5 percent chance of this happening.

The board agreed to go ahead with the plan. The plan involved complex financial structures, such as futures and swaps, to save the company money if the stock price stayed within a certain range of values.

Unfortunately, the worst did happen, when the company announced a major shortfall in its earnings. The stock collapsed 55 percent in a single day.

After making all adjustments, EDS admitted it lost about $100 million on the transaction.

How can you guard against this? It is not easy because such transactions are complex and many global companies use them. You can try reading the footnotes but, unfortunately, there are no glaring red flags to look for.

options expire and they become worthless. So, how was this an expense to the company? Simply put, it was not.

I think the main problem for investors is when top executives get huge option grants. If John's company's stock price increases by $1 and he has an option on 10 million shares, his net worth just increased $10 million (assuming the stock price is above the exercise price). In most cases, the option holder does not even have to pay for the stock but can instead resort to a cashless exercise (borrow money to exercise the option and then immediately use the proceeds of the sale to pay off the loan). Think of options as a leveraged way of making money. It is not as if option holders *own* shares of stock. If this were the case, John would have to put up his own cash to buy the shares, which is actually a very good thing. For more on such "insider transactions," see Chapter 11.

Because huge stock grants can almost be a way for executives to print money, I'm leery of this — as all investors should be when they hear of excessive executive compensation. An executive may be tempted to engage in short-term activities that pump up the stock so as to make a quick killing, even though it leaves the company in terrible shape for the long term. I'll look at this in much more detail in Chapter 10.

Conclusion

We all know the old saying: "If it looks too good to be true, it probably isn't." This saying certainly makes lots of sense in investing — being skeptical is a good trait.

In 2002, the *Wall Street Journal* published a story that was a good validation of the saying. It looked at analysts' earnings estimates, which can literally make or break stock prices. During the 1990s, investors greatly rewarded those companies that could consistently beat the analysts' projections. The implication was that the business was solid and would continue to be so. For this, investors were willing to pay a premium stock price.

But it is the nature of business to not be completely consistent. If a company shows consistently increasing numbers, perhaps it is really not getting consistent results but instead managing the numbers. This appears to be what WorldCom did in 2000 and 2001 — by downright cooking the books. While its competitors were deteriorating, WorldCom was oddly showing surprising strength.

In the article, the advice was to be wary if a company consistently meets its estimate exactly or beats it by a few pennies in earnings per share. There is a chance that the company is using aggressive or even fraudulent accounting. In fact, this is one of the criteria the SEC looks for when investigating potential frauds.

In the next chapter, I will turn to a critical statement — one that is often overlooked but is relatively difficult to manipulate: the cash flow statement.

Sources

1. McKinnon, John, Firms accused of chicanery could get windfall from IRS, *Wall Street Journal*, September 3, 2002.
2. Teach, Edward, The great inventory correction, CFO *Magazine*, September 1, 2001.
3. Sender, Henny, Stormy markets foil bets, *Wall Street Journal*, September 27, 2002.
4. Bryan-Low, Cassell, Meeting expectations too often? Such consistency is now suspect, *Wall Street Journal*, August 15, 2002.

8

Cash Flow Statement

The Lifeblood of the Company

After reading the last four chapters, you may be shaking your head and thinking of stashing your extra cash under the mattress; it's clear that both the balance sheet and the income statement can be subject to considerable manipulation, if not downright fraud. But the third of my Big Three, the cash flow statement, is much harder to play with. Perhaps that's one reason why companies so rarely highlight their cash flow statements.

Interestingly enough, investors often confuse the concept of cash flow with that of profits. In fact, many think they are really the same thing. This is a big mistake. Why? As noted in Chapter 2, public companies calculate profits based on accrual accounting. So sales on credit are counted as sales even though they do not generate immediate cash. Likewise, signing an agreement with a supplier creates an expense — even if no cash changes hands. With the cash flow statement, the accrual accounting aspects are washed out.

The cash flow statement also accounts for changes in working capital, which can be very significant. For example, if a company piles up much inventory, it is using cash to do this. If accounts receivable increase, the company is not taking in as much cash as the sales may indicate. It is really lending money to customers. This drags down cash flow. And if a company makes a substantial capital expenditure, this will also be a hit to the company's cash flow.

Yet savvy investors go beyond the cash flow statement and determine a company's *free cash flow*. This is the cash that is left over after all necessary expense items are paid for. With free cash flow, a company can expand into new markets, pay dividends, pay down debt, or buy back shares. This can be a very powerful tool for the success of a company and, as a result, it can be a very powerful indication of strong gains for investors.

The trouble is, cash flow statements don't indicate free cash flow as a line item. Rather, you need to make a variety of adjustments, described in this chapter, to get the information. Moreover, there is no standard approach. It seems there are a myriad of ways to calculate free cash flows. In this chapter, I show you the approach I take with companies; it has worked for me and is not overly complicated either.

Understanding the Cash Flow Statement

Before diving in, I want to emphasize that, for my investment program, the cash flows of a company are very, very important. Cash is the lifeblood of a company. Microsoft and Dell owe much of their successful performance to their incredible cash management techniques. These companies focus on bringing efficiencies to their organizations — high inventory turnover, quick collection of bills, and so on — that give them a huge competitive edge.

Background: Watch for Divergence

Most companies' net income will differ from their cash flows, but this does not mean it is OK if the figures are far apart. In fact, savvy investors watch out for companies that post high net income but negative free cash flows. This may indicate that a company is playing fast and loose with its books.

On the other hand, emerging companies deserve a little more slack. To be competitive and grow their market share, they will probably be spending lots of money on R&D and other long-term investments. Down the road, these investments should pay off. But in the short run, they will be a drag on free cash flows.

Interestingly enough, even companies that are experiencing super growth in sales tend to have meager cash flows. How can this be? Fast growth typically requires substantial investment in inventories, receivables, and overhead. But some companies do demonstrate high sales growth rates alongside high cash flow rates. These are potentially truly great investments: Dell, Microsoft, and eBay are examples (see Figure 8.1).

For the most part, negative cash flows scare me and I tend to avoid these stocks. (The worst picture combines declining sales and declining cash flows.) If a company hemorrhages cash for too long, it will have no choice but to raise money from an equity offering or debt offering. However, if the stock market is in trouble, this may not be an option, which is why many upstart Internet companies went bust in 2001–2002.

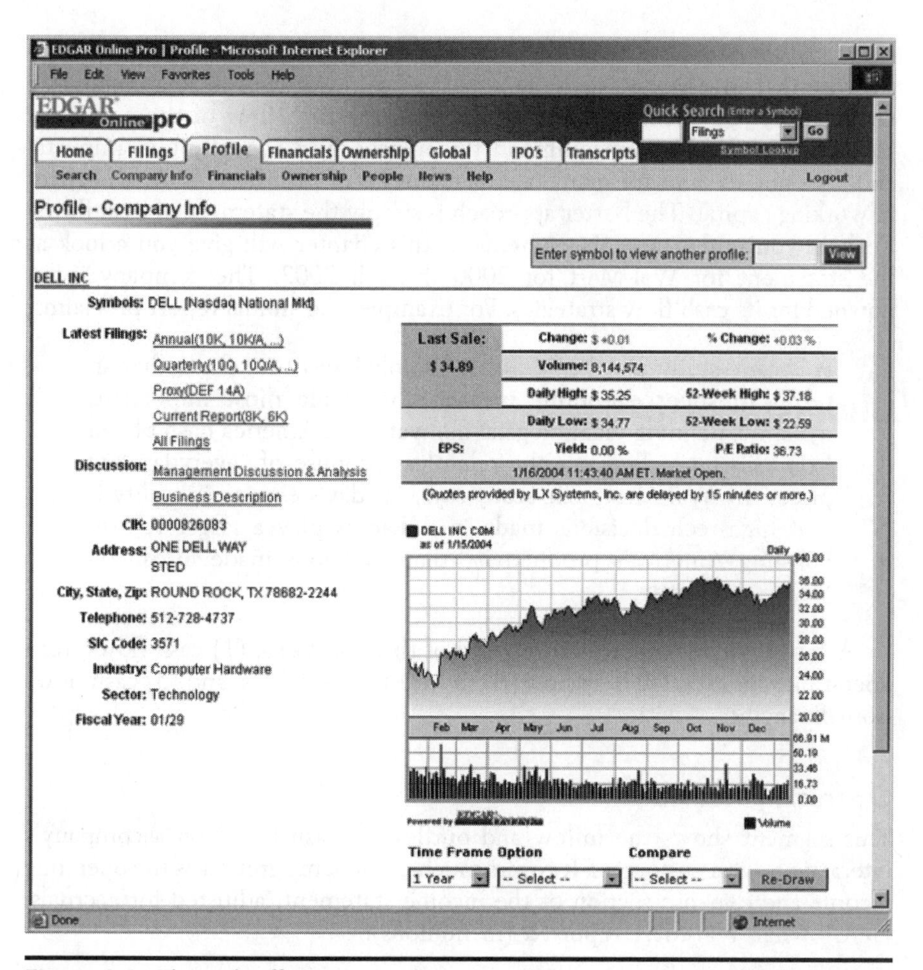

Figure 8.1 Through efficiencies and strong management systems, Dell is able to keep ahead of the pack by posting strong cash flows. It's an element of all great companies. From EDGAR Online Pro (http://www.edgaronlinepro.com).

Cash Flow Basics

Whereas publication of the balance sheet and income statements has been required since the 1930s, it was not until 1988 that the SEC required that public companies disclose their cash flow statements. Before this, investors had to use their own systems to estimate company cash flows. One approach is simply to use the following formula:

$$\text{Net income} + \text{Depreciation} = \text{Estimated cash flow}$$

Many investors still use this technique. Essentially, depreciation is an expense that involves no cash outflow. So by adding it back to a company's net income, you should get a better idea of the cash flow of the company. However, I would not recommend this approach; it is really too simplistic and does not account for many critical elements of cash flow, such as changes in working capital. The better approach is simply the statement of cash flows. To help you understand this statement, this chapter will give you a look at the statement for Wal-Mart for 2000 through 2002. The company is renowned for its cash flow strategies. For example, the annual report proclaims:

> A recent study by the McKinsey Global Institute finds that in terms of sheer economic impact, the single most important, dynamic, defining technological innovation in America hasn't been from Silicon Valley; it's the relentless promise of "everyday low prices" by Wal-Mart. The study says, "Today's economic reality is that high-tech decisions made in Arkansas play a larger role in boosting America's productivity than decisions made in Silicon Valley or Seattle."

A cash flow statement is composed of three sections: (1) cash flows from operating activities, (2) cash flows from investing activities, and (3) cash flows from financing activities.

Operating Activities

This segment shows the inflow and outflow of cash based on a company's interactions with customers. It covers much of the same ground as the operating income and expense section of the income statement, adjusted for accruals. Here's what Wal-Mart reported (in millions):

Cash Flows from Operating Activities	*2002*	*2001*	*2000*
Net income	6,671	6,295	5,377
Adjustment to reconcile net income to net cash provided by operating activities:			
Depreciation and amortization	3,290	2,868	2,375
Cumulative effect of accounting change, net of tax			198
Increase in accounts receivable	(210)	(422)	(255)
Increase in inventories	(1,235)	(1,795)	(2,088)
Increase in accounts payable	368	2,061	1,849
Increase in accrued liabilities	1,125	11	1,015
Deferred income taxes	185	342	(138)
Other	66	244	(139)
Net cash provided by operating activities	10,260	9,604	8,194

The *net income* line of the operating activities section of the form comes straight from the income statement. Then the *depreciation and amortization* totals, being noncash items, are added back in. The following lines make adjustments for changes in current assets and current liabilities. Here's how to determine when these items should be added to or subtracted from net income:

- *Increase in a current asset.* A company increases expenditures of cash to acquire the current asset and this amount is subtracted from net income.
- *Decrease in a current asset.* A company turns the current asset into cash and this added to net income.
- *Increase in current liability.* A company turns the current liability into cash and this is added to net income.
- *Decrease in current liability.* A company uses cash to reduce the current liability and this is subtracted from net income.

If you apply these relationships to the Wal-Mart statement, this is what you find:

- *Increase in accounts receivable.* The increase in accounts receivable means that the company is not receiving cash to cover all of its sales (though it has every hope of getting paid later). Wal-Mart's accounts receivable went up by $210 million and this is subtracted from the company's net income.
- *Increase in inventories.* The increase in inventories required expenditures that amounted to $1.2 billion in 2002. This is subtracted from net income — but note the counterbalancing effect of the next item.
- *Increase in accounts payable.* The increase in payables shows that Wal-Mart didn't actually pay cash for all that new inventory; it was able to defer much of the payment for later. This means the company kept some cash in the bank — about $368 million, which is added to net income. It is an effective strategy for major companies to try to extend the length of time to pay off accounts payable. Because of Wal-Mart's market power, it has the leverage to make these types of deals.
- *Increase in accrued liabilities.* When these current liabilities increase, the company is essentially borrowing money. That produces a positive cash flow — $1.2 billion in Wal-Mart's case. This is added to the net income.
- *Deferred taxes.* The differences between accounting and tax rules sometimes require an expense item called deferred taxes. But these taxes are not paid out when they're recognized; they're literally *deferred*, and that makes them noncash items that must be added back into net income.

Investing Activities

Most companies invest heavily in plant and equipment, which can consume substantial amounts of cash. They also — some to a much larger extent than others — invest capital in the stock market or other areas outside their primary business to make productive use of their cash reserves. Wal-Mart reported a moderately lively investment program (again, in millions):

Cash Flows from Investing Activities	*2002*	*2001*	*2000*
Payments for property, plant, and equipment	(8,383)	(8,042)	(6,183)
Investment in international operations (net of cash acquired, $195 million in Fiscal 2000)		(627)	(10,419)
Proceeds from termination of net investment hedges	1,134		
Other investing activities	103	(45)	(244)
Net cash used in investing activities	(7,146)	(8,714)	(16,846)

Burn Rate

In June 1998, Michael Wolff wrote a prophetic book called *Burn Rate,* which described the giddy experience of his Internet start-up, Wolff New Media. In the book, Wolff notes that he was puzzled to see well-heeled investors jump at the opportunity to invest in companies that were experiencing substantial negative cash flows.

The concept of burn rate is not new. Burn rates, for example, are a common thing with new industries; such was the case with the auto industry or biotech. But the Internet made *burn rate* a mainstream term.

Another prophetic piece came from *Barron's* in April 2000, which had a list of the burn rates of more than 200 Internet companies. Of these, 74 percent had negative cash flows. Moreover, the list also indicated the probable date of a company's bankruptcy (by assuming the burn rate would continue at the current rate). It was done in a very simple way and based on SEC filings.

True, it caused a stir, and companies such as VerticalNet (which was later delisted) said the list was faulty. As we all know, the analysis turned out to be quite accurate.

This is not to imply that you should avoid every company with a substantial burn rate. However, before making the investment, repeat the *Barron's* calculation of time-until-bankruptcy:

Burn rate = Operating cash flows for the last quarter (when negative)

Bankruptcy = (Cash + Marketable securities)/Burn rate

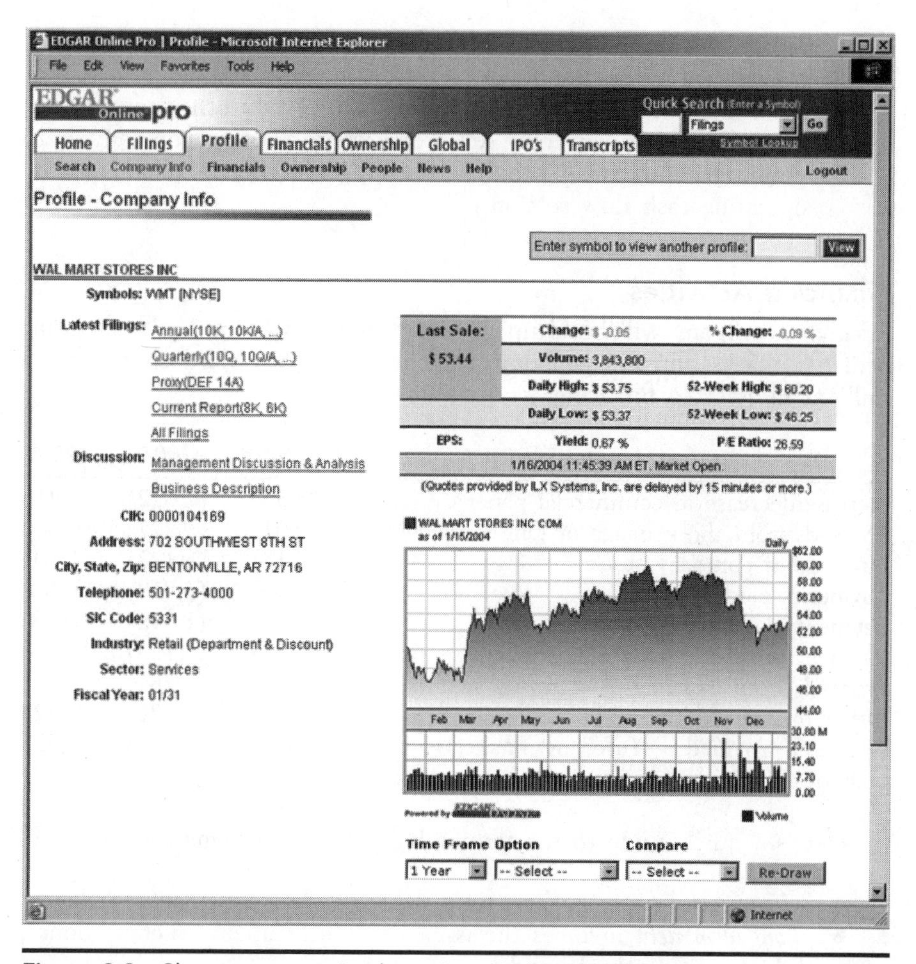

Figure 8.2 Chances are you've been in a Wal-Mart. Well, the company spends a tremendous amount on its stores. When you calculate a company's free cash flows, you certainly need to account for these cap ex items. From EDGAR Online Pro (http://www.edgaronlinepro.com).

The *capital expenditures* (also known as "cap ex") line includes any investment in property, plant, and equipment. For a company like Wal-Mart, which builds its own huge stores, the capital requirements are significant (see Figure 8.2). In 2002, it spent $8.3 billion. The *international operations* line is more or less self-explanatory, and the *investment hedges* represent financial strategies designed to reduce the risk of currency fluctuations. The *other investing activities* line is a catch-all, including activities like these:

- *Investments*. A company may have excess cash and make investments, perhaps in stocks, bonds, or private companies.
- *Acquisitions*. A company may spend cash to buy other companies.
- *Spin-offs*. A company may sell a division to another company or to public shareholders. (Note that this may sometimes be included in the operating cash flow section.)

Financing Activities

Finally, a company will build up its cash through debt or equity *financing activities* (that is, borrowing money or selling stock). Wal-Mart reported more millions in assorted financing:

Cash Flows from Investing Activities	*2002*	*2001*	*2000*
Increase/decrease in commercial paper	(1,533)	(2,022)	4,316
Proceeds from the issuance of long-term debt	4,591	3,777	6,000
Purchase of company stock	(1,214)	(193)	(101)
Dividends paid	(1,249)	(1,070)	(890)
Payment of long-term debt	(3,519)	(1,519)	(863)
Payment of capital lease obligations	(167)	(173)	(133)
Proceeds from issuance of company stock		581	
Other financing activities	113	176	224
Net cash provided by (used in) financing activities	(2,978)	(443)	8,553

Here's a quick guide to the terminology of the financing section:

- *Commercial paper* is short-term debt — relatively small cash loans.
- *Long-term debt* involves the issuance of instruments such as bonds, which are purchased and then traded.
- *Company stock* is new stock issued and sold in a secondary offering to the public or stock from the company's holdings of its own shares.

This section shows how Wal-Mart made use of its cash for shareholder purposes:

- Dividends
- Purchase of company stock
- Repayment of long-term debt
- Payment of capital lease obligations

Free Cash Flow

The *Wall Street Journal* named Joe Arsenio of JP Morgan top analyst for the advanced industrial equipment industry. What was impressive about his performance is that the industry was lackluster yet Arsenio was able to find top performers.

His secret? He looked at many factors, of course, but a very important one was free cash flow. His two top picks, Itron and Flir Systems, generated returns of over 300 percent. When he analyzed the financial statements for these two companies in late 2000, he realized that they were showing great improvements in free cash flow.

As I noted earlier, though, there's a fly in this particular batch of ointment. Useful as free cash flow information is, the statement of cash flow does not provide it. Rather, the analyst must sit down and figure it out.

As an example, take the cash flow statement of AutoZone, the leading auto solutions provider. A contributor to its success has been healthy free cash flow, which has allowed the company to lower its debt and buy back shares.

Cash Flows from Operating Activities	*2001*
Net income	175,526
Adjustments to reconcile net income to net cash provided by operating activities:	
Depreciation and amortization of property and equipment	122,576
Amortization of intangible and other assets	8,757
Deferred income tax expense (benefit)	(46,981)
Restructuring and impairment charges	156,822
Income tax benefit realized from exercise of options	13,495
Net change in accounts receivable and prepaid expenses	10,562
Net change in merchandise inventories	(164,164)
Net increase in accounts payable and accrued receivable	187,801
Net change in income taxes payable and receivable	10,798
Net change in other assets and liabilities	(16,255)
Net cash provided by operating activities	458,937

Cash Flows from Investing Activities	*2001*
Capital expenditures and real estate purchased from Pep Boys	(169,296)
Disposal of capital assets	44,601
Notes receivable from officers	2,552
Net cash used in investing activities	(122,143)

Cash Flows from Financing Activities	*2001*
Net increase (decrease) in commercial paper	(381,853)
Proceeds from debentures/notes	465,000
Net increase (decrease) in unsecured bank loans	(105,000)
Net proceeds from sale of common stock	48,410
Purchase of treasury stock	(366,097)
Other	3,063
Net cash provided by (used in) financing activities	(336,477)

To calculate free cash flow, I take the following four steps:

1. Pick up the cash flow from operating activities, which is $458 million.
2. Reduce the operating cash flow by the tax deduction received from the exercise of employee stock options ($13.4 million) and deferred income taxes (negative $46.9 million). Since the deferred income tax total is a negative number, this is added back to the operating cash flow number to wash out its effect. The reason to exclude the tax benefit of employee stock options is that this is really part of the overall financing of the company (the company gets cash for the exercises of employee stock options). The adjustment for the deferred taxes is not a true inflow of cash, since the company will ultimately have to pay the taxes.
3. Pick up the capital expenditure (cap ex) figure, $169.3 million. Remember that cap ex can be a significant part of any business — and in reality may be an operating expense. Why? If the company has high cap ex every year, then isn't it really part of the ongoing operation, not a one-time thing? Some analysts use sophisticated techniques to divide capital expenditures into two categories:
   - *Required expenditures.* These expenses (also called maintenance expenditures) are essential to continue the company's current operations, so they're really a cost of doing business.
   - *Growth expenditures.* These are capital expenditures that are not necessary but are instead a means to improve the growth rate of the company.

   In theory, I would add the required expenditures to the operating cash flows. But for an individual investor, it is nearly impossible to differentiate between required and growth expenditures. Thus I prefer to assume that most or all of the expenditures are required (which tends to be a safe assumption).
4. Subtract any one-time payments the company has made, such as settling a major lawsuit. Such payments typically are not part of ongoing operations. The resulting total is the company's free cash flow.

The following chart illustrates the calculation based on AutoZone's cash flow statement:

Item	*Result*
Operating cash flow	458 million
Subtract option exercises and deferred income taxes (this is a positive number since the deferred taxes were negative)	33.5
Subtract capital expenditures	–169 million
Subtract one-time payments	0
Free cash flow	322.5 million

Cash per Share

Another way to look at a company is to see how much cash it has for each outstanding share, a productive version of an old daydream: "If only I had a dollar for every..." Calculating this total is easy:

(Cash + Marketable securities)/Shares outstanding = Cash per share

Sometimes a company's stock is selling for less than the cash per share. In a sense, that means investors are getting the operating company for free. Famed mutual fund manager Peter Lynch wrote a classic book on investing called *One Up on Wall Street*. In the book, he uses examples of buying companies that sell below their cash value. One was Ford, which was selling for $38 per share:

> It meant that I was buying the company not for $38 a share, the stock price at the time, but for $21.70 a share ($38 minus the $16.30 in cash). Analysts were expecting Ford to earn $7 a share from its auto operations, which at the $38 price gave it a p/e of 5.4, but at the $21.70 price it had a p/e of 3.1.

That sounds great — but, as always, it is not a good idea to focus on just one factor. For example, suppose that a company is selling at $10 per share and has $10 in cash per share. But also suppose the company is losing $10 million a month or $3 every quarter per share. If this burn rate continues, the company will run out of money in less than a year.

In fact, this was the case with many dot-com companies. They raised substantial amounts of money from their IPOs, so they were rolling in cash for a while. When the NASDAQ collapsed, so did the stock prices of these

Disconnect at Lucent

During the late 1990s, Lucent was a darling of Wall Street. A spin-off from AT&T, Lucent became the premier supplier of equipment to the telecom industry. What's more, it had the incredible advantage of Bell Labs.

While most analysts had "buy" or "strong buy" recommendations on the stock in 2000, there were some doubters. One was Whitney Tilson, portfolio manager of Tilson Capital Management, LLC. In late December of 2000, he wrote several articles (on the Motley Fool) on Lucent and the problems he saw. He made a chart of the company's net income and free cash flows from the first quarter of 1998 through the third quarter of 2000:

	Q1 1998	*Q2 1998*	*Q3 1998*	*Q4 1998*
Net income	1,124	186	518	647
Free cash flow	173	-499	794	–650
	Q1 1999	*Q2 1999*	*Q3 1999*	*Q4 1999*
Net income	1,523	533	819	891
Free cash flow	–1,619	–841	–571	–783
	Q1 2000	*Q2 2000*	*Q3 2000*	
Net income	1,250	818	1,040	
Free cash flow	–1,019	–671	–1,348	

This plainly shows that even though the company posted substantially positive net income, it was also showing substantially negative free cash flow. Yet investors were not looking at the negative cash flows. Tilson received many e-mail messages questioning his analysis.

By 2002, the stock price of Lucent was $1.50 per share, a far cry from its $60 per share in 2000 (at that time, the market capitalization was $275 billion and it was the most widely held stock in America). How was this big disconnect possible? There were two main reasons: (1) very high cap ex and (2) a deteriorating balance sheet (accounts receivable and inventories were soaring).

newly minted dot-com public companies, making them appear — at least on a cash per share basis — dirt cheap. But the water was swirling down the drain; their reserves, big as they were, weren't big enough to carry them through the crisis, and their "cheap" prices turned out to be vastly above their final value.

It's also possible for a company to be selling at or less than cash value but have a big problem: it has no growth potential. Perhaps the company is in

Cash Cows and Moats

Microsoft has used its virtual monopoly power to generate huge profits and free cash flow. One of Bill Gates's friends, the famed Warren Buffett, looks for companies that have monopoly powers. He has a colorful phrase for this kind of power: the *moat.* Yes, he means the kind of ditch that surrounds a castle to protect it from enemies. Here is a memorable quote on the subject from Buffett's 1999 annual shareholders' report:

> The key to investing is not assessing how much an industry is going to affect society, or how much it will grow, but rather determining the competitive advantage of any given company, and above all, the durability of that advantage. The products or services that have wide, sustainable moats around them are the ones that deliver rewards to investors.

A more official way of describing moats is *barriers to entry* — that is, how hard it would be for anyone else to grab a piece of the protected markets. So when you read a company's financial statements, try to find the moats. For example, when Buffett analyzed Coca-Cola, he realized the company had a tremendous moat: its incredible brand that extends across generations. Do you think an upstart company could disrupt this? Most likely not. Other examples of moats:

- *Capital-intensive businesses.* It would be foolhardy to spend the billions of dollars necessary to build, say, a global oil company from scratch these days.
- *Natural monopolies.* These are industries that seem to ultimately have one provider in a marketplace, because it would be too expensive to have many competitors. This is why you see only one utility in a region or, in many cases, just one newspaper in a city. The cable industry is another example. However, because of natural monopolies, the U.S. government takes notice and does not want the companies to gouge customers. Thus it is typical for the government to impose limits on what natural monopolies can charge customers.

a mature industry and cannot raise prices. In this scenario, what is the catalyst that will get investors excited?

Moreover, a company may also have substantial short-term debts, which wash out the benefits of its cash position. If you're going to look at cash per share, here's a better formula:

(Cash + Marketable securities – Current liabilities)/Outstanding shares = Cash per share

The Obscure "Quality of Earnings Ratio"

I've devoted a lot of space to the concept of quality of earnings. Unlike most other investors, I want earnings that are solid, not promoted by gimmicks. However, analyzing the quality is no easy task, as companies have a bag of tricks that they can use to hoodwink investors. But there is a little-known metric called the quality-of-earnings (QE) ratio that can help. Essentially, it uses these formulas to compare free cash flow to reported earnings:

Net income – Free cash flow = Net income differential

(Average total assets for quarter X + Average total assets for quarter Y)/2 = Average total assets

Net income differential/Average total assets = QE ratio

The rule of thumb is that a QE ratio of 0.03 or higher indicates a possible earnings quality problem. Example: Say Problem Corp. generates net income of $100 million but has free cash flow of $10 million. During this time, total assets have gone from $500 million to $550 million. The QE ratio (in millions) looks like this:

1. Net income differential = $100 million – $10 million = $90 million
2. Average total assets = ($500 million + $550 million)/2 = $525 million
3. QE ratio = $90 million/$525 million = 0.17

The QE ratio is almost six times the trouble level indicated by the rule of thumb. Thus it looks as though Problem Corp. may indeed have a problem with the quality of its earnings.

Does the Company Have Cash to Pay Its Debt?

Chapter 5 discussed the way the balance sheet can give you a sense of the overall debt position of a company. Simply put, a high amount of debt can put a company in jeopardy. To gauge the risk, smart investors will compare a company's interest payments to its free cash flow. If there is not enough money in the bank and the free cash flow is falling, it could mean disaster for a company. Yes, a company may be able to raise money by selling stock — but this means existing shareholders' stake is diluted. Besides, when a company is having problems with cash flow, it often finds it difficult to raise money.

Enron and Erratic Cash Flows

One of the many important lessons that Enron provides is the value of cash flow analysis. While the company was posting smooth earnings gains, its cash flow statement was far from steady. If anything, it was a clear example of huge inconsistencies:

Time Period	*Operating Cash Flows*
Q1 2000	–$457 million
Q2 2000	–$90 million
Q3 2000	$674 million
Q4 2000	$4,652 million
Q1 2001	–$464 million
Q2 2001	–$873 million

As you can see, there were wide shifts — from negative to positive and back — from the first quarter of 2000 to the second quarter of 2001. True, the quarterly numbers for many companies show some volatility, but these Enron performance figures should have raised big red flags for investors.

Cash Flow Efficiency

One of my favorite sites is the Motley Fool (http://www.fool.com), which always publishes engaging material that is very helpful for investors. The cofounder of the site, Tom Gardner, has done much work on cash flow analysis and has developed his own metric called *cash flow efficiency*. The ratio looks at cash and assets that can be easily converted into cash (such as marketable securities). Here is the formula:

$$(\text{Current assets} - \text{Cash and cash equivalents})/(\text{Current liabilities} - \text{Short-term debt}) = \text{Cash flow efficiency}$$

The short-term debt includes the short-term part of long-term debt (that is, interest due in a year) and notes payable. Gardner prefers companies with low ratios. He likes to see the number at 1.0 or below.

Conclusion

That finishes the tale of the Big Three. Don't worry if you don't remember everything; there's an awful lot of detail, and all you really need are the highlights of what's important and what may be a red flag. You can return to these five chapters whenever you need information for your investment analysis.

For me, the cash flow statements are the first place I look when investigating a company. As the old saying goes: cash is king. This is very true for investing, and the best investors — such as Peter Lynch and Warren Buffett — have done quite well focusing on a company's cash flows.

The next chapter will explore some of the other ways you can make the numbers in the financial statements disgorge information about how well a company is really doing.

9

Ratio Analysis

Back in grade school, your teacher probably said something like, "One day you will need to know fractions. Trust me." Most likely, you figured this was a ploy to get you to do your homework. But your teacher was right.

Fractions — under their grownup name, *ratios* — are critical for financial statement analysis because they show relationships among the different elements of an income statement, balance sheet, and cash flow statement. This chapter introduces the fine art of ratio analysis, which is something professional investors spend a lot of time with. And for good reason. A correct interpretation of a ratio can shed quite a bit of light on an investment decision.

Of course, like any investment technique, ratio analysis is not foolproof. One ratio or another may well indicate that a stock is dangerous when the company is actually a good investment. Nonetheless, properly used, the technique can do a lot for your long-term prospects.

To make things more understandable, I've grouped the important financial ratios into the following categories:

- Profitability ratios
- Liquidity ratios
- Activity ratios
- Solvency ratios
- Valuation ratios
- Cash flow ratios

Simply put, a ratio is a comparison between two numbers. For example:

$$50/100 = 50 \text{ percent or } 0.50$$

For most investment ratios, that's about as complex as things get. You won't need an advanced degree from Wharton to understand this stuff. But computing ratios can be very time consuming and downright boring. With online resources like Multex.com and Morningstar, you do not have to go through the grueling process of computing ratios over and over again (see Figure 9.1). You just need to know how it's done so as to understand the concepts — hey, just like your teacher told you — so it's worth looking at how these ratios are computed.

Using Ratios

I still remember an introductory finance class I took in college, in which my gruff (and rude) professor wrote on the board

2.0

He asked the class: "Is this a good current ratio?" No one raised their hand but me (I was a glutton for punishment). I remembered that, in my readings, the author mentioned that a 2.0 current ratio is good as a rule of thumb. So I said so.

He almost growled at me and then said, "That's wrong. Ratios are meaningless if not compared to the industry. A 2.0 ratio may not make sense for a bank but could for a manufacturing firm."

While I still think his classroom approach was less than optimal, he was right. When looking at ratios, I do the following: (1) get a sense of the ratios for the industry and (2) track the ratios over time and see if they are improving or getting worse. These two principles can be very powerful in targeting good investments and weeding out the duds.

In the rest of the chapter, I'll be talking about a lot of different types of ratios. But keep in mind the two basic principles. As my professor declared, ratios are meaningless unless put into context, both for the industry and for a given company over time.

Profitability Ratios

You have lots of options for analyzing a company's profitability. With the return on equity ratio, you can compare profits in terms of the investment of capital into a company. Or, with the return on asset ratio, you can see how efficient a company is in driving profits from its asset base.

The main types of profitability ratios are return on equity, return on assets, and net margin/gross margin. Chapter 7 discusses the differences between

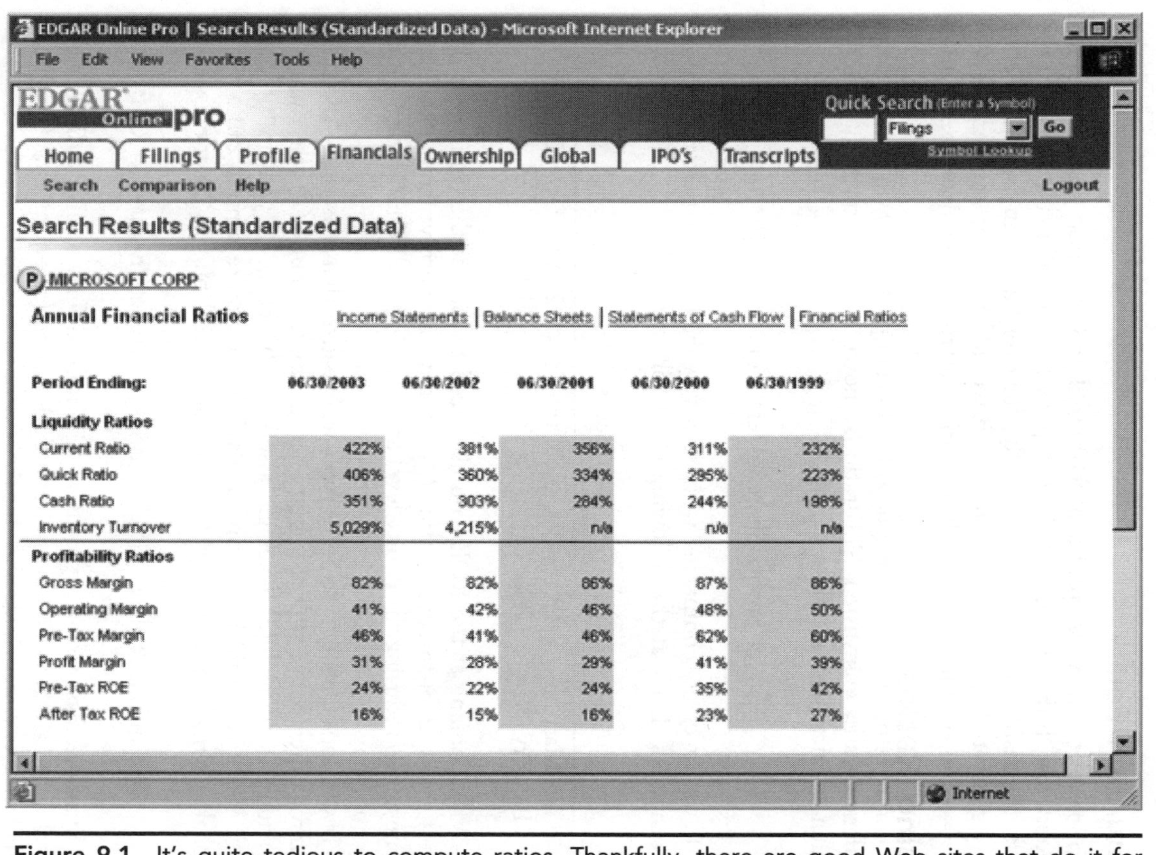

Period Ending:	06/30/2003	06/30/2002	06/30/2001	06/30/2000	06/30/1999
Liquidity Ratios					
Current Ratio	422%	381%	358%	311%	232%
Quick Ratio	406%	360%	334%	295%	223%
Cash Ratio	351%	303%	284%	244%	198%
Inventory Turnover	5,029%	4,215%	n/a	n/a	n/a
Profitability Ratios					
Gross Margin	82%	82%	86%	87%	86%
Operating Margin	41%	42%	46%	48%	50%
Pre-Tax Margin	46%	41%	46%	62%	60%
Profit Margin	31%	28%	29%	41%	39%
Pre-Tax ROE	24%	22%	24%	35%	42%
After Tax ROE	16%	15%	16%	23%	27%

Figure 9.1 It's quite tedious to compute ratios. Thankfully, there are good Web sites that do it for you, such as EDGAR Online Pro. From EDGAR Online Pro (http://www.edgaronlinepro.com).

net margin and gross margin and the need to keep a close eye on them. The following sections take a look at the other two.

Return on Equity

Suppose a company had profits of $100 million in the past year. Sounds like a good year, huh? But what if the company has $10 billion in assets. In this light, the results look terrible. Basically, for every dollar in assets, the company generated only a penny in return. It would have been smarter to invest its assets in a money market fund. And the risk would have been much lower.

For investors, it is vitally important to look at profitability in terms of what shareholders have invested. This ratio is known as return on equity (ROE), which is calculated as follows:

Net profits/Shareholders' equity = ROE

In many cases, companies with relatively high ROEs perform best for shareholders. Look at the following chart for retail sales:

	1998	*1999*	*2000*	*2001*
Wal-Mart	19.1%	21.0%	20.8%	20.1%
Industry	18%	18%	18%	12%

When looking at the ROE, you also need to look at the company's debt levels or the debt-to-equity ratio. A company can borrow large amounts of money, thus reducing the equity level and boosting the ROE. This may mean the company has a higher level of risk.

If you look deeply into ROE, you will realize that it is really the result of three other ratios: (1) net margin: net income/revenues, (2) asset turnover: revenues/assets, and (3) leverage: assets/equity. How? If you multiply the three ratios, you will get a company's ROE (if you're a math buff, you've probably already noticed that the revenues cancel out, as do the assets):

(Net income/Sales) × (Sales/Assets) × (Assets/Equity) = ROE

Example: Fast Co. has profits of $10 million and sales of $100 million. Total assets are $80 million and debt $20 million (so equity is $60 million). The formula would look like this:

($10/$100) × ($100/$80) × ($80/$60)

That is,

$$0.10 \times 1.25 \times 1.33 = 16.7 \text{ percent}$$

This equation gives you an indication where a company's profits are coming from. Is it from its profit margins? Or is the company more efficient because of its turnover ratio? Or has the company taken on debt?

In other words, the ROE is a very powerful ratio, and it measures not only profitability but efficiency, management capability, and leverage. Moreover, if a company has demonstrated a strong growth rate in ROE, it should be able to translate this into strong earnings per share (EPS) and, yes, a strong stock price.

Return on Assets

Return on assets (ROA) is calculated as follows:

$$\text{Operating income/Average assets} = \text{ROA}$$

You may see companies that have a relatively high profit margin but a relatively low return on assets. How is this possible? This is typically the case with capital-intensive companies. For instance, Fast Co. may need $1 billion in assets to generate $500 in sales whereas Slim Co. may only need $100 million in assets to generate the same amount of sales. Thus there is a good chance that Slim Co. will have not only high profit margins but also high ROA.

For investors, finding a company that can make very efficient use of its asset base can mean attractive returns. In the end, the company will need to commit less cash to capital expenditures and more money will flow to the bottom line. This has been the case with Dell, a company with an incredibly efficient operation. As of 2001, it had assets of only $13.4 billion. However, sales were $31.8 billion and the company was able to generate an ROA of 355 percent. New systems to manage inventory and accounts receivable played a critical part in the company's asset management program. With more cash available, Dell was able to expand into new product segments and buy back more shares.

The *DuPont method* offers an alternative approach to calculating ROA:

$$(\text{Net income/Sales}) \times (\text{Sales/Assets}) = \text{ROA}$$

This is the same equation as for ROE, except for the absence of leverage. This makes sense because the return is based on assets, not overall investment (investment may include both equity and debt).

Liquidity Ratios

Liquidity indicates whether or not a company can cover its current obligations. If a company is unable to do so, the consequences can be quite severe for the company — and for its shareholders.

Lenders typically rely heavily on liquidity measures and ratios. Simply put, they want to make sure there is enough cash to pay back the loan. If things deteriorate below certain thresholds, a lender can declare the loan in default and take immediate action, perhaps demanding payment in full at once. The company is almost certain to default at that point, forcing it into bankruptcy; if it was in a position to pay the bill, it wouldn't have gotten into this spot in the first place. The main liquidity ratios include:

- Current ratio
- Quick ratio
- Cash ratio
- Cash-to-current-liabilities ratio
- Working capital turnover

Current Ratio

The current ratio is calculated as follows:

Current assets/Current liabilities = Current ratio

As I tried to point out to my professor, a rule of thumb is that a current ratio of 2.0 is OK. That is, for every $1 in current liabilities, a company has $2 in current assets to meet the obligation. But, as is typically the case with rules of thumb, this one has many exceptions. For very stable industries, a low current ratio may not necessarily be bad. Companies in volatile industries, on the other hand, may need a relatively higher current ratio to maintain liquidity.

The big problem with the current ratio, however, is determining how liquid the assets really are. What if a company has a large amount of inventory that it cannot sell? In this case, the current ratio would be misleading. To adjust for this, look at the quick ratio.

Quick Ratio

The quick ratio is very similar to the current ratio except that it excludes inventories. Here is the calculation:

(Current assets – Inventories)/Current liabilities = Quick ratio

If you see a big change from the current ratio to the quick ratio, it indicates the company has a substantial amount of inventory. If the company is in an industry subject to fast obsolescence, it is a red flag for investors. The rule of thumb for the quick ratio is 1.0 or higher.

Cash and Cash-to-Current-Liabilities Ratios

For ultraconservative investors, the cash ratio is an attractive tool. It's figured like this:

Cash balance/Current assets = Cash ratio

Of course, the higher this ratio, the more liquid the company. But remember that a high ratio may indicate that the company is being too conservative with its cash. If it does not have much to invest the money in, why not just distribute it to shareholders as a dividend?

To be even more conservative, investors can compare cash to liabilities instead of assets, as follows:

Cash/Current liabilities = Cash-to-current-liabilities ratio

This shows what a company can pay off in terms of current liabilities with the cash on hand today. Again, if it's unusually high, it's useful to wonder what the company is doing with all that money lying around.

Working Capital Turnover

Liquidity ratios focus mostly on working capital, which is the difference between current assets and current liabilities. One interesting ratio is the working capital turnover:

Sales/Working capital = Working capital turnover

With this, you can get an idea of how efficient a company is at using its working capital. If the ratio is 5, for example, it means that $1 in working capital translates into $5 in sales.

Activity Ratios

All things being equal, you want a company to be able to collect its receivables quickly, as well as convert inventory into sales quickly. Companies that do this successfully will often become industry leaders — and in the process make their shareholders very happy.

To measure these things, you can use activity ratios, which really give an indication of the company's overall efficiency. There are several types of activity ratios available: inventory ratios, accounts receivable ratios, and asset turnover.

Inventory Ratios

Successful companies have learned that it is vital to keep moving product out the door. It not only reduces overall expenses, but boosts sales. For example, the successful inventory management strategy at Dell has been a significant factor in the company's profits — whether in good times or bad.

Basic Inventory Turnover

Generally, the higher the turnover ratio, the better. The inventory turnover ratio is calculated as follows:

Cost of goods sold (COGS)/Average inventory = Inventory turnover ratio

The COGS reflects the book value of the inventory items that have been sold. In the ratio, this is compared to the inventory on hand. Example: Fast Co. has COGS of $5 million for the past year. At the start of the year, inventory on hand was $1 million, and at the end of the year it was $2 million. That is, the company had an average inventory of

($1 million + $2 million)/2 = $1.5 million

And the inventory turnover ratio is

$5 million/ $1.5 million = 3.33

Thus, Fast Co. was able to turn over its complete inventory 3.33 times per year.

You can convert this ratio into how many days it takes a company to convert inventory into sales:

Ending inventory/Average daily COGS = Days sales in inventory

The average daily COGS is an easy formula:

COGS/365 days = Average daily COGS

Using the latest Fast Co. example, the solution would work like this:

$5 million/365 = $13,698

$2 million/$13,698 = 146 days

If you see the average daily COGS start to creep up over time, it may be an indication that the company is having problems moving its inventory. Note that companies are not required to disclose the COGS figure, and many refrain from doing so. You can use the net sales figure as a substitute if necessary.

Advanced Inventory Turnover

You can play with the inventory turnover ratios to get more detailed information from them. Here are three formulas that can offer some useful insights:

COGS/Average finished goods inventory = Finished goods turnover

Cost of raw material used/Average material in inventory
= Raw material turnover

Cost of goods manufactured/Average work-in-process inventory
= Work-in-process inventory turnover

Accounts Receivable Ratios

Tracking accounts receivable is a good way to see how a company's customers are doing; everyone — including the investors — does better when the company has strong customers that can and do pay their bills promptly. The calculation is as follows:

Net credit sales/Average accounts receivable for period covered in the sales
= Accounts receivable turnover ratio

Note: If net credit sales are not disclosed, then use net sales. Example: Fast Co. has sales of $5 million for the year. At the beginning of the year, accounts receivable totaled $1 million; the corresponding figure was $1.5 million at the end of the year. (Thus the average is $1.25 million.) The accounts receivable turnover ratio would be

$5 million/$1.25 million = 4

That is, in the course of the year, the company was able to turn its accounts receivables into sales about four times. Again, like the turnover ratio, the larger the accounts receivable turnover ratio, the better. It indicates the company is effectively collecting on its sales. You can also calculate the collection period (that is, the time it takes for the company to get paid):

365 days/Turnover ratio = Collection period

or

365 days/4 = 91 days

All manufacturers have an *operating cycle*. This is the time it takes from the creation of inventory to the receipt of money for its sale. To calculate this, just add the days to sell inventory to the collection period. In the case of Fast Co., its operating cycle is 237 days.

Asset Turnover

This is another way of looking at the ROA, discussed earlier in the chapter. Basically, this ratio shows how many times a company turns over its total assets and is an indication of how efficient a company is with its asset base. It's computed by the following formula:

Sales/Average total assets = Asset turnover

Solvency Ratios

Leverage refers to the extra muscle a company can apply by borrowing money. It can be a big advantage, and so it is certainly a common — if scary — part of the U.S. corporate system. If a company has strong cash flows and a substantial asset base, it can borrow money for new products, marketing campaigns, or share repurchases.

The drawbacks of debt include interest payments (which cut into overall profits) and higher risk of default and potential bankruptcy.

With solvency ratios, you can get a sense of whether a company is leveraging its balance sheet so enthusiastically that it may be exposing itself to too much risk. Thes main ratios are debt-to-assets ratio, debt-to-equity ratio, times interest earned, and degree-of-leverage ratios.

Debt-to-Assets Ratio

The debt-to-assets ratio is the most basic ratio for solvency and represents the claims of creditors against a company. All things being equal, the higher

Do Debts Matter?

Professors Franco Modigliani and Merton Miller won the Nobel Prize for their pioneering work on company debt structure. Their findings, which were developed in the 1950s, became known as the Modigliani–Miller theorems.

Assuming the markets are efficient, then it does not matter how much debt a company has. The company will still have the same valuation. Why? Well, the theory looks at value in terms of enterprise value, which is the market capitalization plus debt minus cash. This value is determined ultimately by the future cash flow of the company. The theory was even expanded to dividends and the conclusion was the same: dividend payout has no effect on the value of the firm. But keep in mind that these are theoretical principles. The real world can be quite different; if a company does have a high debt structure, it can mean trouble — especially if the economy or industry falters.

the ratio, the higher the risk of potential trouble for a company. It is calculated as follows:

Total liabilities/Total assets = Debt-to-assets ratio

Debt-to-Equity Ratio

Keep in mind that debt is not necessarily bad (as noted in the sidebar titled "Do Debts Matter?"). Debt can be a very useful way for companies to grow their operations. But if debt levels get excessive — especially in light of the industry standard — a company that begins to falter can crumble very quickly because it is unable to find the cash to meet its debt obligations. The debt-to-equity ratio is a good way to measure potential problems with debt loads. Here's the formula:

Long-term debt/Shareholders' equity = Debt-to-equity ratio

As noted in Chapter 7, a company may have debts that are not on the balance sheet (such as leases and so on). This can distort the debt-to-equity ratio. So it is a good idea to adjust the ratio to account for these debts:

(Long-term debt + Off-balance-sheet debt)/Shareholders' equity = Debt-to-equity ratio

Times Interest Earned

Times interest earned is also known as the *coverage ratio*; it shows a company's ability to meet its interest expenses. Generally, a higher ratio means it is easier for a company to meet its debts. The formula is:

Income before interest and taxes and other income (or expense)/Interest expense = Times interest earned

Degree-of-Leverage Ratios

Leverage is a very important concept in finance, and many academics have studied the complex issues (see the sidebar titled "Do Debts Matter?"). A company has three types of leverage:

1. *Financial leverage*. By increasing debt, a company can increase its return on equity, as noted earlier.
2. *Operating leverage*. Basically, if a company has high fixed costs, it can leverage its earnings when sales surge. Chapter 7 discusses this point in some detail.
3. *Total leverage*. This combines financial and operating leverage.

Here is a useful equation to evaluate financial leverage:

Percent change in EPS/Percent change in earnings before interest and taxes = Degree of financial leverage

When this equation yields a result higher than 1, it indicates positive financial leverage. This means that an increase in earnings before interest and taxes will mean a higher increase in EPS.

As for operating leverage, the calculation is:

Percent change in earnings before interest and taxes/Percent change in sales = Degree of operating leverage

As before, if the result is higher than 1, then there is positive leverage. In other words, an increase in sales will lead to a proportionately higher increase in earnings before interest and taxes. Taking the two together produces the following formula:

Percent change in EPS/Percent change in sales = Degree of total leverage

Basically, an increase in sales will result in a higher increase in EPS. Keep in mind that for all three equations, the opposite is also true. For example, in the total leverage equation, a decline in sales will mean a bigger decline in EPS.

Valuation Ratios

So what makes up a stock price? At the most basic level, the price is simply the amount investors are willing to pay or accept for the stock at the current time. Of course, that succinct statement really provides very little information.

The real question is: What reasons or motivations influence investors' decisions to buy and sell a stock at a certain price? This is a highly complex subject and does not have any right answers. No doubt, academics from many top universities around the globe have tried to answer the question, as have many investors with lots of money riding on these decisions.

To succeed as an investor, you must have some type of discipline for valuing a stock. With this information, you can see if the stock is undervalued. If so, then you should consider buying the stock. Then again, if the transaction is to go through, there must be someone on the other side who thinks the opposite: the stock is at the right price to part with now or, at any rate, not at such a wrong price that it would be better to hang on even if the current owner has another potential use for the money.

Ratio analysis can be helpful in terms of gauging a company's valuation. Here are the ratios that come in handy for this purpose:

- Price/earnings ratio
- Price-to-sales ratio
- Price-to-book ratio
- PEG ratio
- Price-to-EBITDA ratio
- Dividend yield

Chapter 5 discussed dividends. A dividend yield, on the other hand, is the percentage of the payout compared to the current stock price. So, if a company pays $1 per year in dividends and its stock price is $20, then the yield is 5 percent. The following sections take up the other ratios in turn.

For the most part, I think these valuation metrics are not the best in terms of determining valuation. Yet I still look at them, if only to get a sense of other investors' expectations. If the ratios are much higher than others in the same industry, then expectations may be too high.

Price/Earnings Ratio

The P/E ratio is the figure most commonly used for valuation. Interestingly enough, there are two approaches to making the calculation. The first works like this:

Stock price/EPS for the past 12 months = P/E ratio

Alternatively, it can be calculated by looking ahead:

Stock price/EPS forecast for the next 12 months = P/E ratio

The first calculation is fairly easy to do since EPS for the last 12 months will have been reported by the company. The second calculation clearly involves guesswork. Typically, the figure used for the forecast is a consensus estimate from analysts.

What calculation do you usually see? If not specified otherwise, a financial service is likely to be using the first approach. But I actually prefer the second one, because investing is a matter of looking to the future rather than the past.

For the P/E ratio, the general rule of thumb is that if investors believe the growth prospects of a company are strong, the P/E will increase; if they don't, it will fall. It can be an interesting exercise to look at the P/E ratios of different companies in an industry. Here is a chart of industry average P/E ratios:

Industry	*Average P/E*
Basic materials	33
Capital goods	26
Conglomerate	21
Consumer cyclical	22
Consumer noncyclical	24
Energy	23
Financial	21
Healthcare	27
Services	25
Technology	35
Transportation	25
Utilities	14

Investors will often say that you need to be careful with the "E" in the P/E ratio. The reason is that earnings can be quite volatile. For instance, say the earnings of Fast Co. fell substantially to 10 cents per share because of a widespread recession. If the stock price is $10 per share, the P/E ratio would be 100. On the face of it, it looks like the company's stock price is way overvalued. But this is misleading. Perhaps, on average, the company has earnings of $1 to $1.50 per share. In light of this, the company may look cheap over the long term when the economy bounces back.

For instance, look at the P/E chart and you can see that the technology industry has an average P/E of 35. It does seem high. However, the industry has been involved in a significant recession, so it is only to be expected that the current P/E ratios will be high. As things improve, the P/E ratios will look more normal.

To deal with fluctuations in earnings, an investor will *normalize* the earnings, which is what I did in the Fast Co. example. That is, I used a normal or average EPS to calculate the P/E ratio.

One way to look at the P/E ratio is in terms of payback. While a bond requires that the initial investment be paid back, this is not the case with stocks — but investors still look to see if a company will essentially pay back investors over time.

Here's how this works with the P/E ratio: Say Fast Co. has a P/E ratio of 20; then the payback will take 20 years. Why is this the case? It assumes that the growth rate is zero. So if the stock price is currently $20 per share and the P/E is 20, then the current EPS is $1 per share. If a company earns $1 per share for 20 years, then the accumulated earnings will equal $20 per share.

But this is too simplistic. A company will likely grow over 20 years (let's hope so). So a better approach would be to forecast a growth rate to the EPS and then calculate the payback period.

There is something else you can do with the P/E ratio (yes, it is a versatile thing). You can take the reciprocal of the P/E ratio (in other words, divide it into 1):

1/P/E ratio

This is known as the *earnings yield*. Think of it as the interest yield on a bond. Example: If Fast Co. has a P/E of 20, then the earnings yield is 5 percent. So, assuming the EPS stays the same for 20 years, you will be essentially earning 5 percent per year. Again, just as with the payback period, this ratio is flawed because a company is likely to grow over that time. Despite this, many investors still use this ratio. In fact, one technique is to compare the earnings yield to current yields on bonds. If bonds are offering a better yield, then investors may want to shift their portfolios more into bonds.

One of the problems of the P/E ratio is long-term debt. Suppose Fast Co. has a stock price of $20 per share, which equates to a market capitalization of $200 million. But the company also has debt of $100 million. In reality, the company has an enterprise value of $300 million (which is the market capitalization plus outstanding debt). Why is this the case? Think of it this way: If another company wanted to buy Fast Co., in addition to buying in the shares it would need to assume the $100 million in debt, which is a tangible cost.

If Fast Co. has an EPS of $1 per share, the P/E ratio is 20. But what if we use the enterprise value instead of the capitalized value of the stock? In this case, plugging the $300 million enterprise value into the formula and working it backwards, the effective stock price for this calculation is $30 per share and the P/E is now 30. So it is a good exercise to compute the P/E ratio based on a company's enterprise value. It could show that a company has a P/E that's higher than you want to deal with.

On the other hand, the P/E may be actually lower if a company has little or no debt and lots of cash. To understand this, take a look at the formula for enterprise value:

Market capitalization + Debt – Cash = Enterprise value

The reason for subtracting cash is that, if the company were bought out, the acquirer could use the cash to pay down debt or part of the purchase price of the acquisition. Returning to Fast Co., say it has a stock price of $20 and cash of $100 million. There is no debt. The enterprise value would be:

$200 million market capitalization – $100 million in cash = $100 million

The enterprise value stock price — that is, the price as adjusted for the purpose of this calculation — would be $10 and the resulting P/E would be 10.

Price-to-Sales Ratio

It is very simple to calculate the price-to-sales ratio (PSR):

Current market capitalization/Sales for the last 12 months = PSR

Note: As with the P/E ratio, you might want to use the enterprise value instead of the market capitalization. PSR offers some benefits compared to the P/E ratio: (1) it tends to be less volatile than earnings and (2) if a company does not have earnings, you can at least make a valuation based on sales (that is, assuming the company has sales!).

Ken Fisher, who heads his own money management firm, has done extensive studies on PSR, which he published in his groundbreaking book, *Super Stocks* (1984). He tends to stay away from companies that have PSRs of 3.0 or more and prefers companies with a PSR of 1.0 or lower (and he especially likes PSRs of 0.5). You can read Fisher's insightful advice in his column on Forbes.com.

Price-to-Book Ratio

Book value is the equity of a firm. Theoretically, if a company sells all its assets and pays down all its debt, the remaining portion is the book value. Example: Suppose Fast Co. has $10 million in assets and $5 million in liabilities. The book value would be $5 million. If the company has 5 million shares outstanding, then the book value per share would be $1. The price-to-book ratio (PBR) is a simple matter of the following formula:

Current stock price/Book value per share = PBR

Say the stock price is currently $5 per share. That gives a price-to-book value of 5, by this calculation:

$5 stock price/$1 book value per share = 5

Investors like this ratio because book value is likely to be less volatile than earnings. Also, book value appeals to value investors, who tend to focus on liquidation values of a company (see the sidebar titled "Growth Versus Value Investing" in Chapter 7 for more on this topic). But this ratio has particular trouble with historical costing, as discussed in Chapter 2. Over time, the book value is apt to understate the value of a company more and more drastically. For example, property a company bought 10 years ago may have appreciated 100 percent but is still booked at its original cost.

Moreover, some companies — especially high-tech companies — do not have much in the way of tangible assets. For instance, Microsoft has a book value per share of $10 yet its stock price is $60, for a PBR of 6. Obviously, the company's real value goes beyond the physical plant and equipment. But for mature industries — which do have substantial amounts of assets — the book value calculation can be useful. If it is relatively low, it may indicate a good time to buy the stock.

Of course, a company may be selling at a steep discount to book value for a very good reason: perhaps the assets are not worth much. A classic case is Smith Corona, which looked very cheap on a price-to-book-value basis. But so few people were interested in buying typewriters that Smith Corona's factories and equipment were no longer worth anything like the value they carried on the books.

PEG Ratio

One of the problems with growth investing is that you may essentially pay too much for a stock. After all, many investors certainly want to see their companies grow and they will bid up the price of a potential growth company's stock — sometimes to unsustainable levels. With little warning, the price can plunge.

As a result, some investors look at an approach called growth at a reasonable price or GARP. It is not easy to find GARP stocks, but that does not stop investors from trying. GARP investors like to rely on something called the PEG (P/E-to-growth) ratio to help them find the rare jewels they seek. Simply put, to meet the requirements of a GARP adherent, a stock's P/E ratio should be no higher than the company's growth rate. That is, the PEG ratio should be 1.0 or less. Here's how the equation looks:

P/E ratio/Growth rate = PEG

What the PEG ratio attempts to do is counteract one problem with the P/E ratio, which can be misleading on its own. During the 1990s, for example, many investors stayed away from Dell stock because the P/E ratio looked too high. Yet the stock kept going up and up.

As noted earlier, the P/E ratio is an indication of the growth expectations of a company. The higher the growth outlook, the higher the P/E ratio. So why not have a ratio that compares the P/E ratio to the growth rate? The problem, of course, is coming up with a growth rate. Needless to say, this is not an exact science — despite the many analysts who try to forecast EPS.

You could try to estimate growth rates yourself, by looking at the growth of the industry for the past few years and assume it will continue at that rate. Or, you could look at the consensus growth forecasts from Wall Street analysts, which are easy to obtain from financial Internet sites. In fact, quote.yahoo.com has its own PEG numbers if a stock has analyst coverage.

The gang at the Motley Fool like the PEG ratio so much that they call it the Fool Ratio, and they list it on their Web site (http://www.fool.com) for a variety of companies. They believe that it can be a good way to gauge whether a company is overvalued or undervalued (although they do warn that investors should never rely on just one indicator). Here are the guidelines from the Motley Fool:

Fool Ratio	*Tend To*
0.50 or less	Buy
0.50 to 0.65	Look to buy
0.65 to 1.00	Watch (or "hold")
1.00 to 1.30	Look to sell
1.30 to 1.70	Consider shorting
Over 1.70	Short

Price-to-EBITDA Ratio

Many investors are fond of the earnings before interest, taxes, depreciation, and amortization (EBITDA) figure, regarding it as an indication of how a company is really doing. As I said in Chapter 7, I don't much care for this figure. Since the scandals of 2002, many analysts are veering away from it as well. Nonetheless, you'll see references to a variant P/E ratio based on EBITDA, calculated as follows:

Market capitalization/EBITDA = Price-to-EBITDA ratio

Note: Some investors use enterprise value instead of market capitalization in this formula, as with the P/E and price-to-book ratio.

Although EBITDA rarely makes much sense, some industries need to use it. Cable companies, for example, generally have little reportable earnings (because of the substantial depreciation and amortization charges from capital expenditures). Analysts studying those industries rely mostly on EBITDA measures such as this one.

Cash Flow Ratios

I spent a lot of time on this in Chapter 8, but it's worth saying again: The cash flow statement is vitally important to any investor. Over and above the direct readings, it generates several useful ratios:

- Cash flow ratio.
- Cash flow to net income. I've discussed this measure of the quality of a company's profits so extensively that I won't bring it up again here. See the sidebar titled "Disconnect at Lucent" in Chapter 8 for a vivid example.
- Cash return on sales.

Cash Flow Ratio

The cash flow ratio gives an indication of whether a company's cash inflows can cover its outflows, such as financing and investing costs. It is calculated as follows:

Cash flow from operations/Financing and investing cash outflows = Cash flow ratio

Cash Return on Sales

Cash return on sales gives you an idea of the cash earnings a company generates per dollar of sales. It is similar to operating margin, but cash flows are factored into the formula instead of net income. It is calculated as follows:

Cash flow from operations/Sales = Cash return on sales

Intrinsic Value Per Share

A stock's *intrinsic value* is the present value of the company's future earnings stream, figured on a per-share basis. If the current stock price is lower than the calculated intrinsic value, then the analyst preparing the estimate will consider the stock to be undervalued.

It is beyond my scope here to detail the intricacies of calculating intrinsic value (it entails not only lots of math but also crunching lots of fundamental company information, such as earnings estimates). Analysts study the required forecasting and mathematical techniques intensively as they prepare for the Certified Financial Analyst (CFA) exam. But do not be discouraged; there is an alternative. Yes, from the Web, there are resources to help calculate intrinsic value. The one I use is a calculator on the Quicken Web site (http://www.quicken.com and see Figure 9.2).

Here's how it works: You enter the ticker symbol, for example NOK (the symbol for phone maker Nokia). The first screen will show the results instantly. In this case, it indicates that, based on Quicken's model, Nokia's current stock price is $12.43 yet its intrinsic value is $9.44. Thus it appears that Nokia is currently overvalued.

In fact, Quicken then provides some analysis of its conclusions. For example, Nokia needs to grow 18.6 percent for 10 years to justify its current stock price. Can a company of this size do such a thing?

You can change the assumptions for the intrinsic analysis. This can be very enlightening, as a small change in the growth rate may have a big impact on the results. You can also change the discount rate, but I don't recommend it; the default provided by Quicken works better than most alternatives.

With a pull-down menu, I made some changes to the growth rate based on analyst forecasts. With the different types of forecasts, I set up a chart like the following:

Type	*Nokia's Growth Rate*	*Nokia's Intrinsic Value*
Analysts' five-year average forecast	14.77%	$9.44
Analysts' five-year high forecast	25.00%	$19.66
Analysts' five-year low forecast	7.50%	$5.59
Company growth for past three years	3.60%	$4.24

Looking at this chart, it's clear that even if Nokia hits the high expectations of the analysts, the intrinsic value wouldn't be all that high — only $19.66. Then again, if problems persist and the low estimates prove correct, the intrinsic value would be $5.59, and even that seems a bit optimistic compared with the company's growth rate for the past three years. Based on this information, I would probably pass on this stock.

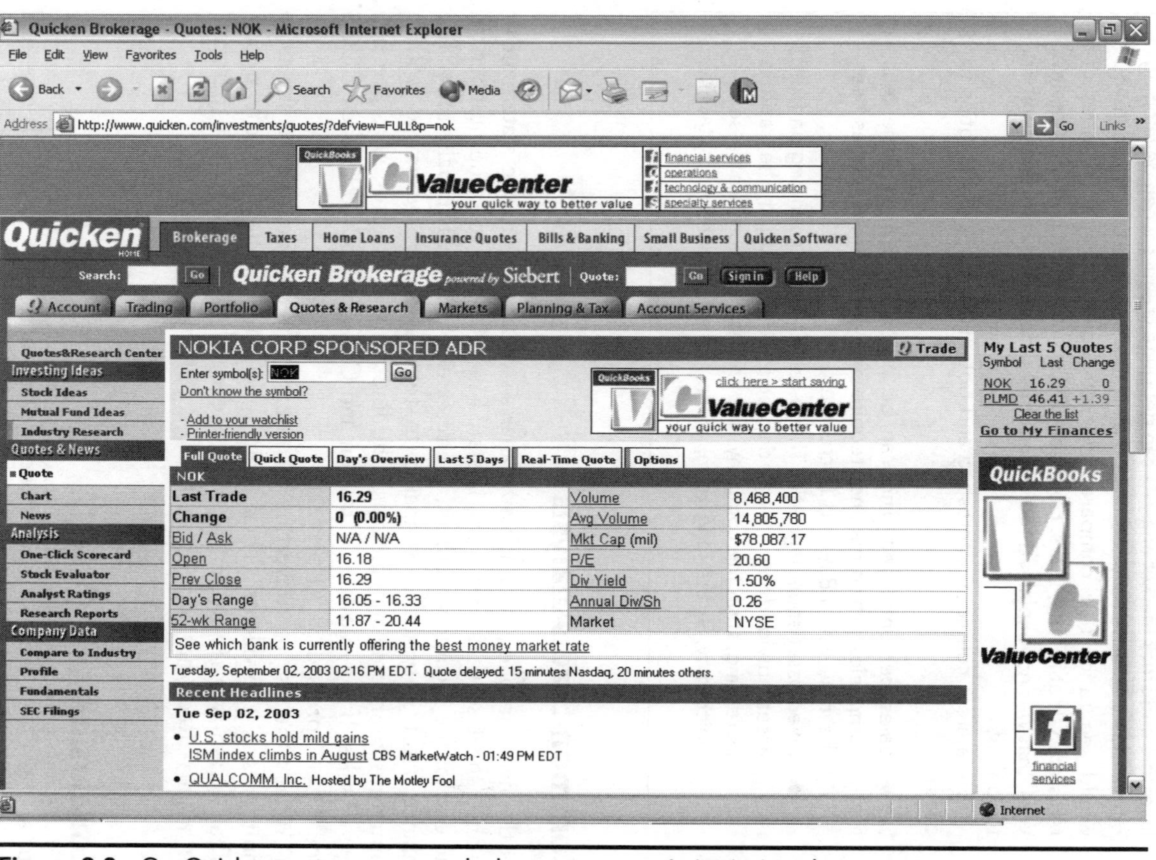

Figure 9.2 On Quicken.com, you can calculate a company's intrinsic value.

Special Ratios

Investors and stock market analysts can get quite creative when developing ratios. This was especially the case during the dot-com boom, when you would see ratios that compared market capitalization to number of registered (that is, free) users. How would this make a company profitable? Well, that was not explained too well, but it made for a comforting number to look at.

Here are a couple of interesting and potentially more useful ratios to consider:

- *Sales per employee.* This can be especially high in some tech companies, which may not require many employees, as has been the case with eBay and Microsoft.
- *Fixed asset spending ratio.* This is calculated as spending on fixed assets divided by annual depreciation charge. If the ratio is increasing, then the company is spending more on fixed assets — which may, in the long term, mean higher growth in profitability.

Common-Size Analysis

As the name implies, common-size analysis recasts an income statement or balance sheet so that everything is stated in reference to some number. In the case of the income statement, the reference number is usually sales. The balance sheet is typically compared to total assets. For example, with a common-size income statement, all the line items are expressed as percentages of sales. If the sales are $1 million and COGS is $500,000, then COGS would be expressed as 50 percent.

What's the use of converting income statements and balance sheets to common-size equivalents? Their main function is to help identify trends. What if cash was 10 percent of total assets and is now down to 1 percent? Or what if R&D has sunk from 10 to 2 percent of sales?

Conclusion

For any investor, ratio analysis is one of the real keys to success. It can shed light on important parts of a company and lead to better investment decisions. That makes this chapter well worth the study until you're comfortable with the terms. It may feel as though there's too much math involved, but you can use these ratios effectively without doing your own calculations. I think the best way to deal with ratios is to use online financial software that uses them to screen thousands of financial statements based — a discussion I'm saving for Chapter 13.

Meanwhile, you also need to be acquainted with several other aspects of investing. The next chapter takes up the wonderful world of proxy statements.

10

Proxy Statements

"A soap opera in black and white" — that's what Hugo Quackenbush, a vice president at Charles Schwab & Co., once called proxy statements. He added, "Management has to disclose all the stuff they don't want to and investors can get more of the texture and flavor of a company reading the proxy statement than the glossy annual report."

In 2000, I decided to attend the shareholders' meeting of a small cap company I owned shares in. The company was in the Internet space and its value had dropped like a rock, along with most of the rest of the sector. Actually, the main reason I attended was that the meeting was local, though it was still an hour's drive, in the middle of the L.A. rush hour.

I was only five minutes late. But the meeting was already over! I shouldn't have been surprised. For small companies, the annual meeting can often be a mere formality, since shareholders rarely show up. I was the only shareholder at the meeting who was not an officer or director or family member. True, they served coffee and donuts — so the trip wasn't a complete waste.

Furthermore, I had face time with the management of the company. They were definitely upbeat and had many initiatives in the works. I got their business cards and was able to keep in contact with them afterward. How did the stock do? In a year and a half, it increased 700 percent.

If you have a chance to attend an annual shareholders' meeting, you should do so. They can even be exciting and tense if the stock price has fallen. I remember a meeting in the early 1990s for a utility company whose stock price had declined steadily over the years. An elderly shareholder went to the mike and started to rail against management's incompetence and excessive salaries. The CEO was curt and dismissed the lady's comments. She left the room and slammed the door. A year later, the stock was down about 25 percent or so.

Structure of the Proxy Statement

If you are a shareholder of a company, you will receive a proxy statement in the mail. You can download proxy statements from EDGAR Online Pro as well, which comes in handy if you're considering buying a company's stock. The official name of the document is a DEF-14.

The purpose of the proxy statement is to provide investors with enough disclosure to make important shareholder votes. Yes, as an owner, you have certain rights — and one of them is the right to vote. What if you cannot attend the meeting? You can vote by signing the proxy card and sending it to the company, and sometimes you can even electronically transmit your vote via a site such as ProxyVote.com.

At least once a year, at the annual meeting, shareholders will be able to vote. But there may also be special meetings, such as for mergers or other mega transactions.

The structure of a proxy statement looks like this:

- Short letter from the CEO, explaining when the annual meeting will be held and the issues to be voted on
- Description of voting rights and the process for voting
- Detailed description of the matters to be voted on
- List of the major shareholders
- Executive compensation
- Audit committee report
- Compensation committee report
- Shareholder proposals (issues that shareholders are putting up for a vote)

The following sections give you a look at the main parts to focus on as an investor.

The Fun Stuff: Executive Compensation

Reading a proxy statement can give you a glimpse into the lifestyles of the rich and famous. In fact, with the landmark securities legislation of 2002, companies will need to make fuller disclosure of executive compensation, which should make the reading even more interesting.

It is not salary but the use of employee stock options that has made many executives superwealthy. Actually, options are a fairly recent development. The concept was signed into law by President Truman in 1950, and it was not until the 1980s that options became a powerful tool for wealth creation. The pivotal event was the option package put together for incoming Disney CEO Michael Eisner in 1984.

As Eisner made his millions, other CEOs took notice, and as a consequence, executive compensation skyrocketed. For instance, the CEO of Coca-Cola, Roberto Goizueta, became the first CEO to make a billion dollars from employee stock options.

True, some executives should be rich because of the results they provide to shareholders — but this does not mean the compensation should be obscene. Of course, the key question is what is obscene. What is over the top? There is no bright-line test, but often the best approach is the famous "smell test."

For example, look at the grant size of the employee stock options. If it is more than, say, 10 million shares, it is probably verging on the obscene. After all, if the stock goes up a mere $1, the executive gets a nice $10 million boost to net worth.

Next, compare the option grants to the current shares outstanding. If last year's grants amount to more than 10 percent of the outstanding shares, be careful. Remember, not only is the executive potentially getting a big payday, but the rest of the shareholders stand to have their holdings reduced in substance as the executive exercises the stock options and floods the market with large amounts of shares.

Try to compare the compensation against others in the industry. This was instructive with the CEO of E*Trade, Christos Cotsakos. The proxy initially disclosed that he pulled in a whopping $88.2 million in 2001, which was well above what executives were getting at much larger financial firms, such as Morgan Stanley and Merrill Lynch. Because of an immediate uproar, he agreed to give back $18 million.

Getting into the Details of Executive Compensation

In a way, executive compensation is a balancing game. On one hand, you want to attract and retain highly motivated and skilled managers to generate profits for the company. On the other hand, you want to make sure that the executives are not draining the corporate treasury.

In the proxy statement, you will have full disclosure of executive compensation — as well as director compensation. However, the statement will only give you a summary of the compensation package. For a complete picture, you need to get a copy of the employment agreements, which you can find on the EDGAR Online Pro service (this is detailed in the sidebar titled "Getting Help on Proxy Issues" later in this chapter). A keyword search will scan across 10-Ks and proxies where these agreements are typically attached as exhibits.

The Corporate Library gets the data by calling the company and requesting the contract. If there is resistance, then it is a danger sign. The Corporate

Library lists what it calls the Corporate Responsiveness Rating to track the ease or difficulty of getting this information.

According to the Corporate Library, an executive's compensation should be tied strictly to the "creation of shareholder value." For example, the firm considers the employment contract of GE's legendary CEO, Jack Welch, to be exemplary. (It also lists GE as one of the best companies in terms of responsiveness.) The contract is short and concise and ties compensation to the growth of the company. Yet the contract Welch received for his retirement appears to be something altogether different, as discussed shortly in the "Perks" section.

Then again, the worst contract was for the CEO of Global Crossing, Robert Annunziata. What was the problem? Here's a look at the main factors:

- He got a signing bonus of $10 million — which he could keep regardless of how well the company did.
- He got two million stock options, at $10 per share (which was below current market value). This he got whether the company did well or not.
- He received a "guaranteed bonus." Sounds strange, huh? Well, it amounted to a minimum of $500,000 per year.
- He got a Mercedes for himself and his wife.
- He got the corporate jet for commuting to the office (until he decided to move).
- His mother got first-class airfare to visit her successful son every month.

Employment contracts often make confusing reading, but you can use EDGAR Online Pro to search for some key terms that indicate that an executive's salary may be on the excessive side. Here are some of the best words to use for queries:

- *Gross-up*. A company agrees to pay the excise tax for, well, huge salaries. If execs get huge salaries, why can't they pay the tax?
- *Lifetime*. This is a dangerous word, but executives love it. For example, the CEO of Cendant gets to use the corporate jet for his lifetime. And if it is being used for business purposes? The company will charter him a plane.
- *Aircraft, car, apartment, country club, helicopter*. You get the picture.

Another danger sign is when executive compensation increases even though the company falters. An example is WorldCom. The CEO, Bernie Ebbers, got a $65,000 hike in his salary and a $10 million bonus. How did the stock do? It fell 70 percent.

Jim Jubak, a widely followed columnist for MSN Investor, wrote an article about how he analyzes proxy statements. He uses a three-strike model. If a company has substantial layoffs, say over 10 percent of the workforce, the company gets Strike One. If there are multiple layoffs, it is Strike Two. If the executives are taking huge compensation while these layoffs are occurring, he gives a Strike Three.

This is a good way to weed out bad stocks. Employee morale is critical for a strong company, and if executives are taking huge pay when the rest of the employees are fearing for their jobs, it is a recipe for disaster.

Perks

Besides salary, options, and bonuses, a company can provide other types of compensation, such as perks. While the word "perk" does not sound very serious, it definitely can refer to a significant cost item. (See the sidebar titled "The Corporate Jet Phenomenon.")

According to the SEC, a company must disclose a perk in its proxy statement if it is worth more than $50,000 or if a perk constitutes 25 percent of the total of all perks. The disclosure is made in a footnote. Despite this

The Corporate Jet Phenomenon

The corporate jet. It is the status symbol of mega executives. Of course, in public, executives try to justify the use of a corporate jet as almost a necessity. How? Here are some of its real attractions:

- It's confidential (no worries about a neighboring passenger overhearing the details of a big deal).
- It's direct and less likely to be delayed.
- It's easier to make frequent trips (especially if your company is global).

But what is the cost? True, a company does not necessarily need to buy a plane but can instead use a fractional ownership system. While this is cheaper, it is still not inexpensive. It can cost several million dollars to use this system. There are also monthly charges and per-hour fees for use.

Corporate jets are, for the most part, luxurious; they make travel quite enjoyable — perhaps too enjoyable. It is certainly tempting for executives to use the jets for personal purposes, and some executive contracts even expressly allow for this.

rule, attorneys are clever in getting around the reporting requirement and investors often do not see the many perks that executives get.

Interestingly enough, when Jack Welch's wife filed for divorce, the world got to see the kinds of perks the former GE CEO continued to enjoy even after he departed. Here are some of the juicy details:

- A consulting gig with GE for $86,000 per year
- The use of a Manhattan apartment owned by GE (a value of about $80,000 per month)
- Satellite TV for his four homes (probably more aptly described as "estates")
- Floor-level seats for the NY Knicks
- Courtside seats at the U.S. Open
- A car and driver
- Security personnel when he travels

Well, there was an immediate uproar, and Welch quickly announced that he would pay for all of these services from his own bank account. But he can afford it; Welch is estimated to have a fortune of about $900 million and he gets an annual pension of $9 million.

Related-Party Transactions

The 10-K, 10-Q, and proxy filings may have a section called "Related-Party Transactions" that is worth keeping an eye on. This means that the company is conducting business with a party that has some type of relationship to the company. For example, suppose Jane is the CEO of Fast Co. and strikes a deal to purchase $1 million in components from Small Co., which is owned by her cousin Jeff. Clearly, this would be a related-party transaction.

Besides regulating disclosure of deals with family members, the related-party rules would also apply to a situation in which, say, Fast Co. conducts business with a company it owns an equity stake in or, as with Enron, where the CFO is a general partner of a partnership that conducts business with the main company.

The big problem with related-party transactions is that they are not at arm's length. That raises the question of whether they are ultimately in the company's interest. For example, is Fast Co. going to Small Co. because Small is the best supplier, or is Jane doing the deal — on better-than-normal terms — to help out her cousin Jeff? Because of this conflict problem, the SEC requires that material related-party transactions be disclosed.

So, if you see many related-party transactions, be wary. This is especially the case if the related party is a major customer.

Also, be wary if the disclosure is vague. (Is the company trying to hide something?) Consider Stellent, a software company, whose proxy statement

A Golden Deal

The buzzwords of executive compensation can be quite colorful — literally speaking. Often, you will see the word *golden* used. Here's a map to the gold:

- *Golden parachute.* A huge severance package due if an executive gets terminated (that is, fired). For example, in 2000, Steve Hilbert was terminated from Conseco (a company he founded) and received a golden parachute of $72 million.
- *Golden bungee.* This uses the same concept as the golden parachute — but is even more lucrative. Besides getting a great severance package, the executive retains some type of position with the new firm (such as after a merger). This happened with several executives at National Commerce Bancorp, who collected $26 million in a golden parachute and were still able to keep their jobs at the newly merged company.
- *Golden hello.* This is a big signing bonus for an executive. It is meant to not only entice the executive but also pay for compensation lost as a result of changing jobs (the departing executive may leave lucrative employee stock options on the table). For example, Gary Wendt received the biggest golden hello on record when he got $45 million (in cash) to become CEO of Conseco in 2000. By 2002, the stock was delisted from the New York Stock Exchange and the company was mired in bankruptcy.

was so complex that it was difficult to keep track of all the different types of related-party transactions.

One of Stellent's deals was with Active IQ Technologies, which purchased $2 million in software from Stellent four days before the end of the third quarter in 2001. This was certainly a material transaction, as Stellent reported $26.6 million in the quarter. More than a month later, Stellent disclosed in its 10-Q that it owned 8.5 percent of Active IQ (even the CEO of Stellent personally owned shares in Active IQ).

Another disclosure said Stellent had loaned $3.5 million to "one of our partners." Which one? The company did not want to say. After much pressure from TheStreet.com columnist Herb Greenberg, Stellent announced several months later that the unknown partner was a major distributor of the company's software products. Stellent did disclose that the distributor paid off the loan. But to do this, the distributor took a short-term loan from an investment firm controlled by the chairman of Stellent. Cozy.

Auditor Independence

In 2000, the SEC required companies to make certain disclosures about their auditors for the proxy statement. Essentially, the SEC was concerned that, with auditors receiving large amounts of consulting fees from clients, the audits might not necessarily be unbiased. In light of the auditing problems at Enron and revealed in other major bankruptcies, the SEC certainly had reason for concern.

The proxy statement must disclose the fees for the audit, IT consulting, and other consulting services from the auditor. Moreover, the audit committee must state whether it believes the auditors were independent in their judgment regardless of the consulting fees. An *audit committee* is a group of a company's directors who review the scope and the procedures of an audit, oversee special investigations, review financial statements filed with the SEC, oversee whether the company is complying with regulations, and review accounting policies.

Investors should be wary if more than half of the auditing firm's fees are for consulting. With that much money on the table, the auditor may be reluctant to question the company hard on the audit. The fear of losing substantial consulting fees is bound to be an inhibiting factor.

Management Team

It is critical to read the management and board bios. This goes beyond looking for inconsistencies of the sort discussed in Chapter 3. Is this the right team? Are they lacking in important areas? Are some of the members questionable in terms of abilities?

Actually, the proxy statement can shed more light on these issues — especially when you read the compensation committee report, which talks about how the board determined executive pay. From this, you can sense the tone of the board. Is it gushing? If so, the company may be suffering from a deadly affliction known as hubris.

This appears to be the case with online broker E*Trade, whose CEO was described in the proxy as a person with "vision, drive and passion...," "one of the visionaries of e-commerce." Oh, yes, he also provided "visionary leadership" — $88.2 million worth in 2001, as noted earlier, if you believe the compensation committee.

Shareholder Proposals

Read this section and see if there is much discontent with the company. Are there proposals to require approval of executive compensation, eliminate a staggered board, or change aggressive accounting procedures? If so, the shareholders may be thinking of bailing out of the stock.

You Have a Right to Vote

As noted at the beginning of this chapter, you have the right to vote at the annual meeting. In most cases, you get one vote for every share you own. Typically, you can vote for such things as directors of the firm, the hiring of an auditor, and mergers. You will also see shareholder proposals, as described in the preceding section. A group of shareholders may put up some issues for vote, such as changing executive compensation or even proposing a new slate of directors. However, shareholder proposals can be an expensive process, requiring legal and marketing expenses (for example, sending letters to shareholders to get support).

Voters in political elections tend to be apathetic these days, and they're models of active participation compared to individual investors with proxy votes. But even if you have only a few shares, you should vote anyway. It is your right. Besides, it is easy to vote. That is, you fill out a proxy card and send it in. Some companies even allow you to use the Internet to vote by entering your vote on sites such as ProxyVote.com (see Figure 10.1).

So you think your measly few votes will not matter? Here's one case where an individual investor's dissent was very important. The company in question runs a chain of cafeterias known as Luby's, which definitely have a homespun environment. But in 1997, the company hired a new CEO who took an aggressive cost-cutting program. Among many other things, he got rid of cloth napkins and replaced them with paper ones. As a result, customers thought Luby's was losing its charm.

Les Greenberg, a retired attorney, owned 5,600 shares of Luby's, a small fraction of the total. But he was a big fan of the restaurants and was very concerned about the direction of the company. He started to post messages on chat rooms to garner support to unseat the CEO and even make a shareholder proposal to elect four board members.

In his fight, Greenberg encouraged shareholders to send letters to management calling for reform and demanding the ouster of the CEO. Soon the CEO resigned. In the end, Greenberg was unable to elect his slate of directors — but the message got through. The new CEO started to reverse the changes at the restaurants. The food was being made from scratch again, and — yes — the napkins were made of cloth.

The CalPERS Effect

One of the country's biggest institutional investors is the California Public Employees' Retirement System (CalPERS), which manages the retirement assets for about 1.3 million members. In all, the assets under management amount to about $151 billion. CalPERS has tremendous influence on corpo-

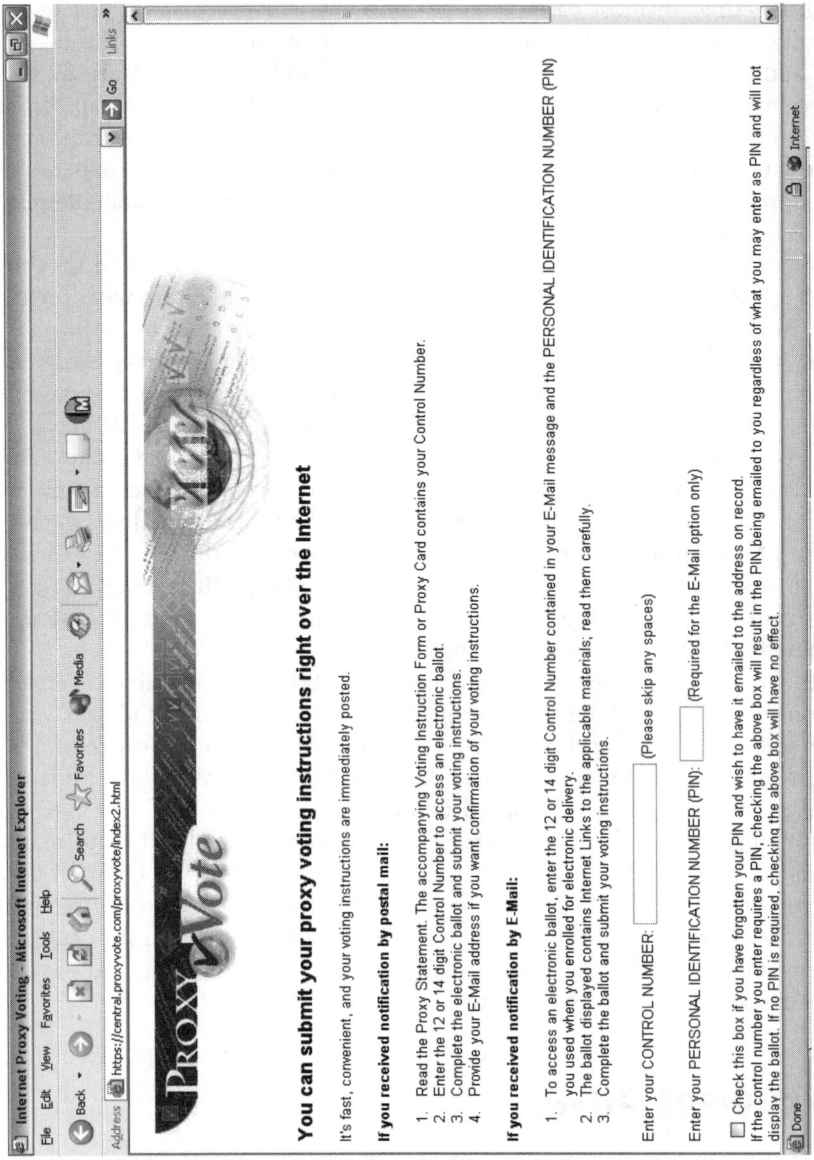

Figure 10.1 As a shareholder, you have the right to vote. Make sure you exercise it. In fact, it is very easy to do — there are even Web sites that streamline the process, such as proxyvote.com.

Getting Help on Proxy Issues

Several Web sites include pages set up to help individual investors interpret proxy statements. Of course, ultimately it is your own decision, but these sites can certainly provide guidance.

- *California Public Employees' Retirement System (CalPERS; http://www.calpers.ca.gov).* This is the mega fund that manages the retirement assets for California state employees. At the Web site, you can find all the recommendations for voting on portfolio companies.
- *The Corporate Library (http://www.thecorporatelibrary.com).* Two well-known experts in corporate governance — Nell Minow and Robert Monks — started this site in 1999. It has a plethora of articles on corporate governance, plus links to the employment contracts and even a list of the worst contracts (the winner was the CEO of Global Crossing, Robert Annunziata, whose company went bust). The site also plans on providing information on attendance for board members.
- *eRaider (http://www.eraider.com).* This is a mutual fund and Web site founded by two professors, Martin Stoller and Aaron Brown. In November 1998, they bought stock in United Companies Financial (UC) for $4 per share. At the time, the company had a book value of $17 per share. Then in March 1999, the company — for no stated reason — decided to file for Chapter 11. Stoller called the company, but there was no response. Not to be deterred, he went to the Yahoo! chat board and generated support from many investors. The bankruptcy judge was persuaded to appoint Stoller to chair the equity committee. With their fund, Stoller and Brown try to generate support from existing shareholders to change the direction of a company. The Web site, in fact, is a great platform for discussing many issues about certain companies that Stoller and Brown have targeted.

rate America, and the fund is not afraid to use its power. On an annual basis, CalPERS analyzes the performance of the lowest performers in its massive portfolio. From this, CalPERS sets up what it calls a Focus List and makes recommendations and proposals to help improve the situation.

A big emphasis is on *corporate governance* — the structure of a company along with its executive compensation, voting rules, board composition, and so on. In other words, corporate governance covers many of the issues discussed in the proxy statement.

Interestingly enough, the research firm of Wilshire Associates has done a study on the CalPERS Focus List. The conclusion was that these stocks outperformed the S&P Index by 23 percent in the following five years — adding about $150 million per year in additional returns to the fund. Wilshire calls this the "CalPERS Effect." You can see the Focus List at the CalPERS site (noted in the sidebar titled "Getting Help on Proxy Issues").

The following are the CalPERS recommendations for effective corporate governance:

1. Board Composition and Structure
   - Board size between 6 and 15 members.
   - Nonclassified board. (This means that all board members are voted in one year rather than for staggered terms; a staggered board is a way to prevent outsiders from gaining board seats.)
   - Separate chair and CEO positions, or appoint a lead director among the independent directors.
   - More than 75 percent independent directors.
   - Nominating committee 100 percent independent directors.
   - Audit committee 100 percent independent directors.
   - Compensation committee 100 percent independent directors.
   - "No members of the board are related to each other, or to senior management."
2. Director Compensation and Stock Holdings
   - Director retainer paid 50 percent or more in stock.
   - Directors and officers own more than 10 percent of the outstanding stock and director options have never been repriced.
3. Management
   - No golden parachutes.
   - Management options have never been repriced.
4. Anti-Takeover Devices
   - Cumulative voting.
   - No supermajority provisions.
   - No unequal voting rights.
   - No poison pill that was not ratified by shareholders.
   - No limited action by written consent.
   - No limitation on ability to act by special meeting.
   - No limitation on ability of shareholders to amend the charter.
   - No limitation on ability of shareholders to amend bylaws.
   - Confidential voting.

Getting Too Personal?

With the proxy statement, you can get some background on the senior managers and board members. And sometimes the information can be very personal. For example, until July 1997, the SEC required that an insider's Social Security number be disclosed in proxy statements. While no longer required to do so, some insiders still disclose their Social Security numbers as well as their birth dates. Why? Perhaps they are using an old SEC form.

However, this can be a dangerous thing to do. A big problem over the years has been identity theft, which is much easier to accomplish if you have a person's Social Security number. If you see such information in the proxy statement, you might wonder about the wisdom of the executives who allow it to be listed.

One of the companies on the 2002 Focus List was Gateway, the PC manufacturer. Recommendations included:

- Conduct a formal governance review using an external consultant.
- Request that the board declassify itself into one class of directors.
- Adopt a resolution requiring that the key committees consist exclusively of independent directors.
- Separate the chair and chief executive officer positions, or consider the appointment of a lead independent director.

So far, there have been no changes at Gateway on these matters. As for the stock price, it has continued to deteriorate since the report.

Conclusion

A corporation, in a way, is like a democracy — with its shareholders as the citizens with the right to vote. Unlike political elections, corporate votes come with a disclosure document called the proxy, which provides a good amount of information to work with. By reading it, as well as looking at the other filings, you will get a much better understanding of the company. You might decide to vote one way or the other — or just might decide to sell the stock!

In the next chapter, we will look at insider buying and selling.

Sources

1. Siskos, Catherine, Shareholders unite! *Kiplinger's Personal Finance,* May 2002.
2. Serwer, Andy and David, Grainger, CEO perks that'll drive you berserk, *Fortune,* July 21, 2002.
3. Fabrikant, Geraldine, G.E. expenses for ex-chief cited in divorce papers, *New York Times,* August 16, 2002.
4. McCaffery, Richard, No substitute for the proxy statement, Fool.com, September 15, 2000.
5. Jubak, Jim, When worker anger boils over, it's time to sell, MSN Investor, May 24, 2002.

This book has free materials available for download from the Web Added Value™ Resource Center at www.jrosspub.com.

11

Insider Buying and Selling

Wouldn't it be great to have access to inside information — the real skinny about what's going on in a company you might like to invest in? In fact, you may already have had such an opportunity. Of course, the problem is that if you act on the information, you may have to pay a fine or even go to prison. That's what happened to a variety of Wall Streeters such as Ivan Boesky in the 1980s. It was also good material for the classic Hollywood film *Wall Street*.

During the 1920s, a tremendous amount of investor activity was based on insider information. It was almost normal operating procedure. Then again, it was not illegal either — that is, until the 1930s and passage of the landmark securities laws.

A big problem with the attempt to regulate insider trading was defining it. Basically, you are not allowed to buy or sell stock if your decision is based on any material, nonpublic information that will affect the stock price. If you find out that Fast Co. is about to buy XYZ Corp. at a big price and you snap up some XYZ shares before the information becomes public knowledge, then this would qualify as insider trading.

However, Congress had a problem: What about the executives and directors of the firm? Aren't they constantly exposed to inside information? One idea was to prevent them from buying or selling any shares in their own company. But this seemed too extreme. If anything, Congress wanted to encourage company management to have an ownership stake. The solution? Congress said that company executives and directors must disclose any purchases and sales of the company stock. This was consistent with the philosophy of the federal securities laws, that is, to rely on disclosure as a means of effective regulation.

Interestingly enough, Congress thus created a great way for investors to get access to inside information in an indirect way. For example, suppose John is the CEO of XYZ. He has been aggressively restructuring the company. One of the latest products has a huge backlog of sales. The CEO knows that profits will, at a minimum, triple in the next few quarters. The result will be a jump in the stock price. So John calls his broker and starts buying shares.

Now, on the disclosure forms, John does not indicate the reason he is buying the shares. But this is really not necessary. The fact that he is buying shares is an indication that he is bullish on them — that is, that he thinks they're going to do well. And he's in a position to know!

In this chapter, I describe the disclosure requirements and show you how to interpret them to make good investment decisions.

Who Is an Insider?

Before looking at the necessary forms for insider transactions, it's necessary to know what the term *insider* means. The word is defined under the Securities Exchange Act of 1934. Essentially, an insider is an executive officer, director, or owner of at least 10 percent of any class of a company's outstanding stock. The implication is that these individuals would likely be privy to inside information because of their positions. But there is certainly controversy surrounding the definition. For instance, according to a *Wall Street Journal* article, companies often have very restrictive views on who is an insider. One of the companies highlighted was ImClone, which had only designated three people as insiders — meaning that no one else in the firm would need to disclose their transactions.

Companies have much discretion in who they classify as an insider, and the temptation is naturally to keep the group as small as possible. That way, if there is major sell-off of the stock, it will not show up as much on the SEC disclosures. Even major companies do this. Disney, for example, only has seven insiders. Despite this, analyzing insider transactions is still a useful tool and, for the most part, companies are not so limited in how they classify insiders. (The number tends to range from 10 to 12 or so, which is enough to be interesting.)

Types of Forms

The 1934 Act has a provision — known as 16(a) — that outlines the necessary forms for insiders. The main ones are Forms 3, 4, 5, and 144, plus schedule 13D (see Figure 11.1). *Form 3* reports new insiders at a given firm. It is filed within 10 days of a person's becoming an insider — regardless of

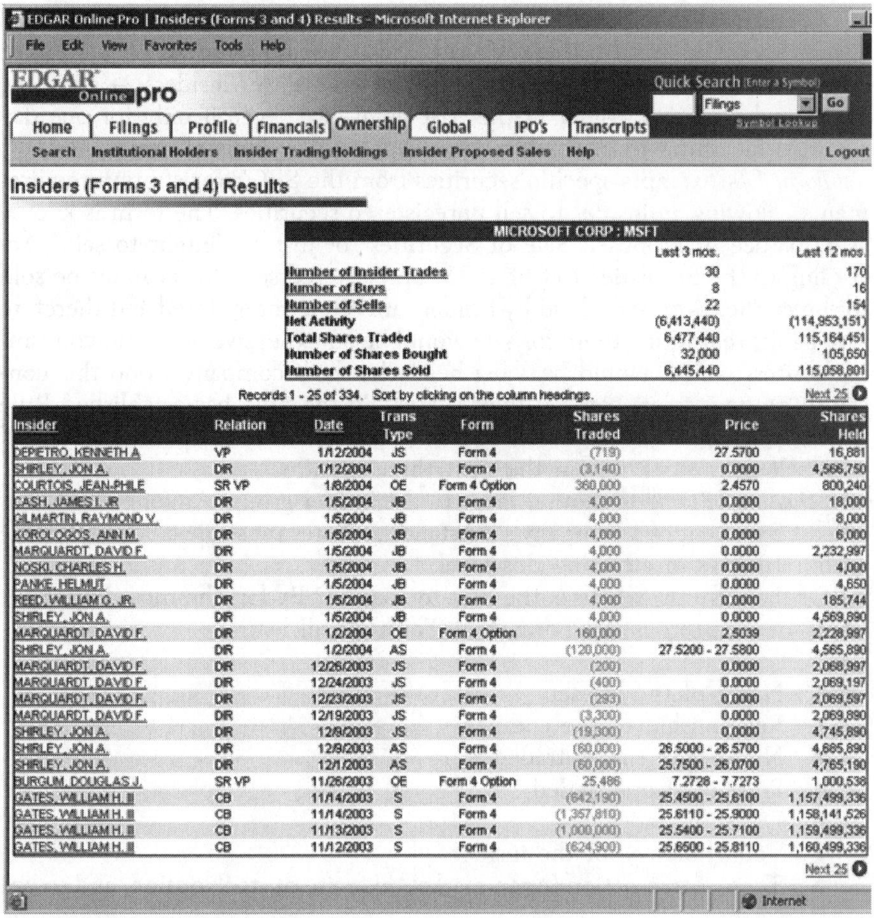

EDGAR Online Pro | Insiders (Forms 3 and 4) Results - Microsoft Internet Explorer

File Edit View Favorites Tools Help

EDGAR Online pro

Quick Search (Enter a Symbol) Filings Go

Symbol Lookup

Home | Filings | Profile | Financials | Ownership | Global | IPO's | Transcripts

Search | Institutional Holders | Insider Trading Holdings | Insider Proposed Sales | Help | Logout

Insiders (Forms 3 and 4) Results

MICROSOFT CORP : MSFT	Last 3 mos.	Last 12 mos.
Number of Insider Trades	30	170
Number of Buys	8	16
Number of Sells	22	154
Net Activity	(6,413,440)	(114,953,151)
Total Shares Traded	6,477,440	115,164,451
Number of Shares Bought	32,000	105,650
Number of Shares Sold	6,445,440	115,058,801

Records 1 - 25 of 334. Sort by clicking on the column headings. Next 25

Insider	Relation	Date	Trans Type	Form	Shares Traded	Price	Shares Held
DEPIETRO, KENNETH A	VP	1/12/2004	JS	Form 4	(719)	27.5700	16,881
SHIRLEY, JON A.	DIR	1/12/2004	JS	Form 4	(3,140)	0.0000	4,566,750
COURTOIS, JEAN-PHILE	SR VP	1/8/2004	OE	Form 4 Option	360,000	2.4570	800,240
CASH, JAMES I, JR	DIR	1/5/2004	JB	Form 4	4,000	0.0000	18,000
GILMARTIN, RAYMOND V.	DIR	1/5/2004	JB	Form 4	4,000	0.0000	8,000
KOROLOGOS, ANN M.	DIR	1/5/2004	JB	Form 4	4,000	0.0000	6,000
MARQUARDT, DAVID F.	DIR	1/5/2004	JB	Form 4	4,000	0.0000	2,232,997
NOSKI, CHARLES H.	DIR	1/5/2004	JB	Form 4	4,000	0.0000	4,000
PANKE, HELMUT	DIR	1/5/2004	JB	Form 4	4,000	0.0000	4,650
REED, WILLIAM G., JR.	DIR	1/5/2004	JB	Form 4	4,000	0.0000	185,744
SHIRLEY, JON A.	DIR	1/5/2004	JB	Form 4	4,000	0.0000	4,569,890
MARQUARDT, DAVID F.	DIR	1/2/2004	OE	Form 4 Option	160,000	2.5039	2,228,997
SHIRLEY, JON A.	DIR	1/2/2004	AS	Form 4	(120,000)	27.5200 - 27.5800	4,565,890
MARQUARDT, DAVID F.	DIR	12/26/2003	JS	Form 4	(200)	0.0000	2,068,997
MARQUARDT, DAVID F.	DIR	12/24/2003	JS	Form 4	(400)	0.0000	2,069,197
MARQUARDT, DAVID F.	DIR	12/23/2003	JS	Form 4	(293)	0.0000	2,069,597
MARQUARDT, DAVID F.	DIR	12/19/2003	JS	Form 4	(3,300)	0.0000	2,069,890
SHIRLEY, JON A.	DIR	12/8/2003	JS	Form 4	(19,300)	0.0000	4,745,890
SHIRLEY, JON A.	DIR	12/9/2003	AS	Form 4	(60,000)	26.5000 - 26.5700	4,685,890
SHIRLEY, JON A.	DIR	12/1/2003	AS	Form 4	(60,000)	25.7500 - 26.0700	4,765,190
BURGUM, DOUGLAS J.	SR VP	11/26/2003	OE	Form 4 Option	25,486	7.2728 - 7.7273	1,000,536
GATES, WILLIAM H. III	CB	11/14/2003	S	Form 4	(642,190)	25.4500 - 25.6100	1,157,499,336
GATES, WILLIAM H. III	CB	11/14/2003	S	Form 4	(1,357,810)	25.6110 - 25.9000	1,158,141,526
GATES, WILLIAM H. III	CB	11/13/2003	S	Form 4	(1,000,000)	25.5400 - 25.7100	1,159,499,336
GATES, WILLIAM H. III	CB	11/12/2003	S	Form 4	(624,900)	25.6500 - 25.8110	1,160,499,336

Next 25

Internet

Figure 11.1 Are the officers of the company bailing out? Or are they buying stock? This is key information that you should investigate before buying a stock. From EDGAR Online Pro (http://www.edgaronlinepro.com).

whether the person owns stock or not. *Form 4* reports the transaction when an insider buys or sells stock in the company. Before July 2002, this form had to be filed no later than the tenth day of the month following the month when the trade was made. So there was a built-in lag in insider data and, yes, many insiders did wait until the last minute to make their filings.

But this all changed after the Sarbanes–Oxley Act. Now, all insiders must report their trades on Form 4 filings no more than two business days from the transaction date. Furthermore, an insider must report any trades made in company stock for six months before becoming an insider and six months after leaving insider status. For example, suppose Joe Bigbucks retires, and a month later he buys 100,000 shares. This must be reported on a Form 4.

Form 5 is an ongoing report on insider status. All insiders — meaning anyone who was an insider in the past fiscal year, even if only for one day — must file this within 45 days after the company's fiscal year end.

Form 144 exempts specific securities from the SEC's registration requirements, allowing an insider to sell unregistered securities. The form is known as a "Notice of Proposed Sale of Securities" or just an "intent to sell." According to the Securities Act of 1933, unregistered securities cannot be sold to the public. But shares held by insiders are often unregistered and therefore unsellable; registering them for sale would be an expensive and time-consuming process, and it would be a big headache for a company to do this constantly so its insiders can sell their shares. So the SEC has established Rule 144, which allows insiders who meet its requirements to file this form and then sell their stock within the next three months.

Schedule 13D adds another layer to the insider group. Anyone who owns at least 5 percent of a company's outstanding shares must file a Schedule 13D within 10 days of attaining this level.

Of these forms, which is the best to analyze? By far, the most important filing for investors is the Form 4. A Form 4 will list:

- Name of the insider
- Relationship to the company
- Number of shares traded
- Price of shares traded
- Dates of trades
- Total holdings of the insider
- Type of transaction (open market, exercise of stock option, and so on)

Filling out a Form 4 is no fun for the insider. As mentioned earlier, it is usually done at the last minute. Consequently, there are inevitably some errors in the filings. But it should not be enough to invalidate the usefulness of Form 4 disclosures for investing purposes.

First of all, keep in mind that Congress placed some restrictions on the types of transactions an insider can make. For example, an insider is not allowed, according to section 16(c) of the 1934 Act, to sell short on stock in the company in question. (Selling short is the process of borrowing shares and selling them on the open market, hoping to buy them back at a lower price. In other words, the investor hopes to make money when the stock falls in value. No doubt, Congress thought it would be unwise for insiders to profit from a tanking stock price.)

Another important rule is found in section 16(b) of the 1934 Act. It is known as the "short-swing rule." This means that an insider cannot make any

History of Insider Trading Rules

Even though passed in the 1930s, the landmark federal securities legislation has lasted very well. But this does not mean there haven't been problems. For instance, during the 1930s, the prime mode of communication was the U.S. Post Office, not the telephone or high-speed electronic communications. That is why there were such long deadlines for filings.

In the electronic age, some of these deadlines look quaint. But it took the scandals of 2002 to get reform efforts started. Now an insider has two business days to report trades to the SEC. And beginning in July 2003, the SEC required companies to file their Form 4s electronically, making them accessible in real time via EDGAR Online Pro. Prior to this point, only 10 to 15 percent of the insider filings were filed electronically, and information companies and ultimately the investing public had the burden of processing paper documents.

profits on transactions within a six-month period. Violators are not fined or sent to jail, however, they just have to give the profits back to the company.

There is an exception to the short-swing rule, though. For instance, let's say Joe Bigbucks has options in his company to buy 100,000 shares at $1 apiece. The stock is now at $10. Suppose he exercises the stock option; that is, he buys the 100,000 shares at $1 apiece for $100,000. He then, in the same day, sells the 100,000 shares for $10, making a cool $900,000 profit. Wasn't this profit made within six months? True. But the SEC considers this legitimate.

Interpreting Form 4

Form 4 is shown in Figure 11.2. Following are the important elements on which to focus.

Transaction codes. These codes are found in Table I, Column 3, as well as in Table II, Column 4. The most critical codes to look for are:

- *P.* Open market or private purchase (sometimes a filing will mistakenly indicate this as "B" not "P").
- *S.* Open market or private sale.

These transactions are true purchases or sales — without assistance. For example, some transactions may involve a loan from the company or buying

MICROSOFT CORP
Form: 4 Filing Date: 8/21/2003

FORM 4

[ ] Check this box if no longer subject to Section 16. Form 4 or Form 5 obligations may continue. *See* Instruction 1(b).

UNITED STATES SECURITIES AND EXCHANGE COMMISSION
Washington, D.C. 20549

OMB APPROVAL
OMB Number: 3235-0287
Expires: January 31, 2005
Estimated average burden hours per response... 0.5

STATEMENT OF CHANGES IN BENEFICIAL OWNERSHIP OF SECURITIES

Filed pursuant to Section 16(a) of the Securities Exchange Act of 1934, Section 17(a) of the Public Utility Holding Company Act of 1935 or Section 30(f) of the Investment Company Act of 1940

1. Name and Address of Reporting Person *
GATES WILLIAM H III
(Last) (First) (Middle)
ONE MICROSOFT WAY
(Street)
REDMOND, WA 98052
(City) (State) (Zip)

2. Issuer Name and Ticker or Trading Symbol
MICROSOFT CORP [MSFT]

3. Date of Earliest Transaction (MM/DD/YYYY)
8/19/2003

4. If Amendment, Date Original Filed (MM/DD/YYYY)

5. Relationship of Reporting Person(s) to Issuer (Check all applicable)
_X_ Director _X_ 10% Owner
_X_ Officer (give title below) ___ Other (specify below)
Chairman of the Board

6. Individual or Joint/Group Filing (Check Applicable Line)
_X_ Form filed by One Reporting Person
___ Form filed by More than One Reporting Person

Table I - Non-Derivative Securities Acquired, Disposed of, or Beneficially Owned

1. Title of Security (Instr. 3)	2. Transaction Date (MM/DD/YYYY)	2A. Deemed Execution Date, if any (MM/DD/YYYY)	3. Transaction Code (Instr. 8)		4. Securities Acquired (A) or Disposed of (D) (Instr. 3, 4 and 5)			5. Amount of Securities Beneficially Owned Following Reported Transaction(s) (Instr. 3 and 4)	6. Ownership Form: Direct (D) or Indirect (I) (Instr. 4)	7. Nature of Indirect Beneficial Ownership (Instr. 4)
			Code	V	Amount	(A) or (D)	Price			
Common Stock	8/19/2003		S		23700	D	$26.4600	1164475636	D	
Common Stock	8/19/2003		S		47900	D	$26.4500	1164427736	D	

Figure 11.2 An insider trader form from the chairman of Microsoft, Bill Gates. From EDGAR Online Pro (http://www.edgaronlinepro.com).

shares at a discount, such as with an option exercise. In other words, the risk level of the insider is lower.

You will also see gift transactions. These have lesser significance for the investor since insiders typically engage in these transactions for tax reasons.

Code	Description
A	Grant, award or other acquisition
C	Conversion of derivative security
E	Expiration of short derivative position
F	Payment of exercise price or tax liability
G	Bona fide gift
J	Other (must be described)
K	Transactions involving equity swaps and similar instruments
L	Small acquisition
O	Exercise of out-of-the-money derivative security
P	Open market or private purchase of security
S	Open market or private sale of security
U	Tender Shares in a Merger or Takeover
V	Transaction voluntarily reported earlier than required
W	Acquisition or disposition by will
X	Exercise of in-the-money or at-the-money derivative security
Z	Deposit Into or Withdrawal From Voting Trust

Figure 11.3 Insider transaction codes take up nearly the entire alphabet.

It's hard to believe, but there are actually 16 different transaction codes. Figure 11.3 shows the list.

Relationship. This is in section 6 at the top of Form 4. The following is a list of the different relationships an insider can have to a firm:

- Officer
- Director
- Beneficial owner (holder of 10 percent or more of a company's stock)

Insiders can be both individuals and corporations and are required to report their direct and indirect holdings. Direct holdings are those that are held in the name of the insider or the insider's bank, broker, or designated nominee for the account of the reporting insider. However, it is also important to pay attention to the indirect holdings as well. These indirect holdings are usually controlled by the insider, yet are held by another entity such as:

- Family member
- Partnership
- Trust
- Corporation to which the insider is affiliated

In many cases, especially in the case of family-owned businesses, the same block of indirect stock may be claimed by several insiders, such as a group of trustees over the same trust or several partners in the same partnership.

You want to focus on the insiders that are likely to have the most intimate knowledge about the inner working of the company. Examples would include the CEO, CFO, and senior executive officers. Board members can be good indicators too, since they have access to critical company information.

Perhaps the best one to focus on is category H. This is an insider who is an officer or director and owner of 10 percent or more of a class of the company's equity securities.

Ownership form. This is section 6 in Table 1. The ownership can be either direct or indirect. The difference is common sense. If Fred Insider owns the shares directly — that is, himself — then they are registered in his name. Otherwise, they are registered in another name, such as that of an immediate family member or a firm or trust that Fred has an interest in.

According to Rule 16–1, an immediate family member can be any of the following:

- Child
- Stepchild
- Grandchild
- Father
- Father-in-law
- Mother
- Mother-in-law

Noise in the Data

Since insiders must make their own filings, there is the potential for errors. How do you spot these? Here are some things to look for:

- *Duplicate filings.* You may, for example, see a sale of 100,000 shares in the CEO's name as well as an item that is in the name of a trust. Chances are good that it is the same trade and it is the result of an administrative mistake on behalf of the CEO (yes, CEO's can get very busy).
- *Stock splits.* Many data providers do not make adjustments for stock splits.

Call the investor relations department if you have any questions. They should be able to help you with any potential problems in the data. Or you can subscribe to an online service that deals with these issues (see the Appendix).

- Son-in-law
- Daughter-in-law
- Brother
- Brother-in-law
- Sister
- Sister-in-law

For the most part, focus on direct ownership. It has the most impact on the insider.

Insider Selling

Despite the much-publicized insider dumping of stock, it's important to remember that insiders may be selling for lots of reasons other than taking a dim view of the prospects of the stock:

- Recently divorced and need to make a settlement
- Need to pay taxes
- Want to enjoy the money and perhaps buy a new car or house
- Want to diversify holdings

Bill Gates, for example, has a program in which he sells a fixed amount of shares in his Microsoft holdings. Interestingly enough, since the IPO, he has never bought one share of the company. Instead, he has been diversifying his holdings, as well as funding his charitable foundation.

Furthermore, you will often see venture capitalists cash out of their holdings. This is a normal process. In fact, many venture funds have requirements in their charter that force them to liquidate their holdings and distribute the proceeds to investors. In other words, this type of selling is not necessarily a sign of problems with a company.

However, that does not mean you should ignore insider selling. In fact, it is something to analyze, especially if you see a large number of insiders dump their holdings. This is especially discouraging if it occurs as the stock keeps falling and falling. When the bubble burst in 2000, many top executives were doing just that.

Fortune, with the assistance of Thomson Financial and the University of Chicago's Center for Research in Securities Pricing, conducted an extensive study on insider selling. The conclusion was that significant insider selling was not just from a few big players like the executives at Enron and Global Crossing. It was widespread and fierce, resembling an epidemic. The study looked at the following considerations:

Hedging for the Rich and Famous

Despite the fact that the Sarbanes–Oxley Act has provided much greater disclosure of insider trades, there are still some gray areas. Perhaps the biggest one is hedging. This is a sophisticated money management technique in which corporate executives use derivatives to lock in a certain amount of gains from their stock options.

Typically, these are for high-net-worth executives and the hedges can be for several hundred million. A notable case was Mark Cuban, who hedged his stock holdings when he sold his company, Broadcast.com, to Yahoo!. The hedge cost him $20 million, but he was able to take several billion off the table as Yahoo! stock plunged. Other well-known biggies who have used these hedges include Paul Allen, cofounder of Microsoft, and Halsey Minor, founder of CNET.

Essentially, with a hedge a person can convert stock holdings — without having to sell any shares. If the stock price moves significantly up or down, then the shares are sold off. In fact, it is possible to even defer taxes on these hedges.

Some analysts believe that hedging is really a form of selling the stock and should be disclosed to the SEC. But so far, it is not clear if these types of transactions should be disclosed — so they mostly aren't.

- The company had a market cap of at least $400 million.
- Stock fell at least 75 percent from its high.
- The insider sales were counted from 1999.
- Only directors and executives were included in the analysis.

The study shows that of the 1,035 corporations looked at, insiders dumped about $66 billion (as of 2002) and $23 billion was concentrated in 466 insiders of 25 corporations. The following is a look at some of the big beneficiaries:

Philip Anschutz	Qwest	$1.57 billion
Ted Waitt	Gateway	$1.10 billion
Henry Samueli	Broadcom	$810 million
Henry Nicholas	Broadcom	$799 million
John Moores	Peregrine Systems	$646 million
Gary Winnick	Global Crossing	$508 million
Steve Case	AOL	$475 million
Sanjiv Sidhu	I2 Technologies	$447 million
Naveen Jain	InfoSpace	$406 million
Charles Schwab	Charles Schwab	$353 million

Of course, not everyone dumped stock on the unsuspecting public. Look at David Filo, the cofounder of Yahoo!. He never sold any shares. Then there is the case of Jay Walker, who used $36 million of his personal funds to create Priceline.com. In late 1999, he purchased $125 million of the stock. He did cash out $276 million, but used most of it to fund private start-ups, which went bust. He also got the $276 million by selling his shares to wealthy investors such as Microsoft cofounder Paul Allen, rather than to the public.

Insider Buying

All things being equal, insider buying is more significant than insider selling. When an insider buys stock, it's only because of a belief that the stock price will go up. It's that simple. And it is a very powerful signal for investors. Following are key factors to look for.

Transaction amount. Simply put, look for large transactions. In some cases, the amounts can be quite large. For example, Richard Ressler (chairman of the board of an Internet company called J2 Global) bought 3.6 million shares at prices between $2 and $3 per share. Within a year, the stock was over $20 per share. But don't wait for such multimillion-dollar trades to come through; they're still unusual. In many cases, the amounts will be anywhere from $50,000 to $100,000 or so.

Cluster buying. Look for situations in which several insiders — say, three or more — engage in heavy buying. This is a very bullish sign.

Buying on the fall or the rise. Suppose the stock plunges from $50 to $25 yet insiders keep buying shares at $25. This would indicate that insiders think the market is overreacting. And if the stock hits new highs and insiders keep buying, it is again a bullish sign. On the other hand, if the stock falls to new lows and insiders sell large amounts, that is a very bearish signal.

Track record. Suppose five years ago the chairman made a significant insider purchase and, within several months, the stock surged. He did this again three years ago and reaped another big gain. In other words, he has demonstrated a good track record. Next time he buys, it might be time to follow suit. Of course, analyzing insider track records can take lots of time and effort. Instead, you might want to use an online service such as Thomson Financial (described in the sidebar titled "More Information on Insider Buying").

Conclusion

I'm a big believer in insider trading analysis and it has been a tremendous benefit in my trading. There are also some nuances. For example, some industries are notoriously difficult to analyze, such as biotech. But what if

More Information on Insider Buying

Compiling and tracking insider transactions can be a time-consuming and tedious process. But there are a variety of services to help guide you:

- *InsiderInsights.com.* This is a weekly newsletter that is distributed online and via e-mail (at an annual subscription of $249.50). The editor is Jonathan Moreland, an expert in the field. With both an MBA and CFA, he started providing analysis on insider transactions in the early 1990s as a writer and analyst for *Individual Investor* magazine. From there, he started InsiderTrader.com, which he sold in the fall of 1998. In his analysis, he goes beyond just looking at the insider sells and buys, taking an in-depth look at the fundamentals of a company. He is also author of the book *Profit from Legal Insider Trading: Invest Today on Tomorrow's News.*
- *EDGAR Online Pro.* In addition to its other features, this site provides fielded data on insider trades and intents to sell. You can track total trades, total sells or total buys, and net activity by company. A view by corporate executive also shows the last 24 months of insider trading activity. Using other features of the service, you can quickly complete your due diligence by viewing news, stock charts, financials, SEC data, and other ownership information. The site is located at http://www.edgaronlinepro.com.

major executives at a biotech firm are buying large amounts of stock? Well, I would definitely take notice.

Insider trading is not foolproof, and there are certainly examples in which heavy buying came right before a major implosion of the stock. But, all in all, it is a good analytical technique for investors.

Sources

1. Gimein, Mark, You bought. They sold, *Fortune*, September 2, 2002.
2. Hallinan, Joseph, Limits on number of insiders, *Wall Street Journal*, September 12, 2002.
3. Bryan-Low, Cassell, Hedging moves by insiders are untouched by new rules, *Wall Street Journal*, September 9, 2002.
4. McMurray, Scott, *Ka-ching* around the collar, *Business2.0*, March 2001.

12

IPOs, Spin-Offs, and Tracking Stocks

During the middle to late 1990s, the initial public offering (IPO) market was red hot. It was not uncommon to see stocks surge 100 or 200 percent or more in the first few seconds of trading. It was almost like printing money for investors. But which investors?

Traditionally, it is the institutions and wealthy investors that get the hot IPOs. And, yes, the not-so-hot (or dead cold) IPOs go to individual investors. In fact, the *Wall Street Journal* did an exposé on how IPOs were used as a method for ginning new business for investment banks. The focus was on Frank Quattrone, the top dealmaker at Credit Suisse First Boston. He set up a system called the "Friends of Frank" accounts, which included about 160 clients.

Of course, CS First Boston was not the only firm to engage in this — rather, just about every firm did. For example, Salomon Smith Barney had special clients who received IPO shares. One was Bernie Ebbers, the CEO and founder of WorldCom, who made about $11 million from IPOs. As for Salomon, it generated hundreds of millions in fees from WorldCom's investment banking business.

However, just as with many other aspects of finance, the federal government has been investigating these tactics, and there is likely to be some sort of reform. In other words, the playing field for IPOs should improve.

But this does not mean you do not have to do your homework. IPOs are full of risks, and analyzing the financial statements is still absolutely critical.

What Is an IPO?

An *initial public offering,* as the name implies, is the first sale of a block of shares to the public. From then on, the shares will trade on a stock exchange. (See the sidebar titled "Different Exchanges" for more detail on the choices.)

Here's an example of how it works: Fast Co. looks at its strong track record over the past 10 years and believes that public investors would be interested in owning stock. Besides, by going public, the company will have many advantages: it will raise substantial amounts of money, it will have more credibility in the marketplace (public companies tend to be taken more seriously), the stock can be used as currency to buy other companies, and the stock (through options) can even be used to attract new employees and provide incentives for current employees.

So Fast Co. hires a Wall Street firm known as an investment bank or underwriter. The investment bank conducts extensive due diligence and concludes that Fast Co. is likely to do well if it goes public. Over several months, Fast Co. and the investment bank draft a prospectus, which is a highly detailed business plan.

A company has the option of three types of prospectus filings with the SEC:

1. *Form SB-1.* SB is an acronym for "small business." To file an SB-1, a company must have less than $25 million in annual revenues.
2. *Form SB-2.* This is another small business form, with the same $25 million annual revenue limit as the SB-1. The SB-2 is further limited, being usable for offerings designed to raise no more than $10 million. Its requirements tend to be less paper-intensive.
3. *Form S-1.* A company will use this filing if it does not meet the requirements for an SB-1 or SB-2. This is the most common choice; see the sidebar titled "The Structure of an S-1 Filing."

While the prospectus is under review of the SEC, Fast Co. and the investment bank will hold *roadshows* across the country to pitch the investment to major investors and institutions. It is at these events that demand can be gauged. If there is more demand than shares available, then the IPO is considered to be oversubscribed and is likely to jump on its first day of trading.

In terms of selling shares to the public, the investment bank will estimate a valuation for Fast Co. For example, suppose it is $250 million and has 25 million shares outstanding. The investment bank believes that, with current demand, it can raise $50 million and this translates into five million shares at $10 apiece.

A critical role of the underwriter is to provide a firm commitment for the

The Structure of an S-1 Filing

The S-1 filing is highly regulated in terms of format. Here is what you will see:

- *Front cover.* Includes the terms of the offering, the underwriters, and the number of shares being issued. Before the final prospectus is filed, the terms won't state an exact price, just a price range (such as $10 to $12). The reason is that the company is in the process of gauging the pricing. If you see the price range increase, it is an indication that the IPO is hot.
- *Prospectus summary.* This is a short background of the company and a summary of the financial statements.
- *Risk factors.* Discloses the risks that investors need to be aware of.
- *Use of proceeds.* Shows how the IPO money will be spent.
- *Dividend policy.* Typically, an IPO company will not pay a dividend because it is young and needs to plow its capital back into the business.
- *Capitalization.* Shows the distribution of equity and debt before and after the offering.
- *Dilution.* This shows the reduction in value to the current shareholders based on the price and number of shares in the offering.
- *Selected financial management discussion and analysis.* A detailed analysis of the company, especially in terms of its finances.
- *Business.* Describes the industry and the business operations and discusses the business opportunities the company is looking at.
- *Management.* Bios of the senior management and directors and also their compensation packages.
- *Certain transactions.* Discloses any related-party transactions.
- *Principal shareholders.* Lists the major equity holders.
- *Underwriting.* Shows the underwriters and their compensation.
- *Financial statements.* Income statement, balance sheet, and cash flow statement.

offering. This means that on the day before the IPO, the investment bank will write a check to the company to buy all five million shares — but at a discount, paying, say, $9.90 per share. The 10-cent difference per share is the profit to the investment bank. That is, on the next day, the investment bank will sell the shares to public investors at $10 per share.

An investment bank can also do the IPO on a *best-efforts* basis. As the phrase implies, this means that the investment bank will not write a check at all but will instead make strong efforts to find buyers for the shares. This typically is the case if the investment bank does not have a lot of capital or is not confident in the IPO. Whatever the reason, it is a major red flag for an IPO investor. In many cases, a best-efforts IPO does not do very well in the aftermarket.

On occasion, a company may not even use an underwriter. This is known as a *direct IPO* because the company is selling directly to the public without using a financial intermediary. For the most part, this is a big red flag for investors. Why? First of all, an investment bank performs independent due diligence on the company. With a direct IPO, you are relying on the company to be truthful — and this can be a big stretch. Next, an investment bank can be very effective in providing aftermarket trading support in the stock by encouraging clients to buy the shares, as well as providing research coverage. Finally, direct IPOs tend to be very small companies with limited growth potential. A big part of this is that, in most cases, the offering raises very little money — and it takes money to make money. Without much money coming in, the company will find it difficult to exploit its market niche.

Factors to Consider When Investing in IPOs

An IPO is just as risky as any other public company investment, and thus it is critical to apply the same analytical tools you use to assess other investments, as presented throughout this book. In addition, IPOs have certain characteristics that tend to separate them from other types of investments:

- IPOs are usually younger companies and as a result can be more susceptible to problems.
- Then again, by being young, the company may have great opportunities for growth (just imagine if you bought Dell or Microsoft or Qualcomm at the IPO).
- IPOs can be subject to quite a bit of speculation — especially in the first few months because of the publicity.
- IPOs are under more scrutiny than existing stocks. This is the result of the Securities Act of 1933, in which Congress wanted to help prevent the hyping of new issues. Thus, the disclosure requirements tend to be tougher, which means investors get more information.

Unless you get an IPO at the initial price, it is probably a good idea to wait awhile before making a purchase. (See the secton on "Getting a Piece of the Action" later in this chapter for info on buying IPOs.) Over time, the hype should subside and you are likely to get a better valuation. Moreover, you need to be aware of the lock-up period. This is a clause in the prospectus that prevents insiders and major shareholders from selling their stock within a certain period of time after the IPO, usually six months, although in special situations it may be shortened. The reason is that the investment banks do not want huge dumping of the stock when a company is going public.

Of course, when the lock-up period expires, there is generally lots of selling, which puts pressure on the stock price. This can be a great time for individual investors to buy the company's stock — assuming the insiders are not leaving the company en masse.

Besides the timing, consider these factors before you buy in:

- *Underwriter*. Stick to offerings with well-known underwriters. As discussed earlier, a strong underwriter can help build a strong investor base and provide continuing research coverage. A small underwriter, on the other hand, is limited in these capabilities and also is likely not to be able to raise as much money for the company.
- *Risk factors*. Read these. You will be essentially looking for the same things that we discussed in Chapter 3, such as competition and litigation. Also look at factors like heavy customer concentration, prior defaults, and history of losses.
- *Selling shareholders*. It is not uncommon for insiders and major shareholders to sell some of their holdings at the IPO. This is not necessarily bad. However, if there is a large amount of selling (say, 20 or 30 percent of the offering is composed of insiders), then be very wary.
- *Use of proceeds*. With the IPO money, the company will have many options. Or will it? In the "use of proceeds" section, a company will specify major initiatives for the money. If the money is mostly being used to pay down debt, then this may crimp the overall growth plans of the company.

Spin-Offs and Tracking Stocks

As companies get bigger, managements consider whether or not they should be in certain business segments. It can be very difficult to manage disparate subsidiaries and may divert attention from a company's core growth areas.

One idea is to spin off a division to shareholders as an IPO. A famous example is when networking computer giant 3Com decided to spin off its fast-growing Palm division. 3Com had acquired Palm through the acquisition of U.S. Robotics in 1997, and it turned out this small division was quite a

IPO Resources

The Web offers many IPO sites. The good ones will list upcoming IPOs, show the aftermarket performance of recent IPOs, and provide an alert for new IPO filings and daily IPO news. My favorite site is EDGAR Online Pro (http://www.edgaronlinepro.com), which provides all three — EDGAR Online Pro service including complex fundamental ownership, IPO and secondary offering datasets, advanced search tools, and much more (see Figure 12.1). For instance, it has management bios, in-depth profiles, and so on. The service also tracks secondary public offerings.

Finally, to learn more about IPOs, you might want to look at my book, *Investing in IPOs Version 2.0.*

gem. In the IPO, Palm raised a staggering $825 million. Initially priced at $38 per share, the stock surged as high as $160 on its first day of trading.

What are the other reasons to do a spin-off? Here's a look:

- *Money*. As in the Palm case, a spin-off can be lucrative. But keep in mind that not all spin-offs raise money. Some will merely distribute shares in the division to existing shareholders.
- *Currency*. The spin-off can use its stock as currency to buy other companies.
- *Deals*. Being part of a big company can make it difficult to do deals. For example, Lucent had troubles getting new clients while it was a division of AT&T. Basically, Lucent found it hard to do business with potential clients that were competitors of AT&T.
- *Incentives*. In a large corporation, it can be difficult to motivate employees with stock options. But with a spin-off, employee actions can have a bigger impact on the stock price, so people have more incentive to make the company prosper.
- *PR*. A spin-off typically gets lots of press and hype.

But are these good reasons for investors? In other words, should you consider buying a spin-off? You definitely need to be careful, as spin-offs may be structured to benefit the parent company at the expense of the division. For example, if the spin-off raises cash, most of the cash may go to the parent.

Another thing to consider is debt. In some cases, the parent may shove a lot of debt onto the balance sheet of the spin-off company. Also, a spin-off may be a way for the parent company to get rid of an underperforming division.

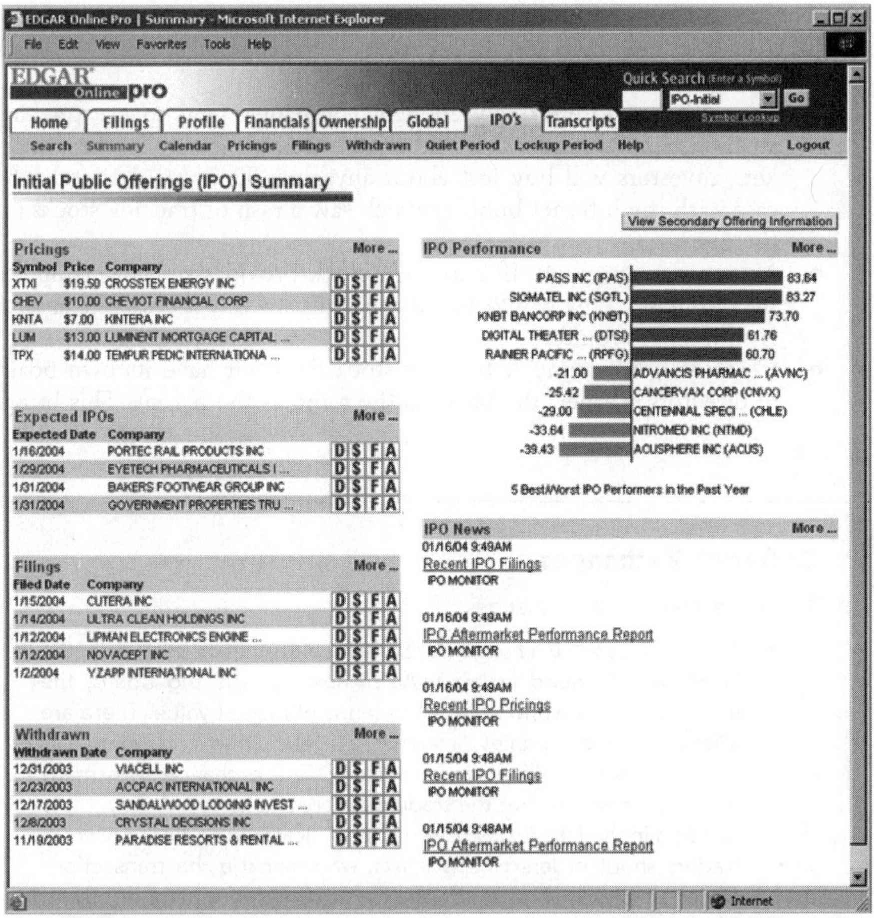
EDGAR Online Pro | Summary - Microsoft Internet Explorer
File Edit View Favorites Tools Help
EDGAR Online pro
Quick Search (Enter a Symbol)
IPO-Initial
Go
Symbol Lookup
Home Filings Profile Financials Ownership Global IPO's Transcripts
Search Summary Calendar Pricings Filings Withdrawn Quiet Period Lockup Period Help Logout
Initial Public Offerings (IPO) | Summary
View Secondary Offering Information
Pricings More ...
Symbol Price Company
XTXI $19.50 CROSSTEX ENERGY INC
CHEV $10.00 CHEVIOT FINANCIAL CORP
KNTA $7.00 KINTERA INC
LUM $13.00 LUMINENT MORTGAGE CAPITAL ...
TPX $14.00 TEMPUR PEDIC INTERNATIONA ...
Expected IPOs More ...
Expected Date Company
1/16/2004 PORTEC RAIL PRODUCTS INC
1/29/2004 EYETECH PHARMACEUTICALS I ...
1/31/2004 BAKERS FOOTWEAR GROUP INC
1/31/2004 GOVERNMENT PROPERTIES TRU ...
Filings More ...
Filed Date Company
1/15/2004 CUTERA INC
1/14/2004 ULTRA CLEAN HOLDINGS INC
1/12/2004 LIPMAN ELECTRONICS ENGINE ...
1/12/2004 NOVACEPT INC
1/2/2004 YZAPP INTERNATIONAL INC
Withdrawn More ...
Withdrawn Date Company
12/31/2003 VIACELL INC
12/23/2003 ACCPAC INTERNATIONAL INC
12/17/2003 SANDALWOOD LODGING INVEST ...
12/8/2003 CRYSTAL DECISIONS INC
11/19/2003 PARADISE RESORTS & RENTAL ...
D S F A
IPO Performance More ...
IPASS INC (IPAS) 83.64
SIGMATEL INC (SGTL) 83.27
KNBT BANCORP INC (KNBT) 73.70
DIGITAL THEATER ... (DTSI) 61.76
RAINIER PACIFIC ... (RPFG) 60.70
-21.00 ADVANCIS PHARMAC ... (AVNC)
-25.42 CANCERVAX CORP (CNVX)
-29.00 CENTENNIAL SPECI ... (CHLE)
-33.64 NITROMED INC (NTMD)
-39.43 ACUSPHERE INC (ACUS)
5 Best/Worst IPO Performers in the Past Year
IPO News More ...
01/16/04 9:49AM
Recent IPO Filings
IPO MONITOR
01/16/04 9:49AM
IPO Aftermarket Performance Report
IPO MONITOR
01/16/04 9:49AM
Recent IPO Pricings
IPO MONITOR
01/15/04 9:48AM
Recent IPO Filings
IPO MONITOR
01/15/04 9:48AM
IPO Aftermarket Performance Report
IPO MONITOR
Internet

Figure 12.1 IPO summaries like this one from EDGAR Online Pro give you a complete picture of the IPO market. From EDGAR Online Pro (http://www.edgaronlinepro.com).

Finally, be especially wary if the spin-off is done as a "tracking stock." On the face of it, it is not easy to see the difference between a spin-off and a tracking stock. After all, both trade on a stock exchange and act just like any other stock. But tracking stocks have some major weaknesses:

- *Ownership*. Basically, the purchaser of a tracking stock owns nothing. That is correct. Nothing. As the name implies, a tracking stock merely tracks the overall performance of the division within the parent. I look at this as a parent company having its cake and eating it too. Investors pay good money to help the parent keep score, but they don't own even the tiny share of the operation that a regular share of stock conveys.

- *Sign of a top.* Interestingly enough, companies tend to use tracking stocks when valuations have reached excessive levels. In these markets, investors will buy just about anything. This was definitely the case with the Internet bubble, which saw a rash of tracking stocks hit the market.
- *No takeover premium.* If a tracking stock provides no ownership for the purchaser, why would an outside company buy it out? The answer is simple: It wouldn't.
- *Corporate governance.* A tracking stock does not have its own board of directors. Rather, the board is the same as the parent. This brings

Different Exchanges

These are main stock exchanges:

- *New York Stock Exchange (NYSE).* The oldest stock exchange, the NYSE was founded in 1792. Also known as the Big Board, the exchange is the world's largest in terms of market value. There are about 2,800 companies listed on the exchange and volume is routinely over a billion shares per day. The exchange uses many computer systems, but the trading is very similar to the way it was handled in the late 1700s. There is a physical trading floor on which traders shout orders to specialists, who manage the transactions of certain stocks. The specialists have the responsibility of buying when others are selling and vice versa so as to maintain liquidity.
- *American Stock Exchange (AMEX).* As at the NYSE, trading is handled on a physical trading floor with specialists. Currently, the NASDAQ owns the AMEX, and the exchange specializes in energy, foreign, and biotech companies.
- *NASDAQ (National Association of Securities Dealers Automated Quotation System).* Founded in 1971, this exchange does not have a trading floor; rather, traders communicate via electronic systems. Nonetheless, each stock has a variety of market makers that perform a function similar to the NYSE and AMEX specialists, that is, to provide liquidity. For the most part, it is smaller companies that list on the NASDAQ, but some of these small companies have, over the years, have become quite large, such as Microsoft, Intel, and Cisco.

up a troubling question: Who does the board represent? The parent? The division? Both? It is not clear — but it is likely that the board would favor the parent.

Getting a Piece of the Action

How do you get IPOs? This is not an easy feat. What's more, even if you get some IPO shares, it is usually a small amount — say 100 to 300 shares or so. Most of the major brokerage firms, such as Morgan Stanley and PaineWebber, provide their clients with IPOs. So ask your broker if there are any upcoming IPOs. Furthermore, a variety of online brokers (such as E*TRADE, HarrisDirect, Friedman Billings Ramsey [FBR], and WR Hambrecht) also participate in IPOs (see Figure 12.2).

- *Over the Counter (OTC) Bulletin Board.* This is not an exchange. Instead, it is a quotation service that provides pricing and volume data on stocks that are not listed on major exchanges. OTC companies are typically very small and have light trading volume. So, as an investor, be careful when investing in these stocks. Regulation of the OTC marketplace is relatively lax, so the chance of fraud tends to be higher here than on the major exchanges.
- *Pink sheets.* If a company is unable to trade on the OTC Bulletin Board, its other alternative is the pink sheets published by the National Quotation Bureau. This has even less liquidity than the OTC Bulletin Board and there is a higher likelihood that a company is a downright fraud.

  Note: In many cases, a company goes public on the OTC Bulletin Board or the pink sheets by a process called a reverse merger. Example: Suppose Fast Co. is unable to convince an investment banker to take it public. Moreover, the company does not feel confident about doing a direct IPO. As an alternative, the company merges into a public company *shell.* This is a company that was once listed on a major exchange but was taken off because it failed to meet the minimum requirements or went bankrupt. Through the reverse merger, the shell company becomes Fast Co. and the company begins trading on the OTC or via pink sheets.

  Reverse mergers can be dangerous for investors. What often happens is that a group of promoters effect the reverse merger and hype the stock, selling the shares at a high valuation. Then the stock price crashes. This is known as a "pump and dump" scheme.

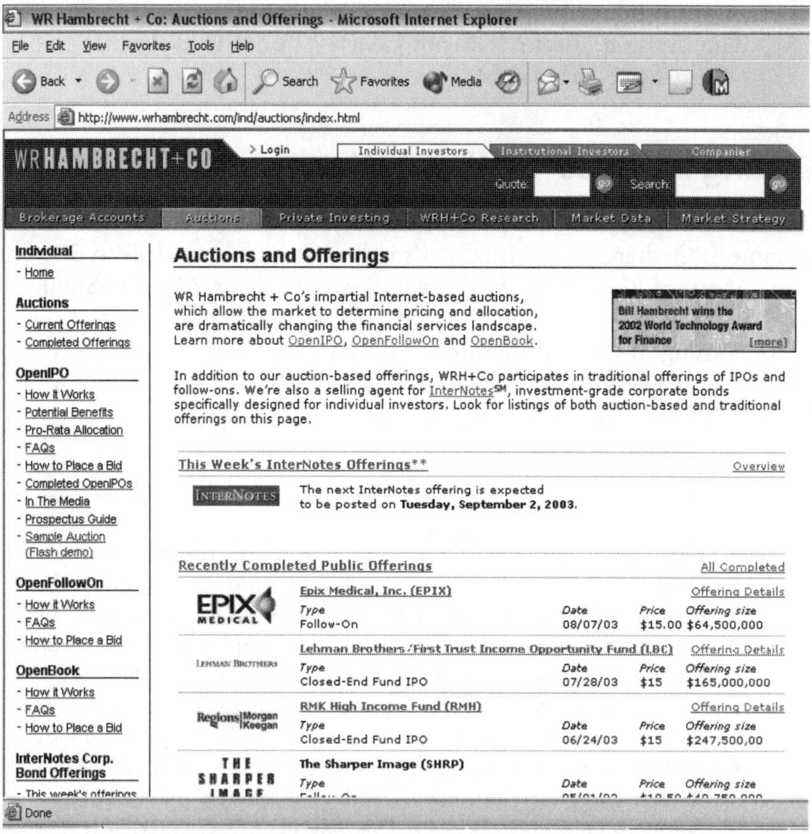

Figure 12.2 WR Hambrecht has a unique system for buying IPOs, called the OpenAuction.

The online systems work like this: You open an account that will have a minimum balance requirement, which can range from $2,000 to as much as $100,000. You will also need to fill out a form that asks about your investment experience. If you are a newbie, the investment firm may not allow you to trade in IPOs. As a result, many investors will overstate their experience. But this can be troublesome, especially if you later want to sue your broker. After all, if you lied about your investment background, the investment firm will have a stronger argument in denying your case.

The online system will have a list of upcoming IPOs and a link to view the prospectuses. If you are interested in purchasing shares of an IPO, you click for an "indication of interest." Under the federal securities laws, an investor cannot buy any shares before the prospectus has been approved by the SEC; rather, you can only indicate if you are interested. Once the SEC

Fun with Ticker Symbols

The roots of ticker symbols come from the days of the ticker tape, in which streams of stock prices were printed on a long strip of paper. To save room, stock exchanges adopted standardized ticker symbols, which of course are used to this day. For the NYSE, the symbols range from one to three letters. In fact, having one letter is a indication of a great company, such as F for Ford or C for Citigroup.

On the AMEX, a ticker symbol is three letters long; on the NASDAQ, four letters. However, the NASDAQ symbols can change as a result of missed filings or bankruptcies. When a company misses a filing or has irregularities in its accounting, the letter "E" is appended at the end of the symbol. This is what happened with WorldCom, which went from WCOM to WCOME.

A bankrupt company, on the other hand, will have a "Q" at the end of the symbol. An example was eToys, whose ticker changed from ETYS to ETYSQ. Not all symbols are bad. Take "Y," for example, which is for foreign stocks that list on U.S. exchanges. Keep in mind that these added symbols are only for NASDAQ stocks, not shares traded on the NYSE.

approves the prospectus, the investment firm will then allocate the shares to investors. Before this time, you can cancel your order at any time.

However, only a few shares are typically available to investors in these online systems. In terms of making an allocation, each investment firm has a different approach. According to HarrisDirect:

> In cases where demand exceeds supply, we allocate the available shares according to a number of criteria. Such criteria include, but are not limited to, the following: client assets held at Harris*direct*, activity, tenure as a Harris*direct* client, and post-offering activity in previous new issues. It is not the policy of Harris*direct* to allocate stock on a first-come, first-served basis. The time your Indication of Interest is received will not influence the allocation decision.

This is E*TRADE's approach:

> Shares will generally be randomly allocated among interested customers after a review of applicants' holding records in prior public offerings, and subject to priority allocation for Power E*TRADE Platinum customers. Accounts with a history of short

The IPO Lexicon

IPOs can be exciting, and so it should not be surprising that there are some colorful terms in the industry. Here is a list:

- *Broken issue.* When the stock price of an IPO falls on its first day of trading. This is certainly bad and usually means the stock will fall further.
- *Flipping.* When an IPO investor buys and sells shares quickly, say within a few days. The investment banks hate this and you may be put on a blacklist if you do it.
- *Spinning.* When investment banks allocate hot IPOs to favored clients so as to get future investment banking business.
- *Bought deal.* Another name for a firm commitment IPO.
- *Book.* The list of investors who want to buy shares in the IPO.
- *Greenshoe.* Disclosed in the prospectus, this is a provision that allows the underwriter to purchase a certain percentage of the IPO (about 10 to 15 percent of the total offering). This is exercised typically if the IPO is hot.
- *Gross spread.* This is the difference between the IPO offering price and the money that goes to the company going public, that is, the profit for the underwriter. And, yes, it can be quite gross.
- *IPO.* Well, I've said what this means, but some investors give it other definitions, such as "immediate profit opportunities" or "it's probably overpriced."
- *Pipeline.* The upcoming IPOs.
- *Pop.* The increase in stock price on the first day of trading of the IPO.
- *Red herring.* The prospectus before it is approved by the SEC. Traditionally, there is a warning on the front cover — in red ink — which indicates that the SEC has not given its blessing on the offering.
- *All hand meeting.* Several months before an IPO, the advisory team will set up a timetable to execute on the offering.
- *Quiet period.* This is part of the federal securities laws and requires that a company may not engage in any promotional activity for 25 days after the offering. This also means that the research departments of the investment banks may not publish any reports either. Of course, when the 25 days have passed, you will see a flurry of hype.

> holding periods will receive a lesser allocation priority in offerings where demand for shares exceeds the supply of shares available for E*TRADE Securities to distribute. The rationale for allocating shares to customers who tend to hold for longer periods is that it helps E*TRADE Securities get access to more offerings and more shares as issuers of new stock seek to build stability in the aftermarket.

And from FBR:

> Unless you cancel your [indication of interest], it will be entered into our computer-generated random selection process. Neither the time at which you place your [indication of interest] nor the number of shares requested will have any effect on the selection process.

One of the most innovative online IPO distribution systems is from WR Hambrecht, which uses an electronic *Dutch auction* to allocate IPO shares to investors. Investors file bids at amounts they choose to offer, and the computer system processes all bids for the IPOs and determines the final price for all shares. If your bid is at this price or higher, you get the shares you requested at the final IPO price.

Conclusion

IPOs are certainly tempting for investors. When markets are bullish, they seem like a guaranteed way to profit. But the IPO markets are extremely volatile and can shut down very quickly. Discipline is critical for being successful with IPOs. It often means just saying no to many of them. True, you may miss out on some big ones, but will probably miss out on many losers as well.

Sources

1. Smith, Randall and Pulliam, Susan, How Quattrone's CSFB unit doled out shares of hot IPOs, *Wall Street Journal,* September 23, 2002.
2. Ceron, Gaston, What a difference a new letter in a firm's stock symbols makes, *Wall Street Journal,* July 2, 2002.

13

Rating System

Well, you've covered a tremendous amount of material in this book — especially in terms of making in-depth analyses of the balance sheet, income statement, and cash flow statement. This is definitely a good start, but you may be scratching your head and wondering: OK, so how do I apply all this information?

It's a great question. After all, there are thousands and thousands of public companies to apply your analytical tools to. But no private investor has enough hours in the day to dive into the detail of all public companies. In fact, not even top-notch Wall Street analysts or investors can cover them all.

How do the pros deal with this pile of data? There are a variety of approaches. First, an analyst may be responsible for a certain industry sector, which narrows the field considerably. Even that may not be enough; an industry can involve hundreds of companies, and as a result, an analyst may focus on an industry subset.

This is not helpful for you, though. From an investor's standpoint, you do not want to have all your stock investments in one industry. That simply puts too much risk into your portfolio.

The next approach is stock screening. Essentially, this means using an online system to query a database of stocks. To do this, you will select several tests. For example, you may want to search the database for companies that have seen earnings per share grow 25 percent per year for the past year and also have seen annual increases in sales of at least 20 percent per year. The computer system will process the tests and provide you a list of companies.

Of course, that list can still be quite long. This chapter covers effective screening techniques that you can use to winnow the list to a manageable number of companies — without sacrificing quality analysis.

After you have your list, you can do more in-depth analysis on each company. You will look at the financial statements, read the press releases, track insider buying and selling, and look for red flags. This chapter will cover this second stage of analysis as well.

In the process, I will show you some ways to monitor your stock picks. In our dynamic capitalist system, a company can easily go from great to terrible in a very short time. Tracking your investments and having a cut-off point where you sell lagging positions is absolutely critical to success in investing.

Screening Programs

People have many great capabilities, and the best investors use this natural intelligence to their advantage. This is the case with Peter Lynch and Warren Buffett, who over the years have developed an innate sense for making excellent investment decisions.

But almost no one does a good job of processing information in bulk when it isn't clear which bits are important and which ones can be ignored. That's where computers and the Internet come in really handy. Computers are perfect instruments for analyzing data, and the Internet brings data by the bushel within easy reach. For any investor, it is a good idea to learn how to use these resources.

All a stock screener does is search through a database, looking at the following relationships: greater than, less than, and equal to. It is really that simple, but it is also extremely powerful. It can give you fascinating results, but if you do not use these relationships properly, it can set you up to make bad stock selections. Computers are quite literal-minded; they will do exactly what you ask for, which may not be what you wanted. "Garbage in, garbage out" is still the watchword!

Background on Screeners

For me, a screening program is absolutely essential for investing. I use the process constantly. I like to experiment with it and refine my search criteria over time. This is something that should evolve.

Interestingly enough, despite the power of screeners, many investors apparently do not use them. I am not sure why; perhaps it is the fact that screening is not mentioned much in the press. You will see many articles about, say, "The Best Ten Stocks to Buy," but you will not read in the article how the authors were able to sift though the thousands of stocks to get at their best ten. Chances are, they used a screening tool.

Lots of online screeners vie for investors' attention; some free, and others require a fee. Regardless of the cost, they are all very similar. All access a database (which can vary in size), and all allow you to set up a test. A *test* is a comparison, that is, one of the three relationships I mentioned earlier, applied to a pair of *variables* — pieces of information in the database, such as profits, sales, and so on. If you apply one or more tests, you have a stock screen.

As you look at all the different screeners on the market, it can be somewhat overwhelming. Don't despair. True, many of these screeners have lots of variables you can test for. But for the most part, you will not need all this firepower for these tools to greatly improve your investment results. Actually, if you get too convoluted in your screening process, it could hurt your results!

Regardless of the power of screening, it is far from foolproof. Then again, no investment technique is perfect. Yes, the screener will overlook some stocks. But in the end, you will be able to efficiently analyze thousands of public companies.

However, I do not want to imply that screening should always be the first step in the investment process. If you read a magazine article on a stock or

Screening Books

As you look at the different screening programs on the Web, you will learn different techniques. But if you want to get more detailed information on the subject, here are several books to consider:

- *Online Investing.* The author, Jon Markman, writes for MSN Investor and is an expert in designing investment models. This book goes beyond screening and looks at many other online resources, such as EDGAR Online Pro.
- *The SmartMoney Stock Picker's Bible.* Again, this book is not just about screeners, but looks at the many strategies for good investments. In terms of screening advice, it focuses mainly on the SmartMoney online system.
- *Screening the Market.* This is the only book that is devoted to using stock screening techniques, such as setting up search criteria, refining searches, and putting the results into action. The author, Marc Gerstein, provides a four-step process for screening and uses many examples to help understand his techniques. And he knows what he's talking about — he is the director of investment research at Multex and has over 20 years in the investment industry.

hear a stock idea on TV or know about a local company, go ahead and analyze these stock ideas in depth if you think they have potential. The best investors are constantly looking for stock ideas.

Choosing a Screener

Before looking at the different screeners available, it is important to consider a few things. First, many screeners have predefined sets of tests. For example, there may be a "growth company" screen that takes into account strong earnings and sales over time. These predefined screens can be very helpful since they were probably constructed by professional investors who know just which comparisons are apt to produce the most interesting results.

Other elements to look for in a screener include the size of the database (most range from 7,000 to 9,000 stocks) and how often the database is refreshed (you want at least daily, so the information is current). You also want to be able to save screens you have created (rather than just use the preselects) and be able to export the results to a spreadsheet, such as Excel (so you can play with them further).

Here are some screeners to consider:

- *MSN Investor*. To better understand screens, Jon Markman writes a weekly column on the subject. It is well worth the reading. Price: free. Available from investor.msn.com.
- *SmartMoney*. What makes this program stand out is the ease of use, as well as the ability to make very innovative reports. You can also perform stock charting. The help system is comprehensive. Price: $59 annually; $5.95 monthly. Available from www.smartmoney.com.
- *Morningstar*. A nice feature with this system is that it provides a breakdown to see how stocks are being screened out. This can be helpful in terms of refining your search. Price: $109 annually; $11.95 monthly. Available from www.morningstar.com.
- *Quicken*. This screener has unique preset screens based on well-known investors or investment approaches. Examples include the Motley Fool's Foolish 8 Strategy to identify fast-growing small cap companies, the Warren Buffet portfolio (this is based on Robert Hagstrom's book, *The Warren Buffett Way*, which is actually well worth reading), the National Association of Investors Corporation (NAIC) approach (this is a system that has been in use since 1951), and the Weiss approach, based on the highly ranked investment newsletter *Investment Quality Trends*. Price: free. Available from www.quicken.com.
- *Multex*. This is a full-featured screener. Moreover, the site has a tremendous amount of useful information about screening techniques. Price: free. Available from www.multex.com (see Figure 13.1).

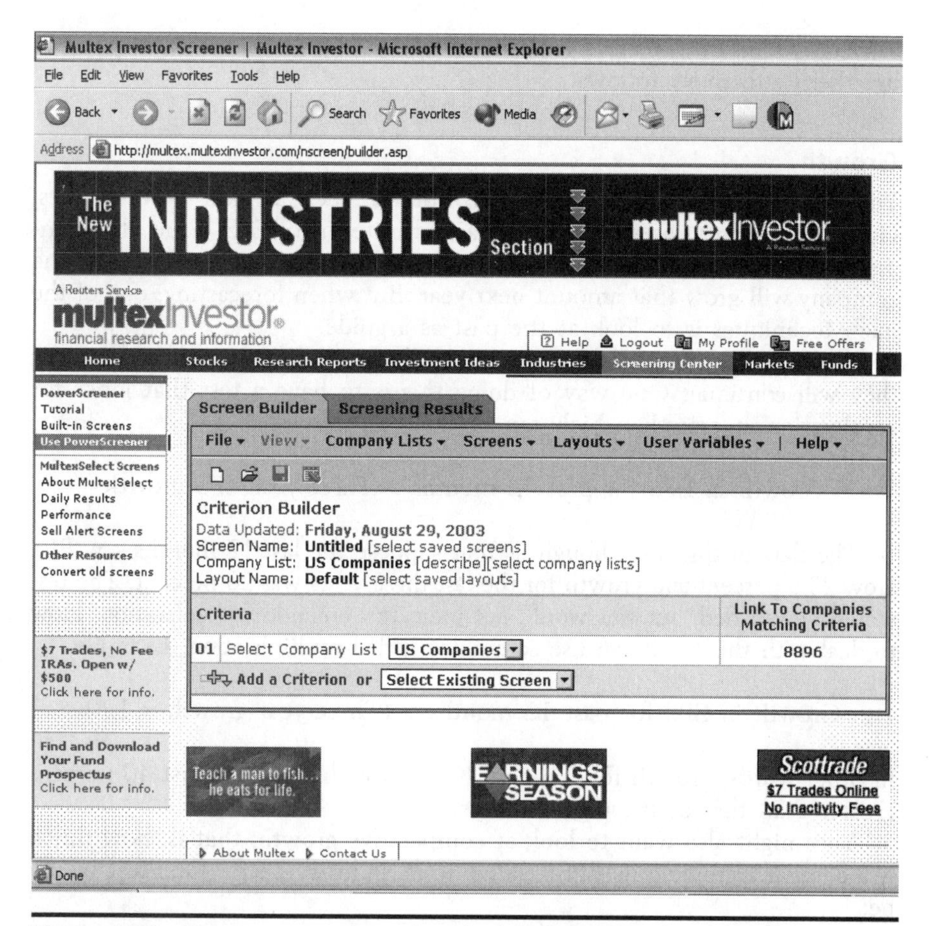

Figure 13.1 There are a variety of tools to help screen the thousands of stock on the markets. One of the better ones is Multex.com.

Tips and Strategies

Spend time looking at the different systems and you will begin to see the differences. Perhaps you will like the ease of use of one system or some of the variables that you can use in the tests. No doubt, the process will take time — but it is well worth it.

Which system do I use? I look at several from time to time, but for the most part, I focus on the Morningstar system. To me, it is easy to use and I think it has enough features for any stock investor.

Most screeners will base the analysis on different categories. For example, there may be a growth category that looks like percentage gains in sales or earnings per share (EPS). A look at the typical categories and how you can use them effectively follows.

Growth

You can look at the growth of many things, such as cash flow or sales. However, in most cases, growth is tracked in terms of EPS. True, if a company grew 25 percent in EPS last year, it does not necessarily mean the company will grow that amount next year. But when forecasting, one of the main techniques is to look at the past as a guide.

With the growth category, you can look at past growth rates and assume they will continue. One way of doing this is to have a test that looks for acceleration in growth, which can be done as follows:

Growth in EPS for past 12 months > Three-year EPS growth

The flaw in this test, though, is that suppose the last 12 months saw EPS grow 20.5 percent and growth for the last three years was 20 percent. The test would be satisfied, but this would not indicate tremendous acceleration. How to deal with this? You can use something called multiplication. Example:

Growth in EPS for past 12 months > (Three-year growth × 1.4)

In other words, growth for the past 12 months must be at least 40 percent greater than that of the past three years.

You might also want to look at comparative growth; that is, how much is a company growing its EPS relative to its industry peers? One test would be:

Growth in EPS for the past three years
> (Three-year industry average EPS growth) × 2

In this case, a company that met this test would have twice the industry growth rate in its EPS. This may indicate that the company is better managed than its peers. A screener may also make the following industry comparison:

Three-year EPS growth is in the top 10 percent of the industry

As you can see, you can get very creative in how you construct the tests.

Quality

This indicates how well the company is managed. One of the best indicators of this is the return on equity (ROE), which I explained in Chapter 9. Besides

ROE, you can also look at turnover ratios as well as profit margins as measures of company quality. A test can be as basic as this:

ROE for the past 12 months ≥ 20 percent

However, what is the appropriate percentage rate to look for? This is a matter of judgment. One guide, though, is to look at the ROE of the S&P or an industry. This can be done with the following test:

ROE for the past 12 months ≥ Industry average ROE for the past 12 months

Or you can use multiplication:

ROE for the past 12 months ≥ (Industry average ROE for the past 12 months) × 1.20

Also, you can test for companies that have shown improvements in ROE:

ROE for the past 12 months > Three-year industry average

Investor Sentiment

This is an indication of the overall bullishness or bearishness of a stock. Interestingly enough, some investors are happy to see a lot of bearishness in a stock, which may mean it is a bargain (see the sidebar titled "Value All the Way" in Chapter 5 for more information about one successful analyst who prefers downbeat stocks).

Other investors believe in momentum investing and will only focus on stocks that have a very bullish sentiment on the Street. Whatever your predilection, you can use a screener to gauge investor sentiment.

One way to get a sense of truly informed investor sentiment is to screen for insider activity (the topic of Chapter 11). Insider selling has many possible inspirations, so it is not necessarily a good indicator — but insider buying definitely is. Here's one useful test:

Net insider buys for the past month > 0

A screener can filter based on short interest. Basically, *short interest* is the current outstanding number of shares being shorted. As described in Chapter 6 (in the sidebar titled "Going on the Short Side"), short sellers make money when the stock falls; if there is a big short position in the stock, it typically means investors are skeptical. A test could be as simple as this:

Short interest ≥ 5 percent of the outstanding shares

Finally, institutional activity can be an indicator of investor sentiment. Over the years, institutions have become very influential in the movement of stock prices. Moreover, institutions typically have professional investors who perform strong research for them. If institutions are dumping a stock, it could mean a storm is brewing. If institutions are buying, it could mean brighter days. Here is a commonly used test:

Net institutional purchases for the past quarter > 0

Riskiness

Too much debt on the balance sheet can be very limiting for a company. You can use a screener to filter out companies whose burdens are too high. This is usually done by looking at the debt-to-equity ratio:

Debt-to-equity ratio ≤ 0.50

Where did I come up with the 0.50? I made it up. Perhaps a better approach would be to make an industry comparison:

Debt-to-equity ratio ≤ Industry average

Most screeners also allow you to look at other liquidity ratios, such as the current ratio and quick ratio, which were described in Chapter 9.

Analyst Expectations

True, analysts are not necessarily the best indicators of the future performance of a company's stock. Nonetheless, looking at average forecasts can be a very useful addition to an investor's toolbox. Most screeners allow you to use analyst expectations. Following are some of the techniques you can try out.

Discrepancy hunting. Be wary if you see a significant discrepancy among analyst forecasts. This usually means that it is difficult to forecast a company's results and indicates the possibility of a big surprise — either on the upside or downside. You can check for discrepancies with the following test:

High forecast estimate/Low forecast estimate > 1.50

This formula looks for a 50 percent difference in the forecasts.

Revision tracking. If analysts are revising estimates upward, this can be a very bullish sign. Here's a test:

> **Getting the Terms Right**
>
> Before using a test, make sure you read the screener's glossary of terms to see how it calculates the various ratios. For example, with the ROE, what does the screener consider to be the return? Is it operating profits? Or is it net income?
>
> Also, it can be easy to confuse terms. Is there a difference between ROE and ROI? There certainly is. The ROE shows the return on the equity invested in the company, whereas ROI shows return on the total investment in the company, which includes both equity and debt.
>
> Or look at margins. Are you testing for gross margins or operating margins or EBITDA margins?

Consensus estimate > (Consensus estimate for the past month) × 1.2

This will report if there was a 20 percent increase in the consensus estimate.

What Should You Include in Your Screen?

Screening stocks is ultimately about your investment philosophy. If you are a growth investor, you will focus on EPS and ROE. If you are a value investor, you might look at relative P/E. As stated earlier in this chapter, screening is about experimentation. Over time, you will hit on a system that you like and can work with.

After you conduct the screen, your job is still not over. The next step is to take a hard look at the companies that pass the screen. What I like to do is look at a variety of parts of the financial statements and get reality checks. Screens are far from perfect and you certainly need to continue with the winnowing process.

Reality Check #1: Business Model

Getting a feel for the business model is essential. True, a company may be showing strong growth — but if you cannot easily describe the reason for the growth, then you should stay away. After all, Enron was a profitable company for several years. It was also nearly impossible to comprehend, and the people who took it on faith eventually saw their investment crash and burn.

Once you understand the business model, the next step is: Can the business model be sustained with continued growth? Or is competition threatening? Can it easily be replicated? As Warren Buffett says, look for moats.

Reality Check #2: Listen to the Company

What is the vision of the company? Its attitude? Its town? Yes, these are quite vague concepts. But they can shed light on the power of a company — or lack thereof. From the letter to the shareholders, conference calls, TV interviews, and other messages, you can hear the vision and attitude of the CEO and other senior managers. Does the team appear confident or strong? Or does the team seem almost cocky? Do people blame others for problems or take responsibility? Does the company keep changing its vision or business model? Is management evasive?

Reality Check #3: Ratio Comparisons

Chapter 9 took an in-depth look at ratio analysis. However, as explained in that chapter, ratio analysis is worthless unless put into context. I like to use these two approaches:

1. Look at the trends in the ratios: Are they worsening or improving?
2. Compare the ratios to the industry: Does the company come out above its peers year after year?

An effective way of doing this is to use EDGAR Online Pro or Multex.com. These services provide industry-by-industry averages for the most common ratios.

Reality Check #4: Red Flags

In this book, I've mentioned many red flags. The ones I am particularly concerned about (where the appearance of even two or three will make me avoid the stock) are the following:

- Late filing of a required document with the SEC
- Change in auditor because of a dispute
- Resignation of a top executive without a replacement in the wings
- Press releases that hype the business
- Highlighting pro forma numbers over GAAP numbers
- Potentially major litigation exposure, such as for environmental liabilities or patent battles

- A "qualified opinion" or "going concern" statement from the company's auditor
- Incorporation in an exotic locale such as the Caribbean
- Labor dispute
- A variety of related-party transactions
- Loan default
- Several insiders dumping substantial amounts of stock
- A major write-down for inventory or goodwill
- Large salaries and option grants
- Major product recall

Reality Check #5: Green Flags

Just as there are red flags, there are green flags (for money, of course!) that give you the go-ahead on a stock. The following are particularly bullish:

- Company buy-back of shares (assuming the company is in healthy shape)
- Use of innovative management techniques, such as Six Sigma
- Large amounts of insider buys
- Several insiders buying stock (that is, cluster buying)
- Insider buying when the stock hits a new low or a new high

Reality Check #6: Information Is Everything

For investors, the most valuable commodity is information — the right information. One of the biggest mistakes, in fact, is to ignore information. Besides reading the financial statements, you need to be constantly aware of information around you and how to get an edge on your investments.

- Talk to experts.
- Read trade publications.
- Attend trade shows.
- Join an investment club.
- Read local newspapers.

Reality Check #7: Analyze the Cash Flow Statement

The great companies have all been tremendous cash generators. So make sure you focus intently on the cash flow statement.

- Are cash flows erratic? If so, there may be problems.
- Beware of companies with negative cash flows. In most cases, avoid the stock.

- Calculate a company's free cash flow and compare it to its interest payments. You want some margin of error for being able to meet these obligations.

Reality Check #8: Analyze the Income Statement

The income statement is prone to manipulation. If you spot any indication that someone is trying to make the income statement look better than it should, it is a danger sign and it is probably best to stay away from the company. Also, look carefully at sales trends as well as industry trends.

- Is the revenue mix changing? Is it changing to lower margin products or services? If so, the company may see lower profits and a lower stock price.
- Is the industry maturing or falling into a slump? If so, you probably want to avoid or sell the stock.
- Is the company engaging in many acquisitions? This may be a way to keep pumping up sales and profits while the underlying business is deteriorating.

Knowing When to Fold 'Em

Investor Warren Buffett has said many times that he wants to own a stock forever. He looks for the types of stocks that can supercharge a portfolio over the long term, and he has largely been successful in finding them.

Chances are that you do not have the stock-picking abilities of Buffett, so perhaps holding onto stocks forever may not be wise. Interestingly enough, Warren Buffett has, on occasion, sold stock. Even the Sage of Omaha can blunder sometimes, too.

I think one of the hardest decisions for investors is selling. I have to admit that, in the early 1990s, I owned shares in Dell and did make 300 percent on the stock. As the old saying goes: You don't go broke taking profits. But then again, you do not get rich selling too soon, either.

On the other hand, we have all made the mistake of buying a stock and seeing the company deteriorate, as well as the stock price. We somehow believe things will turn around, but they rarely do. The stock falls further and further. Do not become disappointed; there are some approaches to make you a better seller.

Monitor. With your checklists, you need to monitor your stocks whenever there is an EDGAR Online Pro filing or new press release. Are you seeing

- An immediate jump in revenue after a merger is a sign that a company is engaging in accounting shenanigans.
- Track a company's days sales outstanding. If the number is increasing, the company may be having trouble with sales growth.
- A decline in backlog is a sign of slackening growth.
- Vendor financing casts doubts on the quality of sales.
- Sudden changes in revenues cast doubts on the quality of sales.
- Track the allowance for doubtful accounts. If sales are increasing but this is staying the same, it could mean problems in the future.
- Are accounts receivable growing faster than sales? It could mean that growth is slowing down. This is also the case if inventories grow faster than sales.
- Watch out for practices such as "unbilled revenues" and "bill and hold."
- Significant cuts in R&D, say 25 percent or more, indicate that the company may be damaging its ability to generate new revenue streams in the future.
- Changes in accounting polices, such as capitalizing expenses and lengthening the period for depreciation or amortization, generally indicate a wish to look better than the actual condition justifies.

worsening trends? Have advantages suddenly become disadvantages? Are the original reasons you purchased the stock no longer valid? If you answer yes to these questions, then you need to seriously consider selling the stock or lessening your position. A key question you need to keep asking yourself: Why do I own the stock?

Getting expensive. In Chapter 9, I looked at approaches for valuation. Is the price looking, well, pricey? Can the company continue to grow to justify the higher price?

Better opportunity. As you do continual research, you are likely to find great opportunities. These opportunities may be better than some of the stocks you currently own. So, you might want to sell these less favorable stocks and add the new opportunities.

Don't allow emotions to take control. In the markets, crowd reflexes can take over even though investors can't actually see each other. Bad news often sends prices in a swoon, taking down the good companies with the bad ones. It is tough to hold onto stocks when everyone else is selling. But it can be a mistake to go with the crowd. If the company is still meeting your requirements, then selling would be a mistake. In fact, you might want to consider buying more of the stock.

Reality Check #9: Analyze the Balance Sheet

The balance sheet involves many moving parts. But some key areas are worth keeping an eye out for:

- Increasing debt levels combined with slowing growth
- Using optimistic estimates to pump up returns on the pension fund assets
- Using operating leases as a way to get debts off the balance sheet
- Using special purpose entiries and other techniques for off-balance-sheet debts
- Convertible financing maneuvers that involve "resets" or "floorless" features

Conclusion

More than anything, it is important to keep in mind that even the great investors have different approaches. Tom Marsico is a growth investor, while Bill Miller is a value investor. And Bill Miller practices a different type of value investing from, say, Warren Buffett. In other words, approach this book as a guideline, that is, a rough framework to get you started in building your own investment discipline. As when you try out anything new, you will make mistakes — but that is the only way to learn. Even the great investors make big blunders. But by screening for stocks and taking a strong look at the financials, you will be able to greatly minimize your mistakes. You will also greatly increase your chances of hitting the big trades.

This book has free materials available for download from the Web Added Value™ Resource Center at www.jrosspub.com.

Appendix: Financial Statement Resources

Both online and on paper, you can find a wide variety of assistance as you sit down to analyze that pile of financial statements. Here is a selection of the best Web sites, ratings services, and books available to you today.

Web Sites

Web resources are, of course, only as good as the people who provide the information. But some of those people are truly first rate!

EDGAR Online Pro (http://www.edgaronlinepro.com)

EDGAR Online Pro is a professional research tool that provides a complete view of the "financial life cycle" of over 12,000 public companies including complex fundamental ownership, IPO and secondary offering databases, call transcripts, an events calendar, and advanced search tools.

Motley Fool (http://www.fool.com)

Whitney Tilson is a managing partner for a money management firm in New York. He also writes a regular column for the Motley Fool and focuses heavily on financial statement analysis. You can find all his writings at http://www.tilsonfunds.com.

Wall Street Journal (http://www.wsj.com)

Richard Rampell and Art Berkowitz write a column for the online edition of the *WSJ* called "By the Books." The articles are always clear and very informative. Both Rampell and Berkowitz are veteran CPAs. For a solid and interesting read, see Berkowtiz's book *Enron: A Professional's Guide to the Events, Ethical Issues, and Proposed Reforms.*

TheStreet.com (http://www.thestreet.com)

TheStreet.com has a wealth of great articles for financial statement analysis. Notable authors who are not afraid to delve into the 10-Qs and 10-Ks include:

- *Herb Greenberg:* Every CEO's nightmare is to have a company profiled in Greenberg's column. Greenberg digs deep into a company's financials, looking for anything that does not quite add up. He also relies on independent research analysts and hedge fund managers for information. Here's a quote from one of his articles:

  > If you look closely at the SEC filings of ACLN, no stranger to readers of this column, you're bound to say one thing: Something doesn't add up. Belgium-based, Cyprus-incorporated ACLN, which is in the business of shipping new and used cars to Africa from Europe, is a story of inconsistencies, skimpy disclosure and a wide range of discrepancies.

- *Glenn Curtis:* He was an equity analyst at worldlyinvestor.com and InsiderTrader.com. He also worked at Cantone Research, a New Jersey–based brokerage. Curtis looks for value and tends to focus on smaller companies.
- *Odette Galli:* She has been on Wall Street since 1983, when she was an equity research analyst at L.F. Rothschild. She eventually worked as a research analyst at Morgan Stanley.

The subscription is $19.95 per month or $199.95 per year.

BusinessWeek (http://www.businessweek.com)

Anne Tergesen writes a periodic column on financial statement analysis called "The Fine Print." The articles are comprehensive and filled with useful examples.

Association for Investment Management and Research (AIMR; http://www.aimr.org)

AIMR is a professional association of 54,000 financial analysts, portfolio managers, and other investment professionals. To become a member, a person must take three rigorous exams. A member is then known as a Certified Financial Analyst (CFA).

The CFA exam focuses heavily on financial statement analysis. Also, AIMR has a site for individual investors at http://www.aimr.org/investorservices. The organization offers a free newsletter that provides helpful hints for financial statement analysis.

Center for Financial Research and Analysis (CFRA; http://www.cfraonline.com)

Howard Schilit has spent much of his career poring over financial statements. In fact, his specialty is trying to determine whether a company is using creative accounting to hide problems. Perhaps that is why he is known as both the "fraud detective" and the "most hated man on Wall Street."

He got a Ph.D. in accounting and was a professor from 1978 to 1995. He was starting to get bored teaching, so he spiced up his classes by looking at uncovering accounting fraud. Then in 1993, he wrote the best-selling *Financial Shenanigans: How to Detect Accounting Gimmicks and Fraud in Financial Reports*. In 2002, he published a revision to the book.

It did not take long until investment firms wanted him to write up research reports. Business expanded quickly and he formed CFRA in 1994.

He certainly had good calls. He uncovered problems at Microstrategy, Cendant, and Sunbeam. Unfortunately, his service is focused on institutions that can pay the thousands of dollars for the research. Despite this, the CFRA Web site is a good resource. You can find sample reports that demonstrate Shilit's methodology.

Ratings Services

If you do not have the big bucks to pay for an institutional service like CFRA, there are alternatives. In fact, several high-quality independent rating services are affordable for individual investors.

The following services are based on sophisticated computer models, research, and testing. Despite this, it does not mean a system is without problems. There is no perfect system. A ratings system could potentially underperform for many years or it could outperform. So do not rely exclusively on a system. You should always do your own homework.

Another downside is that these services may neglect small companies. This is a big drawback, since the opportunities in this sector can be great.

Morningstar.com (http://www.morningstar.com)

Known for its ratings of mutual funds (for over 20 years), this firm began to rate stocks in August 2001 (covering more than 3,000). The analysis focuses mostly on "competitive advantages, cash flows, and economic moats." What are economic moats? These are barriers to entry, such as significant market share, brand, or patented technologies.

The rating system tries to determine the fair market value (FMV) of a stock. Part of this is based on sophisticated computer modeling called "Economic Margin," which is based on the systems developed by the stock research firm of Applied Finance Group, in Chicago. Also, a variety of Morningstar analysts provide their own subjective input in establishing the FMV. These analysts have no positions in the stocks they cover.

The lower the current stock price is compared to the FMV, then the better the ultimate rating. The rating system ranges from one to five stars (with five-star stocks being the most undervalued). However, a stock may have a five-star rating and still be very risky. To deal with this, Morningstar has a risk rating, which ranges from low to medium to high. Eight risk factors are considered:

- How cyclical is the company's industry?
- How innovative is the company relative to its industry?
- How likely is it that the stock could lose half its value in a three-month period?
- How does the company's debt-to-equity ratio stack up against other companies in its sector?
- How does the company's free cash flow compare with its sales?
- How sustainable is the company's operating cash flow?
- How big are the company's revenues relative to all other companies?
- Is there some nonfinancial issue looming in the future that could materially affect the company's fortunes?

These ratings can change quickly. For example, an analyst may lower the FMV or the stock price may surge. Thus it is a good idea to use the alert system from Morningstar, which sends an e-mail notice when a rating changes.

For free, Morningstar.com has a university section that offers several great online courses dealing with the fundamentals of investing.

The Morningstar ratings service is free for the first 30 days. If you purchase it, you can choose the $11.95 monthly rate, $109 per year, or $189 for two years.

Yahoo! Finance (http://quote.yahoo.com)

Yahoo! Finance is a favorite site of mine (I use it on a daily basis). It is easy to navigate and has a wealth of information. You have access to news stories from diverse sources (*Investor's Business Daily, Motley Fool, Business Week,* and so on), as well as valuable financial data. You can view balance sheets, income statements, and cash flow statements. There is also information on insider transactions, management bios, and financial ratios.

MSN Investor (http://moneycentral.msn.com/investor)

This site offers a free service known as StockScouter. The system is based on the extensive research of Camelback Research Alliance, which is an independent research firm. The StockScouter system tracks about 6,200 stocks using computer-based research; that is, it has no subjective analyst input. The computer system is updated on a daily basis. Stocks are ranked from 1 to 10, with 10 being the best. The system looks at four main areas:

- *Fundamentals.* A company should have earnings that beat brokerage analysts' consensus estimates consistently.
- *Ownership.* Executives should be accumulating shares in the company.
- *Valuation.* The current stock price meets certain standards compared to sales, earnings, and expected earnings.
- *Technical.* The system analyzes a company's chart patterns. Basically, the stock price should be generally increasing.

The rating system is also adjusted for risk. For example, if the risk is higher, it will mean a lower ranking.

Standard & Poor's (http://www.standardandpoors.com)

Standard & Poor's was founded in 1860 with the goal of providing independent research and analysis (the first reports covered railroads and canals). The mission was simple: Satisfy "the investor's right to know." Currently, the firm has about 1,200 analysts. They cover about 6,000 stocks.

S&P has two parts. There is the STARS stock recommendation system, which is based on the subjective work of analysts. The ranking goes from one to five (with five being the best rating). Next, there is the Fair Value Model, which uses quantitative measures to find a company's FMV. These range from one to five as well.

The analysis is comprehensive: fundamentals of the company, industry trends, and major economic trends.

Each report costs $5. If you subscribe to *BusinessWeek* magazine, you can get three free reports every month. If you want unlimited reports, the cost is $995 per year.

Investor's Business Daily or IBD (http://www.investors.com)

William O'Neil, a former stockbroker, founded the company in 1984. As a stockbroker, he did extensive study of the markets and found characteristics of winning stocks. He then formulated an investment strategy called CAN SLIM, which he described in his bestseller, *How to Make Money in Stocks*.

In his newspaper and Web site, he has a rating system — which covers more than 10,000 stocks — that incorporates his strategies. It is a purely quantitative approach and looks at fundamental factors, as well as technical analysis. The ratings go from 1 to 99. A rating of 80 or more is considered bullish.

A subscription costs $197 per year.

Value Line (http://www.valueline.com)

Value Line was founded in 1931 and currently has almost 300 employees, of whom 70 are analysts. In all, the firm rates about 1,700 stocks in more than 90 industries.

The firm has a Timeliness Ranking System, which forecasts relative stock performance for six months to a year. This system has been in place for more than 35 years and is updated on a weekly basis.

A 13-week trial subscription costs $65 and an annual subscription is $598.

Schwab Research (http://www.schwab.com)

Schwab has been a great innovator in brokerage services. In May 2002, the company announced that it would provide clients with its own rating service for about 3,000 public companies. The stocks are rated on a scale from A to F (Schwab recommends buying stocks that are rated between A and B). How does the system work? Schwab is keeping it a secret, but it was the result of the acquisition of a research firm called Chicago Investment Analytics, which has developed a very sophisticated statistical system for stocks.

To use the service, you must be a client with Schwab.

Books

While the book you're reading will be a great start for any investor, there are certainly other good financial statement books to consider. Here's a quick selection to start with:

- *Quality of Earnings* (Thornton L. O'Glove). Even though more than 10 years old, the book is a classic. The author is a great innovator in financial statement analysis.

- *The Financial Numbers Game: Detecting Creative Accounting Practices* (Charles Mulford and Eugene Comisky). This is a very comprehensive book that looks at the intricacies of GAAP — in an understandable way.
- *Financial Accounting: An Introduction to Concepts, Methods and Uses* (Clyde P. Stickney and Roman L. Weil). This is a classic textbook that makes use of real-world examples and also delves into international issues. But like most textbooks, this one has a big price tag: $115.95. (You might access it via interlibrary loan.)

Glossary

Accelerated Filer: A company that has a market value of more than $75 million. This type of company must abide by shorter deadlines for the filing of financial statements.

Accounts Payable: Money that a company owes its suppliers and other short-term creditors (usually with terms of less than three months).

Accrual Accounting: A method of accounting that records transactions in terms of when revenues are earned and expenses incurred — not when cash changes hands.

Allowance for Doubtful Accounts: An estimate of the uncollectibility of outstanding accounts receivable.

Amortization: A process that expenses the value of an intangible asset over time.

Annual Report: A financial disclosure of the results of a company for the past year, although it is usually a marketing piece to entice shareholders.

Balance Sheet: A financial statement that includes a company's assets, liabilities, and equity.

Bankruptcy: A process that is managed by a federal judge to restructure a company's operations.

Best Efforts Offering: An IPO in which an investment bank will not guarantee any proceeds to the firm, but will instead make its best efforts to raise capital.

Bond: A loan that is issued to the public in an offering similar to an IPO (except an IPO is an offering of stock).

Cap Ex: Short for capital expenditures. See Capital Expenditures.

Capital Expenditures: Investments in property, plant, and equipment.

Capital Lease: After a lease term expires, a company may get ownership in the underlying property if it meets a variety of criteria (although this is beyond the scope of this book). A capital lease is reported as a liability on the balance sheet.

Cash Equivalent: A very liquid asset. That means it's available right now or is in an account with a maturity no longer than three months.

Cash Flow Statement: A financial statement that adjusts the balance sheet and income statement to see how much money a company has generated or spent during a certain period of time.

Chapter 11: Provides a company a breather to attempt to turn things around.

Chapter 7: The filing a company makes when it decides to liquidate its operations.

COGS: See Cost of Goods Sold.

Common Stock: The most basic form of ownership in a company, which provides the investor with the potential for dividends and certain voting rights.

Conference Call: Many companies will put on a conference call, in which the executives explain and take questions regarding the most recent prior quarter.

Corporate Governance: The structure of a company along with its executive compensation, voting rules, board composition, and so on.

Cost of Goods Sold (COGS): The costs that are directly related to a company's sales.

Coupon Rate: The rate of interest on a bond.

Covenant: Terms in a loan contract.

Credit Line: When a bank allows a company to borrow a certain amount of money for a set term, say two or three years.

Current Assets: Assets likely to be used up, converted into cash, or sold within the company's operating cycle or within one year, whichever is greater.

Current Liabilities: Debts that must be paid off within a company's operating cycle or within one year, whichever is greater.

Depreciation: A method that expenses the value of an asset over time because of wear-and-tear and obsolescence.

EBITDA: Earnings before interest, taxes, depreciation, and amortization.

EDGAR: The Electronic Data Gathering, Analysis, and Retrieval database run by the U.S. Securities and Exchange Commission (SEC). Public companies, executives, and institutional investors are required to report material news to the U.S. SEC via the EDGAR system.

EDGAR Online (http://www.edgar-online.com): A financial information company that specializes in making complex regulatory reporting by public companies actionable and easy to use. The company is traded on the NASDAQ under ticker symbol EDGR and is not affiliated with the U.S. Securities and Exchange Commission.

8-K: A company must file this for certain material events, such as acquisitions, change of auditors, and even bankruptcy.

Entity Concept: A principle in accounting which requires that there must be a separately defined entity in order to formulate financial statements.

Extensible Business Reporting Language (XBRL): A set of standards that makes it easier to digitally transmit and analyze financial statements.

FASB: See Financial Accounting Standards Board.

FIFO: See First In, First Out.

Financial Accounting Standards Board (FASB): A private organization, established in 1973, that promotes accounting and reporting standards.

Finished Goods: Products ready to be sold.

Firm Commitment Offering: An IPO in which the investment bank guarantees capital for a company.

First In, First Out (FIFO): A method for valuing inventory that uses the cost of the first items in the inventory.

GAAP: See Generally Accepted Accounting Principles.

Generally Accepted Accounting Principles (GAAP): The underlying standards and principles for accounting and financial statements. All public companies must report their financials pursuant to GAAP.

Going Concern Opinion: An opinion from a company's auditor that indicates the company is in jeopardy of going bankrupt.

Goodwill: The value of a company that goes beyond its hard assets. These intangibles include reputation, customer loyalty, brand recognition, and so on.

Gross Profit: The difference between revenues and the cost of goods sold.

Gross Profit Margin: The percentage of gross profits as of total sales.

Historical Cost Method: An accounting principle that requires that a company report its assets at the amount paid for them.

IASB: See International Accounting Standards Board.

Income Statement: A financial statement that shows the profitability of a firm.

Initial Public Offering (IPO): The first time a company issues stock to the public.

Insider: A director, officer, or major shareholder of a public company.

Intangible Asset: An asset that is not physical, such as a patent, trademark, or copyright.

International Accounting Standards Board (IASB): The agency was founded in 1973 and has as its mandate to establish a single standard for all companies in terms of financial reporting.

Inventory: Raw goods, work in process, or finished goods that have yet to be shipped to customers.

IPO: See Initial Public Offering.

Last In, First Out (LIFO): A method for valuing inventory in which the costs of the last items manufactured are used.

LIFO: See Last In, First Out.

Lock-Up Period: A clause in an IPO that prevents corporate insiders from selling their shares for a certain period of time, usually six months.

Management's Discussion and Analysis (MD&A): A narrative in a financial statement that explains the financials.

Market Capitalization (market cap for short): The total value of a company based on the current stock price and the number of shares outstanding.

MD&A: See Management's Discussion and Analysis.

NASDAQ: See National Association of Securities Dealers Automated Quotation.

National Association of Securities Dealers Automated Quotation System (NASDAQ): A stock exchange that is based on an electronic computer system.

Net Income: The profits of a company, after adjusting for taxes and dividends.

New York Stock Exchange (NYSE): The oldest stock exchange in the United States. The exchange has a physical floor, based in New York, and tends to trade the securities of major companies.

Nontrade Receivables: The same as accounts receivable, but they are not from customers. Rather, they are from employees, officers, directors, and stockholders. The category also includes interest and dividends due from investments.

NYSE: See New York Stock Exchange.

Operating Lease: A contract that provides for use or occupancy of property, not ownership. This does not appear as a liability on a company's balance sheet.

OTC Bulletin Board: See Over the Counter Bulletin Board.

Overfunded Pension: A corporate pension fund that has more than enough capital to meet future retirement obligations.

Over the Counter (OTC) Bulletin Board: A quotation service that provides pricing and volume data on stocks, usually for very small companies.

PCAOB: See Public Company Accounting Oversight Board.

Periodicity: An accounting principle which requires that financial statements be completed on a regular basis, such as every year or every quarter or even every month.

Preferred Stock: A security that is a hybrid of a bond and stock. A preferred typically has a fixed amount it pays in dividends, but has a higher priority of claims in a bankruptcy situation.

Prepaid Expenses: Companies prepay certain types of expense, such as insurance, rent, and service fees. These expenses are accounted initially as assets.

Prime Rate: The rate of interest that banks charge their top customers.

Pro Forma Earnings: An earnings report that is not in accordance with generally accepted accounting principles. Rather, it is based on the discretion of the company.

Prospectus: A detailed document sent to investors who are interested in investing in an IPO.

Proxy Statement: An extensive disclosure form for important shareholder votes.

Public Company Accounting Oversight Board (PCAOB): An entity that has a broad mandate to deal with setting standards for auditing, quality control, and accounting ethics. The agency also has the power to inspect registered accounting firms and even bring disciplinary action.

Qualified Opinion: An auditor's opinion that a company is not in compliance with generally accepted accounting principles.

Raw Materials: Ingredients required to produce a product, such as outsourced parts and bulk chemicals.

Realized: A stock or other security has been sold at either a gain or loss.

Restatement: When a company changes a prior financial statement, because of a change in accounting policy or even fraud.

Revenues: Represent the cash and promises to pay from customers for either services provided or goods delivered.

S-1: The form for filing for an IPO.

SEC: See Securities and Exchange Commission.

Securities and Exchange Commission (SEC): Has the authority, under the Securities Exchange Act of 1934, to establish and enforce accounting and reporting standards for public companies.

10-K: A financial statement that shows the results for the whole year, including the periods covered by the preceding 10-Q filings as well as the fourth quarter.

10-Q: The report filed to the SEC that discloses the financials and other material information for the first, second, and third quarters (the fourth quarter is in the 10-K).

Trading Securities: Stock or bond holdings that a company intends to sell within a short period of time (usually less than one year). These are accounted for as current assets on the balance sheet.

Treasury Stock: Stock that a company has repurchased on the open market.

Unearned Revenues: A customer will pay for a product before the product is shipped — or sometimes even built. The company has the money in the bank but has not officially earned it, so the amount is considered a liability. This reflects the product owed to the customer.

Underfunded Pension: A corporate pension plan that does not have enough capital to meet future retirement obligations.

Underwriter: An investment banking firm that manages a company's IPO.

Unrealized: A stock or other security has yet to be sold, even though the value of the security has changed.

Warrant: Gives a person or company the right to buy a certain number of shares of a company if the stock price rises above a fixed price.

Work in Progress: Partially finished product (that is, in the process of being manufactured).

XBRL: See Extensible Business Reporting Language.

Index

C

D

T

U

V

W

X

Y

Z